Dedication

This book is dedicated to all the open source developers and Joomla community. Without you this book would not be possible.

Acknowledgements

When we first conceived of this book, we knew it would be a challenge to cover everything we wanted to cover yet keep the book from becoming too technical or overwhelming. As always it took many people to get this book into your hands, and we would like to extend our thanks to all.

First, thanks to our editors, Nancy, Bob, and Darren. Nancy who patiently pushed us to stay on schedule. To Bob for helping us to better explain the more obscure and vague concepts, and to Darren for having such a keen eye. To Danielle for laying out the book so splendidly and putting up with our constant changes.

We would like to extend a very special thank you to our friend and instructor David McFarland for those simple words that started it all, "You should look into Joomla!"

And finally to all of our friends and family who always believed we could do it.

Joomla!

Second Edition

MARNI DERR • TANYA SYMES

 Peachpit Press

Visual QuickStart Guide
Joomla!
Second Edition
Marni Derr and Tanya Symes

Peachpit Press
1249 Eighth Street
Berkeley, CA 94710
510/524-2178
510/524-2221 (fax)
Find us on the Web at peachpit.com
To report errors, please send a note to errata@peachpit.com
Peachpit Press is a division of Pearson Education
Copyright © 2011 by Marni Derr and Tanya Symes

Project Editor: Nancy Peterson
Development Editor: Bob Lindstrom
Copyeditor: Darren Meiss
Production Editor: Becky Winter
Compositor: Danielle Foster
Indexer: Jack Lewis
Cover compositor: Alan Clements
Cover Design: RHDG / Riezebos Holzbaur Design Group, Peachpit Press
Interior Design: Peachpit Press
Logo Design: MINE™ www.minesf.com

ISBN 13: 978-0-321-77298-5
ISBN-10:   0-321-77298-9

9 8 7 6 5 4 3 2

Printed and bound in the United States of America

Table of Contents

Introduction

Over the last decade, the web has seen monumental changes. Today, everyone has a web presence and, to some extent, everyone is a web designer. Social web sites and new media have changed the way we use the web and interact with each other; and also how we locate, consume, and share information. As the web became more accessible, the ability to create a web site needed to become more accessible for users.

In 2005, free, open source content management systems such as Joomla, Drupal, and WordPress made creating, updating, and maintaining a web site as easy as using a word processor.

Today, with a web browser, a domain name, a web server, and the latest version of Joomla, you can have your own dynamic, socially integrated web presence. You can offer services, write a blog, sell products, or create a stunning portfolio in as little as a few days with little or no web design, development, or coding skills.

This book is your complete start-to-finish guide on installing, using, extending, and maintaining a fully functional Joomla web site.

What Is a Content Management System?

A *content management system* (CMS) is a web-based application that manages your content by storing it in a database and then displaying that content using a template. A CMS provides a graphical user interface (GUI) that you use to input your web site content and create links; the system then writes the code needed to display that content as a web page. When using a CMS, you do not need to be a web coder or designer to create a fully functional and interactive web site—the system handles this for you.

All content management systems contain core management functions: a menu system to create links, default templates to present your content, editors to create that content, and small functions such as search engine optimization (SEO) options, user registration, and so on. To add functionality that is not included in the core CMS, you can acquire free or commercial third-party extensions. Joomla has one of the largest communities of extension developers on the market today.

For example, if you needed interactive forms to collect user information, you could do a web search for "forms for Joomla" and find numerous extension options to enable form creation using Joomla. These extensions provide an interface for you to enter information and then generate the form for your web site. The extension developers have written the code for you; you simply enter the information to create a fully functional form in minutes.

Who This Book Is For

This book is for creative professionals, covering the spectrum from web designers and developers to small and medium businesses and sole proprietorships. Even large corporations have implemented Joomla web sites.

It is not necessary to know HTML, CSS, PHP, or JavaScript, or to understand databases to create a complete Joomla web site. You can complete this book and have a fully functional web site at the end. If you are a web developer or designer with coding skills, this book walks you through all the features Joomla has to offer, including creating custom templates. As always, a good understanding of web site usability and design is extremely helpful.

What Version of Joomla Does This Book Discuss?

This is the second edition of the Joomla Visual QuickStart series. Our first edition taught how to use Joomla versions 1.5.0 through 1.5.x. Joomla 1.5.x will be supported by the Joomla development team through April 2012.

In January 2011, Joomla 1.6.x was released for use on live production sites. At the time of its release, the Joomla development team decided to implement *short-term releases* (STS) and *long-term releases* (LTS). We will not detail the particulars of these release cycles here. For information on the new Joomla release cycles and what each new version means, go to www.joomla.org.

This book was written using the newest Joomla 1.6 release. However, a new release—whether a STS or LTS—might contain minor or major changes and added features. To that end, we have written and constructed this book to be as useful as possible for Joomla versions 1.6.x and above. Even if future releases change the interface and functionality, the core concepts of Joomla will remain as taught in this book.

Companion Web Site

You will find this book's companion web site at www.writingyourdreams.com. There you can provide feedback and also view the demo site used throughout this book. The authors maintain a section for additional information, book updates, addendums, errata, and a forum for feedback and questions.

About This Book

No one book can cover all aspects of a topic; however, we aimed to explore every core feature and function of Joomla, beginning with the basics and advancing into real world examples that you can use on your site. This book is designed to help you rapidly grasp Joomla's functionality and serve as a quick reference guide as you continue to use Joomla.

Chapter 1: Installing Joomla

Review Joomla server requirements and how to set up the Joomla database. Then, walk through installing Joomla on a live or local server.

Chapter 2: Getting Started

You'll start with an investigative tour of Joomla's administrative back end, and continue on to its navigation and key features.

Chapter 3: Creating Categories

Learn how to create and manage your category structure and how to create menus for categories.

Chapter 4: Adding Articles

Create content, text, and media using Joomla; and understand how to assign articles to categories; and how to create menus for articles.

Chapter 5: Managing Menus

Beginning with an explanation of Joomla menus, the chapter then teaches how to create menus and place them on your site.

Chapter 6: Controlling Content Layouts

Understand how to control the display of your content on the site, how to set global content options, and how to use menus to control what content displays on a page.

Chapter 7: Working with Templates

Use both administrative (back-end) and front-end templates in Joomla. You'll also discover how to identify and use template positions.

Chapter 8: Working with Modules

Learn to create and position modules on your site.

Chapter 9: Utilizing Components

Create and use components and their associated modules.

Chapter 10: Managing User Access and Permissions

Create your own user groups, set the appropriate permissions, and control access to site content or administration.

Chapter 11: Building Your Site Structure

Learn how to plan and set up a Joomla site using your categories and menus.

Chapter 12: Creating Portfolios and Galleries

Combine everything you have learned and apply it to real world web sites. You will learn how to create a business portfolio and an artist photo or image gallery.

Chapter 13: Going Social

Walk through the creation of a blog page and integrate social media (such as Facebook and Twitter) to your site.

Chapter 14: Creating Joomla Templates

Explore how to create and customize Joomla templates.

Video Training

You can view free video lessons that demonstrate some of the Joomla tasks described in this book. To access video lessons, register your book at www.peachpit.com/register.

1

Installing Joomla

Installing Joomla is easy and takes about five minutes. Download the Joomla package to your computer, upload the files to your web server, and then enter your site information using the Joomla installation wizard.

Even if you have installed previous versions of Joomla, we still recommend you follow the procedures described in this chapter because a few key changes and improvements have been made to the installation process.

This chapter begins with a quick checklist to help you get through the installation process without errors. Then, we walk through the entire Joomla installation wizard screen-by-screen, and finally show you how to log into the back end, the administrative interface of Joomla.

In This Chapter

Joomla Technical Requirements

To run properly, Joomla requires that specific software versions be installed and loaded on your web server. Consult the following checklist when preparing to run a local or remote (hosted) site. When selecting a hosting company to host your Joomla web sites, make sure their server configuration meets these minimum requirements.

Apache PHP Extension Recommendations

- mod_mysql
- mod_xml
- mod_zlib
- mod_rewrite (must have for using SEO URLs)
- Mbstring enabled
- cURL support
- mcrypt support
- File uploads ON
- Upload and php memory between 32 - 50MB

  The maximum file size should be 50MB. Larger uploads should be transferred using an FTP program, and not uploaded through Joomla, although there are some exceptions such as streaming video files. If you experience issues when uploading media or installing extensions, consult with your hosting provider about upload limits.

JOOMLA 1.6 AND ABOVE

Software	Version
PHP	5.2+
MySQL	5.0.4+
Apache	2.x+
For Microsoft IIS:	
Microsoft IIS	7

Notes: Use Apache mod_mysql, mod_xml, mod_zlib.

To use SEO URLs, apache mod_rewrite extension must be installed.

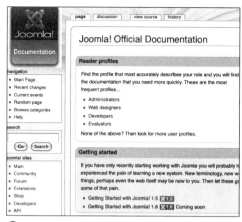

Preparing to Install

You can find all of the information contained in this chapter on the Joomla web site. If you are new to Joomla, take the time to read through the information at http://docs.joomla.org Ⓐ.

To install Joomla, you will need:

- An internet connection
- A web browser
- A domain name
- A local or remote web server
- A database and database user with full permissions
- An FTP program or cPanel if using a remote hosting service

To obtain a domain name:

1. Find a domain registrar.
2. Search and find an available domain name.
3. Purchase the domain name.

A domain name and hosting are entirely separate services—even if your domain name registrar offers free hosting with the purchase of a domain name. A domain name is the URL of your web site. Hosting is performed by a web server set up to run your web site. You do not need to host your site at the same place you register your domain name. In fact, we strongly recommend that you search for a hosting provider that specializes in CMS systems.

Two popular domain name registrars are:

- www.godaddy.com
- www.networksolutions.com

To find a reliable hosting service:

Do your research before choosing a hosting company. Do not make your choice by choosing the lowest price and "unlimited" offers. Although you can install Joomla on any server with any hosting company, not all hosting companies are optimized for Joomla. Find a hosting company that meets all Joomla security and configuration requirements. Talk to a representative and ask if they have servers configured especially for content management systems. The Joomla.org web site has a list of Joomla-friendly hosting companies.

Avoid permission issues caused by improperly configured servers. Using the FTP layer and changing your files and directories to 777 to avoid these issues is a huge security vulnerability for your web site. Even extensions that require read and write access to files and directories do not need to have permissions changed if your server is configured correctly.

- Locate a host that has servers configured just for Joomla, such as Rochen or Host Gator.

- Use a Linux OS server.

- Pay the small extra fee for cPanel server administration, which is well worth it for easy access and configuration of your Joomla files and creating your database information.

- Research the list of recommended hosting services at www.joomla.org.

To use a local web server:

It is best practice to use a local server, running on your computer, when first creating your Joomla web site. If you do not already have a local server installed, you can easily do so using prepackaged software such as MAMP for the Mac or XAMPP for Windows.

The benefits to working on a local web server are:

- Faster to create and test the site

- Reduce the risk of bringing down your live "production" site

- Allow you to test third-party extensions, before deployment on a live site

To set up and configure a web server that is compatible with your operating system, you can use the following software:

- Windows—WAMP (www.wampserver.com/en)

- Macintosh—MAMP (www.mamp.info/en/mamp.html)

- Linux or Unix distribution—LAMP (www.lamp.com)

- Multi-platform—XAMPP (http://apachefriends.org)

A The cPanel database wizard icon. Select the wizard unless you are familiar with creating databases and users.

B Creating a new database

Creating the Joomla Database

Joomla uses a database to store site information and content. Before installing Joomla, you need to create a database and a database user with full privileges.

Use one of the following methods to create the Joomla database:

- **Use cPanel:** cPanel has a very friendly interface for managing and maintaining your web server.

- **Use phpMyAdmin:** Ask your provider how to access your phpMyAdmin account. If you are working on a local server, you may access phpMyAdmin through the web server.

- **Your hosting provider:** In some cases the hosting provider creates the database and user for you. In this case, the provider should issue an email address with your database name and database user name.

To create your database and database user using cPanel:

1. Log in to your cPanel account.
2. Select the MySQL Database Wizard **A**.
3. Enter a name for your database and click Next Step **B**.

   All hosting providers use a prefix for your databases and user accounts. The prefix cannot be changed; you simply append the prefix with the desired information. This helps keep your database secure.

   continues on next page

4. Enter a username for this database and a password, and then click Create User 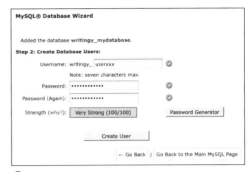.

   You will need this information only once during the Joomla installation process so it is recommended that you use a password generator to create a secure password.

5. On the privileges screen, choose ALL Privileges, and then click Next Step 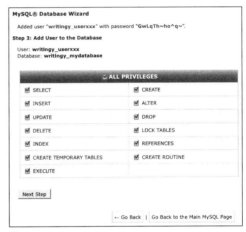.

   The database user created here must have full privileges to read, write, and execute to the database. This is mandatory for Joomla to operate without permission issues. You are essentially giving Joomla full privileges to do what it needs to do to create your web site.

To create a database using phpMyAdmin:

1. Open the phpMyAdmin start page.

   You can access phpMyAdmin through your web server or your hosting account, if available.

   To access the start page when using a local web server such as MAMP or XAMPP, click Open Start Page.

   The phpMyAdmin page displays all databases contained on the server. You can add, delete, and modify databases using phpMyAdmin. We need to create a new database for Joomla to use.

2. In the "Create new database" field, enter a name for the new Joomla database.

   The database can be named anything, but you should choose a secure, hard to hack name to increase database security 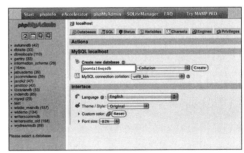.

C Creating a user for the database

D Selecting all privileges for the new database user

E The phpMyAdmin interface allows you to create, edit, modify, and manipulate server databases and users.

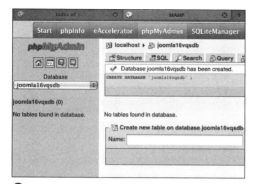

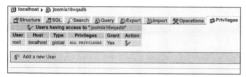

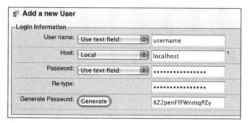

F The new database has been created.

G The privileges tab gives you access to create users for your database.

H The add a new user fields.

3. Select the appropriate collation options.

   The collation options depend on your individual requirements, and we cannot advise you here. However, the most common collation to use on a Joomla site is UTF8-Bin. This is a universal standard using Unicode formatting for the web.

4. Click Create.

   The new database is created and ready to use when you install Joomla **F**.

5. Click the Privileges tab at the top of the page.

   The Privileges tab is where you create user accounts for your database **G**.

6. Choose Add a new User.

   Here you add a user with all privileges to the database. On a local server an initial user is already created: User-name: root, Password: root. On a production site you will need to create a user with all privileges.

7. In the User name field type a user name.

8. In the Host field, choose localhost.

9. In the Generate Password field, click the Generate button.

   Using the password generator will create a secure password, making your database much harder to access or hack **H**.

   Make sure you write down and store your new database, database user name and password, you will need this information during the Joomla installation process.

continues on next page

10. Under Database for user, make sure Grant all privileges on database "your-databasename" is selected.

11. Under Global privileges, select Check All.

The initial database user must have all privileges so Joomla has full read/write access to the database ❶.

12. Scroll to the bottom of the page and select Go.

You have added a new user with all privileges to this database. To ensure the user was created, simply select the privileges tab for your database. You should see the user name listed ❶.

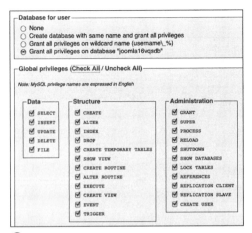

❶ Assign ALL privileges to the new user.

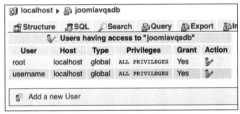

❶ The new user is now applied to the database.

Downloading Joomla

The files you need to install and run Joomla are contained in a single compressed file package. Generally, compressed files are available in three formats: .zip, .tar.bz2, or .tar.gz. You can extract any one of these files by using your web server. If you are extracting (unzipping) the files to your computer, the .zip file type is the safest choice because all operating systems can extract .zip files.

To download the Joomla package:

1. Go to www.joomla.org.

   The Joomla site is updated regularly, and it may not look the same as the figures in this book. However, the Download button always appears on the home page.

2. On the Joomla home page, click the Download or "Download Joomla Get The Latest Version" button Ⓐ.

   Doing so will take you to the file repository containing *all* Joomla files, including current and previous versions and available software patches. This book covers Joomla 1.6.x and later, so make sure you download a Joomla 1.6.0 (or later) file.

3. Click the current Joomla 1.6 package, and save the file to your desktop.

Uploading Joomla to Your Web Server

In this book, we use the Linux/Apache cPanel web server interface. You could also log in to your web server using an FTP program—such as Cyber Duck for Mac or Filezilla for Windows—to upload, move, or delete files. The most important thing is to have root access and know the location of your root folder.

On a hosted server, you do not need to create a folder (directory) to contain the Joomla files. The files should be placed in your /public_html folder, which is your web server's root folder.

On a local server, you will need to create a folder (directory) inside the root folder— such as /htdocs/*mysite*—and place the Joomla files there. The mysite folder becomes the root folder containing the Joomla files and folders.

For example, on a local Apache web server using MAMP or XAMPP, the root folder is the htdocs folder, and it will look like this: /htdocs/*mywebsite*/. On a local Windows IIS web server, the folder is generally named *www* or *webroot*, and it will look like this: /www/*mywebsite*.

A Joomla files extracted to the web server

To upload and extract the Joomla files

1. Log in to your hosting account using cPanel or an FTP program.

2. Using the file manager, navigate to your public_html root folder and upload the Joomla package.

3. Extract the files.

   You can now see all of the Joomla core files and folders **A**.

After you have uploaded and extracted the Joomla package, you need to immediately run the installation wizard. Why? Because Joomla is a web site, it is also a web site application. This means it is fully functional to anyone typing in your web address. If you do not complete the installation, anyone who comes to your web site will be able to access the installation wizard.

Running the Installation Wizard

The installation wizard runs within your web browser and includes seven screens. The wizard checks your server configuration, connects to your database, and installs the Joomla tables you will need to run your web site. It will also help you enter your site information and create your first Super User administrative account.

You can move backward and forward among the screens. If anything fails during the installation, you can exit the installation, correct the problem, and then restart the wizard. Joomla will not be fully installed until everything is functioning correctly.

To complete the installation, you will need:

- Your MySQL database name, user name, and password
- A valid email address for the Super User account

Generally, you'll have few problems when installing Joomla. The only two issues for an installation failure are the following:

- An improperly configured server
- An incorrect database name, user name, or password

To launch the installation wizard:

1. Open a new tab in your web browser and type in the address of your web site.

   The first screen of the Joomla installation wizard opens. As mentioned earlier, you should complete this installation immediately.

A Language selection screen

B The pre-installation check screen

To select your back-end language:

The first screen allows you to select the language you want to use for the administrative back end. Select your language, and then click Next **A**.

To pass the pre-installation check:

The pre-installation check verifies that your server configuration can properly support and operate Joomla. The items listed under the pre-installation check must pass or else your Joomla installation will fail or not function correctly. You needn't choose the items under recommended settings for Joomla to function correctly, but they are desirable because they are set appropriately.

1. Verify that all items in the pre-installation check are marked with a green Yes **B**.

    If any of the items in the pre-installation checklist are displayed in red, the Joomla installation will fail. To correct these settings, contact your hosting company to get help performing a proper setup of the web server.

2. Review the recommended settings.

    Recommended settings are just that, recommended. If your settings differ and some items are marked in red, Joomla will install and function normally. For administrative and security reasons, however, we highly recommend that you use server settings to conform to this list whenever possible.

3. If all settings are green, click Next.

To accept the license agreement:

Yes, this is yet another licensing screen. However, if this is your first Joomla installation, you should read through these terms. Joomla is open source software that operates under the GPL/GNU licensing standards, and they take their licensing requirements seriously. It is very important that you understand what this means if you are a designer, or an extension or template developer, using Joomla for commercial purposes.

1. Read through the license agreement.

2. Click Next **C**.

To configure the web site's database:

On this screen, you'll enter the information Joomla needs to create and write to your web site's database. All site content, media, components, modules, templates, and user information is stored and retrieved from this database. A database makes the site dynamic—retrieving specific information and then compiling it to present a web page to the user.

1. Select an option from the Database Type menu: MySQL or MySQLi **D**.

   In most cases you will want to select MySQLi because it takes advantage of the speed and newer configuration of MySQL version 5. The MySQL option is fine, but it won't leverage the new MySQL 5 features, speed, and optimization.

C The Joomla GPL/GNU licensing agreement

D The database configuration screen

2. In the Host Name field, type **localhost**.

   This name should almost always be localhost, whether you are working on a local server or a hosted server. If this is not the case, you will need to check with your hosting company.

3. In the Username field, type your database user name.

   This is the user name assigned to you by your hosting company, or the one you created in your cPanel setup.

4. In the Password field, type your database user password.

   This is the password generated when you created your database user name.

5. In the Table Prefix field, type a three- to four-digit database prefix.

   The database prefix should not exceed four characters. You can leave the default prefix of *jos_* or change it. Changing the prefix creates a more secure Joomla site.

6. For the Old Database Process, select Backup or Remove. (This step is optional.)

   Do this only if you have an existing Joomla database populated with tables and want to replace them. For a new installation, this should not be necessary.

To configure the FTP settings:

The FTP layer was created to solve server permission errors when installing or using Joomla. It can be used to complete a successful installation or to address the installation of extensions and templates when folder write permissions become an issue. If you have trouble installing due to permissions. Contact your hosting company to resolve these issues.

When your server is configured correctly, you should never need to turn on the FTP layer. In fact, using the FTP layer can result in serious security risks. Enable the FTP layer only if you are having permission issues. Then disable it again, after you're through troubleshooting. You can enable and disable the FTP layer after Joomla is installed.

If you do not know your server FTP information, contact your hosting company.

1. In the Enable FTP Layer pop-up menu, choose No to disable the FTP system layer **E**.

To configure the main site settings:

On this screen you will enter your site information, the site name, and—new to Joomla 1.6—your metadata information. You will create your first Super User account and choose whether or not to install the sample data.

All of the information you enter here, with the exception of the sample data, you can change or modify after installation.

1. In the Site Name field, type the name of your web site **F**.

2. In the Meta Description field, type a short sentence that best describes your web site.

E FTP configuration screen

F The main configuration screen

The Configuration.php File

During installation, Joomla creates a file called configuration.php. This file stores key pieces of information about your web site and database connection that Joomla needs to operate correctly.

If during installation Joomla says it cannot create the file, it will instruct you on how to copy the file and upload it to your server. Problems here are generally caused by permission issues that should be corrected on your web server.

This configuration file can be modified at any time after a successful install.

G Successful installation of the sample data

H After a successful Joomla installation, you are asked to remove the installation folder from your web server.

I The front end of the newly installed Joomla web site

J Remove the installation folder by clicking the Remove Installation folder button.

3. In the Meta Keywords field, type your site's keywords.

This information is used by search engines and search results.

4. In the Admin Email field, type the main email address to be used for this site.

This address is considered the web site's main email address. All email generated from the site will be delivered here.

5. In the Admin Username field, type the user name for this Super User account.

New to Joomla 1.6, and far more secure, is the ability to create a Super User name prior to completing the installation. Earlier versions used *admin* as the default user name, which can cause security issues.

The Super User account created here allows you to log in to both the front and back ends of Joomla.

6. In the Admin Password and Confirm Admin Password fields, type in a password for the Super User account.

7. Click Install Sample Data **G**.

You don't have to install the sample data. However, for the purposes of this book and when first learning Joomla, installing the sample data gives you real-world examples to follow while you learn.

8. Click Next.

The next screen lets you know that Joomla has been installed successfully. But before you can view the site, or log in to the back end, you need to remove the installation folder **H**.

9. Click the Remove Installation folder button to remove the installation directory **I**.

10. Click the Site link **J**.

Accessing the Administration Interface

The Joomla administrative interface is referred to as the back end of your site, whereas the web site displayed for the public is referred to as the front end. The back end is where you create content, install and configure extensions and templates, create users, modify system settings, and so on.

You can add content and perform various functions from the front end of your site; however, most of your work will be done through the administrative back end.

To log in to the back end:

1. Open your web browser and type your web site's URL address.

   In the next step you have two options: If you installed the sample data, a Super User link was already created. Simply click the Site Administrator link in the menu in the left column Ⓐ.

2. If you did not install the sample data, enter your web site URL address in your browser followed by **/administrator**—such as **www.mywebsite.com/administrator**. This opens the administrative login screen.

3. Type the admin user name and password that you created during installation, and then click Login Ⓑ.

   The first screen that appears is the administrative back-end control panel Ⓒ.

Ⓐ The administrator login link

Ⓑ The back-end administrative login page

Ⓒ The administrative back-end interface for Joomla 1.6

Planning a Joomla Site

Web sites are constructed in two forms, static and dynamic. Static sites place content on a single page with a single link to that page. Static web sites—or dynamic sites not using a content management system—require developers with coding and database skills and a full update and maintenance team. Applying a content management system to a dynamic site means that all content, menus, text, media, forms, and so on are contained in a database and can appear on a single page or multiple pages with a simple click of a button.

Content management systems give you a framework with all of the coding in place. You simply add content and create your menus to produce a fully functional web site. So, even though you can start adding content and functionality immediately, don't do it! All web sites require advance planning. If you don't at least plan the fundamental requirements of your site, you will spend many frustrating, wasted hours that can lead to a sense that your web site architecture is too complicated to use.

You should answer these questions before you begin:

- What are the main categories (pages or sections) of your site?

  Identify the main pages of the site and their purpose. Is your site a blog? A catalog? A service? The main categories you create are generally displayed at the top of your web pages and become the main source of navigation.

continues on next page

- What functionality does the site need?

  Do you need registered users? Do you need forms? Do you want a forum? Do you want to integrate social media, and if you do, on which pages?

- Where are you getting your content, and what is the nature of that content?

  Will you have a large number of images or videos? Do you have content planned? Who is writing the content and how should it be organized?

- What branding do you want? Are you going to create a template yourself, or use an existing template? What kind of colors and layout are important to this site?

With Joomla you can create, edit, modify, or delete anything with a single click. You can change the look and feel in an instant. Even so, having this freedom doesn't mean you want to go back and forth undoing and redoing your site. Make a plan, sketch it out, research your site's needs, and then begin.

If you plan well, and learn how to use Joomla correctly and efficiently, creating your web site will be a painless and satisfying experience.

Getting Started

Joomla is not hard to learn, and this book is going to let you in on a little secret: You already know most of what you need to use it. You use the web every day. You use menus to navigate pages. You enter information into forms and submit them. You upload photos and videos to share with friends and family. You know how to interact with web sites, and Joomla is a web site—two sites, actually, the back end for administration, and the front end as displayed to your users.

Learning to use Joomla effectively, you simply need to know where and how to create your site's content and then how to correctly display it. It really is that simple.

This chapter provides a quick tour of the back end to help you become familiar with how to move around and understand the concepts used in Joomla.

In This Chapter

Logging In to Joomla

The first thing you do to begin working with Joomla is log in to the back end. During the installation process, you created the first Super User account when you entered your site admin user name and password. User accounts in the Super User group have full permissions and access to any function that can be performed from either the back or front end.

Joomla installs with eight pre-defined user groups: Public, Manager, Administrator, Author, Editor, Publisher, Registered, and Super User. These groups will be explained in detail in Chapter 10.

To log in to the back end of Joomla:

1. Open your web browser and type your web site address.

   The front end of the web site opens **A**.

   If you installed the sample data during the installation process, the site already contains menus and content.

2. In the This Site menu, click Site Administrator **B**.

   If you did not install the sample content, add **/administrator** to the end of your web site URL.

   The back-end administration login screen appears **C**.

A The front end of the web site

B A link from the front end of the web site to the back end

C Joomla's administrator login form; this logs you in to the back end of Joomla, where you perform site administration.

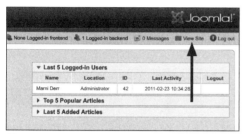

D The Control Panel page

E The View Site button takes you to the front page of your web site in a new window or tab, depending on your browser setup.

3. Type the administrator user name and password you created when installing Joomla, and then click "Log in."

   You are now logged in to the back end of Joomla. The first page that appears when you log in is the Control Panel **D**. This page gives you easy access to the most common tasks you will perform here.

4. To log out of the back end, click Logout on the toolbar.

TIP Although you are logged in to the back end as a Super User and did so by going through the front end, you are not actually logged in to the front end. Joomla, which is a single content management system, functions as if its back and front ends are separate web sites. To log in to the front end, you will need to log in using the web site's login form.

To log in to the front end of Joomla:

1. Log in to the back end of Joomla.

2. In the top toolbar, click the View Site button **E**.

   A new window will open to the front end of your web site. Whenever you are working in the back end, you can quickly view your changes in the front end by clicking the View Site button. This opens a new window or tab in your browser, but does not take you out of the back end.

continues on next page

3. From the front end, enter the Super User name and password in the Login Form, and then click the Log in button **F**.

You should notice a few changes to the front end of the site:

▸ The login form now displays your user name and a "Log out" button **G**.

▸ All the articles have an edit icon (small paper and pencil) above them indicating you have permission to modify them **H**.

Because you are a Super User with full privileges, you can edit, add, or delete content from both the back and front ends of the site.

4. To log out of the front end, click the "Log out" button.

F Front-end login form

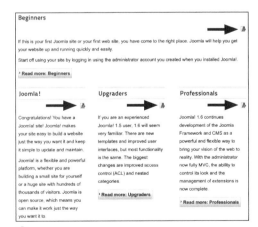

G The login form changes to display the user name and the "Log out" button.

H The front page changes and displays edit icons above each article you can modify.

Using the Control Panel Page

The Control Panel page is always the first page displayed when you log in to the back end of Joomla. Like any web page, the Control Panel consists of menus, toolbars, icons, and site information. The icons are shortcuts to the most common content management tasks and will be explained in detail in later chapters **Ⓐ**.

To return to the Control Panel page at any time:

1. Log in to the back end.

2. Choose Site > Control Panel.

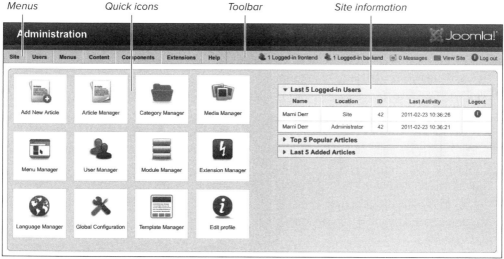

Menus   *Quick icons*   *Toolbar*   *Site information*

Ⓐ The Control Panel page showing the top menu, the toolbar, quick icons, and site information

Viewing Site Information

Site information, as viewed on the Control Panel page, can change depending on which version of Joomla you are using, and what extensions you have installed. The information provided here is just a quick look at your site's status when you first log in.

If you have a site with many different content creators or administrators, this site information can be a handy way to glimpse what is new on the site, what is doing well, and who is contributing most often.

More detailed information can be found under the User and Article managers.

To view the last five logged-in users:

1. Log in to the back end of Joomla.
2. Click the arrow next to "Last 5 Logged-in Users" **A**.

   A list of the five *current* logged-in users appears with the following columns:

   ▸ The Name column displays the user name.

   ▸ The Location column tells you whether the user is logged in to the Site (front end) or Administrator (back end) areas.

   ▸ The ID column displays the user ID number used by the database for this user.

   ▸ The Last Activity column displays the date and time the user logged in.

   ▸ The Logout column allows you to log out the user. Note that you cannot log yourself out of the back end.

TIP The back end toolbar displays the total number of users logged into the front and back ends of the site.

A Last five logged-in users and where they are logged in

B Top five most popular articles on the site based on hit count. The hit count can also be viewed by opening the article.

C Last five articles added to the site through the front or back end based on the date the article was created

To view the top five most popular articles:

1. Log in to the back end.

2. Click the arrow next to "Top 5 Popular Articles" **B**.

   ▸ The Popular Items column displays the name of the article.

   ▸ The Created column displays the date the article was created.

   ▸ The Hits column displays how many hits the article has based on page views.

To view the last five added articles:

1. Log in to the back end.

2. Click the arrow next to "Last 5 Added Articles" **C**.

   ▸ The Latest Items column displays the name of the article.

   ▸ The Published column displays whether the article is published or unpublished.

   ▸ The Created column displays the date and time the article was created.

   ▸ The Created By column displays who created the article.

Using the Main Toolbar

The main toolbar, located at the top of the administration page, is always visible. It displays the number of users logged in to the front and back ends of the web site, displays the number of messages you have, provides a link to view the front end of the web site, and displays the "Log out" button for logging out of the back end.

To view logged-in users:

1. Log in to the back end.

   The top toolbar displays the total number of users logged in to the front end and back ends of your web site **A**.

To view, create, or edit messages:

Joomla's back-end messaging system can be used to communicate with other back-end users and administrators of the web site.

TIP Do not use this messaging system to email all the registered users on your site. Doing so can create serious system performance issues and potentially crash the site.

1. Log in to the back end.

   The top toolbar displays the number of messages waiting in your inbox.

2. Click Messages.

   The Private Messages Manager opens **B**.

TIP Notice the new toolbar. All Joomla managers have their own toolbars. Any options, also referred to as *settings* or *parameters*, are now found by clicking the Options button on their respective manager toolbars.

A The top toolbar with one user logged in to the back end and no users logged in to the front end.

B In the Private Messages Manager, you can view any messages that other administrators send to you from the back end.

In the Write Private Message editor, you can write and send messages to other back-end users.

A pop-up dialog opens to modify your back-end message options.

3. On the toolbar, click New.

   The Write Private Message screen opens ○. Choose a user to send a message, enter the message subject, write the message text, and then click Send. The next time this user logs in to the back end, the message will be waiting.

4. Click Cancel to return to the Private Messages Manager.

5. On the toolbar, click the My Settings button.

   You can customize these settings to manage your messages ○.

6. Make any desired changes to your message settings, and then click Save and Close.

TIP You have the option to click **Save**, which saves your edits but keeps the current screen open, or to click **Save and Close**, which saves your edits and closes the editor window

7. On the toolbar, click the Options button.

   You will find these new access control levels (ACL) options throughout Joomla. Using them, you can create your own groups and user levels and control access to every front- and back-end feature.

TIP You can also access the internal message system by choosing **Components > Messaging.**

Using the Back-End Menus

You can click the quick icons on the Control Panel page or the toolbar menus to navigate through the back end. As you use Joomla, you will develop your own routine for quickly completing tasks. The menus are grouped in a logical manner, giving you immediate access to related tasks within a single menu.

Each menu provides access to managers. Each manager has its own toolbar, setting options, and shortcut links to related managers. Each manager also has options to sort and filter its listed items **Ⓐ**.

> **TIP** Toolbars and menus can change when you install third-party extensions. For example, if you install a new component, the component name will be added to the Components menu.

Manager toolbar   Items   Search filters   Sort columns

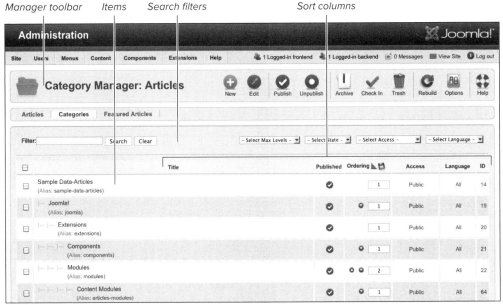

Ⓐ Example of the Category Manager. In managers you create, edit, delete, and view your content, components, templates, and so on.

B The Site menu

C The Users menu

Menus

Menu Manager ▶
User Menu ▶
Top ▶
About Joomla ▶
Australian Parks ▶
Main Menu ⭐ ▶
Fruit Shop ▶ **D** The Menus menu

Here's an overview of each menu and its function:

- Site menu: Manage and configure site maintenance and administration tasks such as viewing your profile, managing global configuration settings, checking in articles, purging the system cache, and displaying system information **B**. The site menu is covered in detail later in this chapter.

- Users menu: Add, edit, and manage your users; create groups; and control access levels on a global level **C**. This menu is new to Joomla 1.6 and later.

- Menus menu: Create and manage all of your menus *modules* and menu *items*. All menus are modules. For example, the first menu is automatically created for you and is always named the Main Menu. You can create an unlimited number of menu modules such as user menu, footer menu, legal menu, and so on. As you add new menu modules, they are added to this list. If you installed the sample data, you will see six menu modules **D**.

TIP The only menu created when you install Joomla without sample data is the Main Menu. All other menus are created by the back-end user.

continues on next page

- Content menu: Create and manage categories, articles, and media 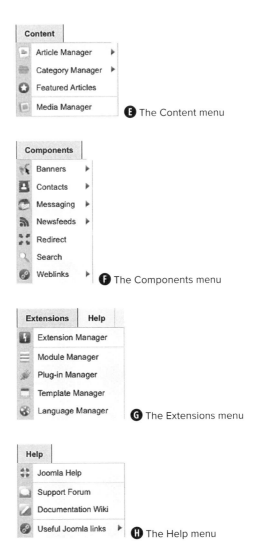.

- Components menu: Access all the components installed on the site, such as banners, newsfeeds, contact lists, and so on. When you add third-party components to Joomla, they are added to this menu 🅕.

- Extensions menu: Install, uninstall, and manage extensions for Joomla, including modules, plugins, templates, and languages 🅖.

- Help menu: Links to help pages on the Joomla.org web site and associated documentation wiki 🅗.

🅔 The Content menu

🅕 The Components menu

🅖 The Extensions menu

🅗 The Help menu

A The Global Configuration screen with links to each of the global configuration setting screens

Modifying Global Configuration Settings

In this section, you will work with several categories of global settings and administrative tools, and learn what they do, and when you need to adjust them. As a general rule, global settings should be configured immediately after installing Joomla. Only permissions and site messages may need to be modified or adjusted later.

Joomla includes four types of global configuration settings: Site, System, Server, and Permissions. It is not common to modify these settings more than once. These global settings for your site control the communication between Joomla, your database, and your web server.

To access the Global Configuration pages:

1. Log in to the back end as a Super User.

2. Choose Site > Global Configuration.

   The Global Configuration Manager opens **A**. A toolbar at the top lets you Save, Save & Close, Cancel, or Find Help.

   Notice the four links on the Global Configuration page: Site, Server, System, and Permissions. These global configurations are directly related to each other. Instead of returning to the toolbar menu each time to change managers, you can switch between related managers using these buttons.

To set or modify site settings:

Site settings are used to manage back-end display settings, site-level metadata, search engine optimization (SEO) URLs, and cookie settings.

1. Choose Site > Global Configuration.

   The site settings page is the first page displayed; the Site link is highlighted .

2. Note that the first field is your Site Name. This name was created when you installed Joomla, but you can change it at any time.

   Joomla uses this name to identify your site in your browser's title bar and site offline message.

3. Select Yes next to Site Offline, and then click Save.

   A message appears, indicating that your changes have been saved .

4. Click View Site.

   Notice the web site now displays the site offline page .

   To view the front end when a site is offline, you must log in. The site will not be available to any user who does not have back-end access.

   This level of security is extremely help-ful when you are first creating a site or when you are updating your site and want to restrict public access.

5. Return to the back end, and select No next to Site Offline, and then click Save.

6. Enter the message you want to appear on your offline page, and then click Save.

   You can customize this page by adding your logo, or you can create a custom offline page. However, building a new page requires knowledge of HTML and CSS.

B The Global Configuration page with Site selected and highlighted to show where you are

C This message shows that your settings have been saved successfully.

D The front end of the web site showing that it is currently offline and cannot be viewed unless you log in as a user with permission to view the site. This is essentially the same as logging in to the front end.

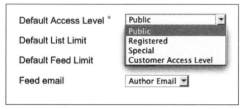

E An image of the TinyMCE editor window

F Selecting the access level for the front end of the site.

7. Click the drop-down list next to Default editor, and you will see three editor choices installed with Joomla. Editors are *plugins* that you can turn on or off through the Plugin Manager.

   The editor you select here becomes the default editor used for both the back and front ends of your web site. You can specify editors on a user level by selecting an editor assigned by user group, or under individual user profiles.

   CodeMirror and No Editor are for those users who are comfortable hand coding their content in HTML.

   TinyMCE is the default editor and looks similar to a word processing program. You do not need to know any HTML to use it. Simply type your text, select a style, and save **E**. Unless you will be hand coding your content, leave this field set to TinyMCE.

8. Click Save when you are done.

TIP You can find more-robust editors in the Joomla extension directory. The editors we recommend most often are JCE Editor, JCK Editor, and CK Editor.

To set the site access level:

1. Choose Site > Global Configuration.

2. Click the Site link.

3. In the Default Access Level field, select the access level of the site.

   Most web sites are available to the public, so this field should not be changed. If however, you have a site that should not have any public access, such as a company intranet, you can change the access level here **F**.

4. On the toolbar, click Save.

To set the default list length for the back end managers:

1. Choose Site > Global Configuration.

2. Click the Site link.

3. In the Default List Limit field, choose the number of items you want to display in the back end managers 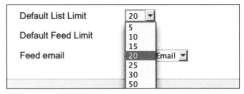.

   Each manager contains a list of items created for the site. If you have hundreds of articles, the Article Manager lists can become quite long. The default setting for all manager lists displays only 20 items. By using the pagination at the bottom of each page, you could view the next 20, then the next, and so on .

   You can set the default value up to 100 items. In the individual managers, you will find an option to display All items.

4. After setting the global default list length, click the Save button.

To set a default feed limit and feed email for your site:

1. Choose Site > Global Configuration.

2. Click the Site link.

3. In the Default Feed Limit field, choose the number of articles, from 5 to 100 feed items, that you want to display in a subscriber's feed lists.

4. In the "Feed email" field, choose the email you want assigned to the feed. Joomla allows you to choose the site email address, or to use the articles author's email .

G The default list length options

H The article manager page pagination using the default list display of 20 items.

I The feed limit and default article feed email

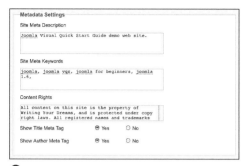

Metadata Settings

Site Meta Description

Joomla Visual Quick Start Guide demo web site.

Site Meta Keywords

joomla, joomla vqs, joomla for beginners, joomla 1.6,

Content Rights

All content on this site is the property of Writing Your Dreams, and is protected under copy right laws. All registered names and trademarks

Show Title Meta Tag   ⊙ Yes   ○ No

Show Author Meta Tag   ⊙ Yes   ○ No

J The global (site-wide) metadata settings

To set or modify metadata settings:

1. Choose Site > Global Configuration.

2. Click the Site link.

   Below the site settings, you will see fields in which you can enter your site's default metadata **J**.

   This information is placed in the header of your HTML pages as your global meta-data and indexed by search engines. You can also insert metadata at the content level, so keep the information set here to concise, descriptive summaries.

3. In the Site Meta Description text field, enter a one or two sentence description of your site.

   This information is used by search engines and normally is the short description displayed beneath your site's title search results.

4. In the Site Meta Keywords text field, enter site keywords, separated by commas.

   You can enter as many keywords as you want; however, search engines and Joomla usually index only the first 30 keywords from this field.

5. In the Content Rights text field, enter a brief message describing content copyright information required for your web site.

6. For Show Title Meta Tag and Show Author Meta Tag, do one of the following:

   ▸ Select Yes to show your site's title metatags and/or author metadata when viewing content on your site.

   ▸ Select No if you do not want titles and author information to be included in the metatags when viewing content on the site.

7. Click Save when you are done.

To set or modify SEO settings:

These settings control how your URLs look to search engines and your viewers.

1. Choose Site > Global Configuration.

2. Click the Site link.

3. Under SEO Settings, select Yes or No for the following options **K**:

   ▸ Search Engine Friendly URLs: Select Yes to create a URL in your browser's address bar that is more easily read by search engines

     For example, choosing this option would change this URL—http://joomlavqs.writingyourdreams.com/index.php?option=com_content&view=article&id=22&Itemid=437—to this URL: http://joomlavqs.writingyourdreams.com/index.php/getting-started.

   ▸ Use Apache mod_rewrite: Set this to Yes to allow the Apache rewrite script to transform your URLs into search engine-friendly addresses.

     You can choose this option only if your server configuration has Apache mod_rewrite turned on and if you have renamed your htaccess.txt file to *.htaccess*. Talk with your hosting provider if you turn this feature on and receive "404 Page not found" or "500 Page not found" error messages.

   ▸ Adds Suffix to URL: Setting this to Yes most commonly adds *.html* to the end of your pages instead of *.php*.

     For example, the previously mentioned URL would be changed to

     http://joomlavqs.writingyourdreams.com/index.php/getting-started.html.

SEO Settings

Search Engine Friendly URLs
  ◉ Yes   ○ No

Use Apache *mod_rewrite*
  ○ Yes   ◉ No

Adds Suffix to URL
  ○ Yes   ◉ No

Unicode Aliases
  ○ Yes   ◉ No

Include Site Name in Page Titles
  ◉ Yes   ○ No

K The global SEO settings

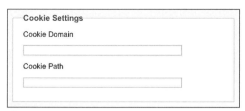

Cookie Settings

Cookie Domain

Cookie Path

L The global cookie settings

| Site | System | Server | Permissions |

System Settings

Secret *   DrYa7rGE5reCkrNt

Path to Log Folder * /home/writingy/public_html/joomlaVQS/logs

Help Server *   English (CB) - Joomla help wiki

M The global system settings

- ▸ Unicode Aliases: Set this to Yes to use Unicode aliases rather than transliteration aliases.
- ▸ Include Site Name in Page Titles: Set this to Yes to include your site name in the URL along with the page titles.

4. Click Save when you are done.

To set or modify cookie settings:

1. Choose Site > Global Configuration.

2. Click the Site link.

3. Under Cookie Settings, enter the cookie domain and path **L**.

Enter these URLs only if you're confident that you understand what will happen.

To set or modify system settings:

1. Choose Site > Global Configuration.

2. Click the System link.

The Global Configuration Settings page opens, in which you can set system, debug, cache, and session settings.

3. *Do not* change the Secret field! This field is auto-generated by Joomla and used as an extra security measure to protect your site. Only advanced users who are moving, fixing, or trouble-shooting a broken site should alter this field **M**.

4. The Path to Log Folder stores Joomla error logs. To add another layer of security to your site, you can create a different folder to contain your log files. You will need to create the directories to change this field.

5. Only one help server is available at this time. Leave the Help Server field at the default setting.

To set or modify the debug settings:

1. Choose Site > Global Configuration.

2. Click the System link.

3. Under Debug Settings, select Yes if you want Joomla to display debugging errors and information .

   Doing so will display a debugging report in the Debug position on both the back and front ends of your web site. This is useful when your site is experiencing problems because it can alert you to the cause. Generally, you want to turn this on only to identify and troubleshoot a problem issue. Other-wise, turn off this setting.

4. If you are using language packs in the back end, you can set Debug Language to Yes.

   Set Debug Language to No when you're not troubleshooting.

To set or modify system cache settings:

The correct cache settings can speed up the load time of your site. When users are viewing the site, their browser's cache retains specific information that can accelerate navigating and loading your site because not all of the system files are loaded from the server.

Always leave the cache turned off when you are developing your site or else changes you make in the back end may not display on the front end due to the system cache.

You can also turn on a system-cache plugin—located in the Plugin Manager—when your site is completed.

1. Choose Site > Global Configuration.

2. Click the System link .

Ⓝ The debug settings

Ⓞ The system cache settings

P The system session settings tell Joomla how long a logged-in user can be inactive before being automatically logged out of the system.

Q The server settings. Most of these settings should never need to be modified. Doing so can cause you to lose communication with your database.

3. Set the Cache field to "Off - no cache," or "On - progressive" or " On - conservative" cache modes.

4. The Cache Handler menu cannot be changed at this time. Leave the default value, File.

5. In the Cache Time field, set the number of minutes you want the site files to be cached. An acceptable value is 15 minutes.

To set or modify session settings:

Session settings set the length of time a user can be inactive on the front or back end of the web site before being logged out.

1. Choose Site > Global Configuration.

2. Click the System link.

3. In the Session Lifetime field, enter a number of minutes until a user is automatically logged out due to inactivity **P**.

4. Leave the Session Handler menu set to Database.

To set or modify server settings:

Server settings configure communication between Joomla, your database, and your server. These settings were configured when you installed Joomla and should not need modification.

1. Choose Site > Global Configuration.

2. Click the Server link **Q**.

continues on next page

3. The Path to Temp Folder setting determines where Joomla stores temporary information to aid in installing or uninstalling new extensions or scripts. To add another layer of security to your site, you can create a different folder to contain your temp files. You will need to create the directories before you change this field.

4. Set the Gzip Page Compression setting to Yes to improve site performance if supported by your server configuration.

5. For Error Reporting, select the level you want Joomla to perform to alert you to possible problem issues.

6. Set Force SSL to On if you are selling products or collecting information from your users that must be protected. You will need to have an SSL certificate installed on your server.

7. Set the Server Time Zone to the time zone where your server is located.

8. Do not use the FTP Settings unless you are forced to do so as a result of permission errors. The appropriate FTP information can be provided to you by your hosting company. Turning on the FTP layer can cause security vulnerabilities to your site.

9. Do not change the Database Settings. These are needed by Joomla to communicate with your database.

10. The Mail Settings fields identify emails sent from the system. You will need to check with your email provider to change these settings.

A The global check-in page

Performing Site Maintenance

Site maintenance is performed for checking in articles and clearing your system cache. When you have more than one user managing your site, items such as modules, categories, and even articles are locked if someone is currently modifying them. As a result, two people cannot make changes to the same thing at the same time. Sometimes modified items are not correctly saved or are left in a "locked" state. When this occurs, and you are sure no one is working with those items, you can go to the Maintenance menu and check everything in at one time.

Clearing your system cache is important whether you have caching turned on or off, because even with caching turned off, some items become cached. Changes you make while working on your site may not be reflected on the front end. If this happens, go to the Maintenance menu and clear the entire system cache at once.

TIP We recommend that you leave caching turned off while a site is in development. Once a site is live, turning on the system cache helps speed up page load times.

To check in items:

1. Choose Site > Maintenance.

2. Click Global Check-in.

3. Select all items, or select specific items from the list.

   Notice the column on the right. This column displays the number of items that are still checked out for any of the content tables in your database **A**.

continues on next page

4. On the toolbar, click the Check In button.

5. On the toolbar, click the Options button.

   You can set permissions to identify which user groups have permission to check in items.

To purge the system cache:

1. Choose Site > Maintenance.

2. Click Clear Cache.

3. Select those items you wish to clear from the systems cache.

   Clicking Clear Cache will list all items contained in the Joomla system cache. Clicking Purge Expired Cache will delete all items that are still cached but have reached or exceeded the cache time limit **B**.

4. On the toolbar, click the Options button to assign permissions to users who are allowed to delete the systems cache or expired cache.

B The Clear Cache page

A You can view your entire server configuration from the System Information pages.

Viewing System Information

If you have come this far and Joomla is installed, chances are your server is configured correctly. At times, however, another server package or configuration is needed to run additional extensions. If you need to check your server configuration and verify your settings at any time, you'll want to review your current system information.

To view your current system information:

1. Choose Site > System Information.
2. Click the buttons to view the following information **A**:
   - System Information: Display your server software versions and configuration.
   - PHP Settings: Display any relevant PHP settings currently residing on your web server.
   - Configuration File: Display the information contained in your Joomla configuration.php file. This file contains all the necessary information for Joomla to communicate with your server and database, your Super User account, and all other information in your Global Configuration settings.

continues on next page

- ▸ Directory Permissions: Display your directories and files to verify that they have the proper settings. If you are having trouble installing or using extensions and a permission issue is reported, you can look up those permissions here.
- ▸ PHP Information: Display all the information necessary to discover any php.ini settings or .php web server configuration settings. This comes in handy if an extension requires a .php package or mod that is not turned on or installed on your server.

Creating Categories

Categories in Joomla help organize and control your site structure and content (articles). With the introduction of nested categories in Joomla 1.6, a single category can contain multiple children or subcategories each with its own subcategories. However, a single category cannot be assigned to more than one parent (root) category. Before adding a lot of content to your site, you should create your categories.

This chapter shows you how to create, edit, remove, and manage categories and how to control category page layouts. Then you will create menu items so they display on your web pages and help you further control category layouts.

TIP If you installed the Joomla sample data, numerous category examples are already available to you.

In This Chapter

Using the Category Manager

Using the Category Manager, you can create, edit, and organize all categories on your site. The category options in the Category Manager allow you to set global layout options and control what, if any, category information is displayed on a page. Once a category is created and published, you can assign subcategories and articles to it.

Although categories can organize your articles, they do not automatically become menu items. You need to manually create category menu items before a category or its articles will appear on a page.

To open the Category Manager:

1. Log in to the back end of the site.

2. Choose Content > Category Manager, or on the Control Panel page, click the Category Manager quick icon.

   The Category Manager displays a toolbar, links to the Article and Featured Articles Managers, and a list of every category created on the site **Ⓐ**.

Ⓐ The Category Manager shown with the sample data installed

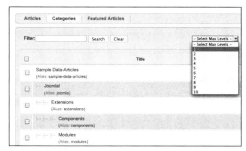

B Category Manager pagination and display options

C Sorting by Max Level tells Joomla to display only level 1 or root categories in the Category Manager.

D The list sorted to display only level 1 categories

To sort, filter, or search categories:

1. Open the Category Manager.

2. Scroll to the bottom of the Category Manager screen.

   All manager lists are controlled by the site global configuration settings. The default list length for all managers is 20 items. This means that the page will display only 20 categories at a time. Using the navigation controls at the bottom of the screen, you can either change the total number of categories displayed, or navigate using the pagination buttons **B**.

   If the Joomla sample data is installed, you have 25 categories. To view all the categories at once, you need to change the display options to All.

3. In the Display # field, choose All.

   The Category Manager now displays all the categories, published or unpublished.

4. From the Select Max Levels drop-down list, choose 1 **C**.

   The Category Manager now displays only level 1 or root categories, even though the list display number is set to All **D**.

continues on next page

All managers have the ability to sort or filter what appears on the page, which makes it easy to navigate very large sites with long lists of content. The category filter options are:

▸ **Max Level:** Filter by the categories level, relative to all other categories.

▸ **Access:** Filter by access level: public, registered, or special. Included in this group are any custom user groups you create.

▸ **Language:** Filter categories by language type. Any language installed and active will appear in this list.

5. Return the Select Max Levels drop-down list to Select Max Levels so that all categories are displayed.

6. In the Category Manager, click the Title column heading.

   In addition to filtering categories, you can sort categories by clicking the Title column, which displays the categories by title in ascending order **E**. This is helpful when you're trying to locate a specific category in the list.

7. Click the Ordering column heading.

   The category list is once again sorted by the actual ordering of the categories **F**.

   Notice that the ascending icon has moved from the Title column to the Ordering column. The icon indicates which column is currently controlling the sort order of the categories. Any column can be used to sort the categories.

TIP Click a column heading a second time to toggle the sort order from ascending to descending (or vice versa).

E You can sort categories in ascending or descending alphabetical order by clicking the Title column.

F Category Manager Ordering column

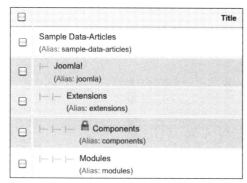

G The Components category is currently locked and cannot be edited.

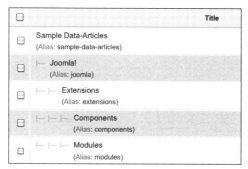

H The Components category is checked in and available for editing.

I The batch process fields allow you to move or copy selected categories in the Category Manager.

To check in categories:

1. Open the Category Manager.

   Two people cannot work on the same category simultaneously. If someone else has a category open, a locked icon will appear next to the category title **G**.

   Occasionally, when you open a category and exit your browser or your session times out, the system may leave the category in a locked state.

   To remove a lock on a category, you need to check in the category.

2. Select the checkbox next to any category with a lock symbol next to its title.

3. On the toolbar, click the Check In icon.

   The Component category is checked in and made available for editing **H**.

   The only time you want to check in items is when they were accidently locked and you are sure no one else is currently working on them.

To move or copy one or more categories:

1. Open the Category Manager.

2. Scroll to the bottom of the screen to the area titled "Batch process the selected categories."

   You can copy or move a category or a selection of categories to another place in the category structure **I**. This can save time when you want to duplicate category details and settings without using an existing category, or when you choose to move subcategories to another parent.

continues on next page

3. Select the checkbox next to the Recipes category.

When moving or copying categories, you must select them from the list.

4. Under "Batch process the selected categories," leave the Set Access Level at "Keep original Access Levels" (the default value).

Access-level batch processing allows you to change the access levels of multiple categories at once.

5. From the "Select Category for Move/Copy" drop-down list, choose "Add to Root."

The selection field is used for selecting the category or categories to be moved or copied. This field tells Joomla where to move or copy the categories marked in the list **J**.

By choosing "Add to Root," you will copy or move the category to the root, that is, make a level 1 parent category.

6. Click the Copy radio button.

7. Click Process.

The category Recipes is copied and becomes a level 1 root category **K**.

Leaving the category name and alias the same as an existing category is not a good idea, so you would normally give the copied category a new name and alias.

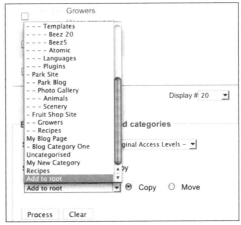

J Choosing "Add to Root" and clicking the Copy radio button copies the category selected in the list and creates a root or parent category.

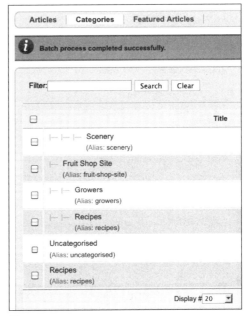

K The Recipes category copied and added as a root category

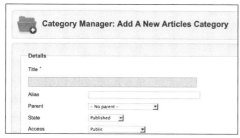

A The Add a New Articles Category details screen

Creating a New Category

When first creating your categories, map out a site plan in advance. Think about the names. Do they help define the articles they will contain? Are they short but descriptive enough to be used for search engine friendly URLs? If they will be used for menus, are the titles clear enough for a user to understand?

Changing a category name (title) and alias is easy and your articles and links will update automatically; however, the name change will not be reflected if you used the category name as the menu name. If you change a category's title here, you will need to change the menu item of the same name.

Modifying categories and menus during the initial stages of development is expected, but the clearer your site map, the fewer changes you will have to make later.

To create a new category:

1. Log in to the back end.

2. Open the Category Manager.

3. On the toolbar, click New to open the Category Manager: Add A New Articles Category screen Ⓐ.

4. In the Title field, type a name for the new category.

5. Leave the Alias field blank. Joomla will use the category name as the alias.

   If you want to create your own alias, you can enter it in this field. An alias is used with the SEF URL feature in Joomla. An alias must be in lowercase letters with the words separated by a hyphen (-).

6. Leave Parent set to "No parent" to create a root category, or select the parent of this category to create a subcategory.

continues on next page

7. Set the State to Published.

Unpublished categories do not appear on the site.

8. Set the Access to Public.

Setting the access level for a category determines who has access to *view* this category and all articles assigned to it.

The Set Permissions button determines who can *change or edit* this category.

TIP **Access levels and permissions affect all categories assigned to a parent category.**

9. Leave the Language set to All.

10. Note the ID field, which is filled in by Joomla and identifies this category in the database. The ID is automatically created when you save a new category.

11. Click Save.

The new category is saved, the user-name of the person who created the category is filled in under Publishing options, the Created Date is set by the system, and this category is assigned an ID **B**.

Title is the only required field when creating a category. All other fields are automatically filled in by Joomla, or are optional to use the category.

12. On the toolbar, click Save & Close.

This saves the new category and returns to the Category Manager. The newly created category appears in the list **C**.

You also have the option of choosing the following:

▸ **Save & New:** Saves the category, closes the editing window, and then opens a new category editing window in which you can create another category.

B The category details fields

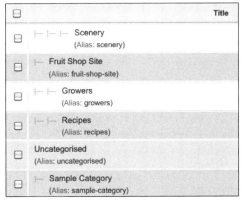

C The newly saved category listed in the Category Manager

D The category description uses the core Joomla TinyMCE editor, which functions like a basic word processing program.

E The Extension category description displays at the top of the page.

F Selecting the word "Joomla!" and then clicking the B (Bold) button in the editor will write the HTML code necessary to style the word as boldface.

▸ **Save as Copy:** Saves the current category and then creates a copy with all the same category settings.

▸ **Close:** Closes this category without saving the most recent changes and returns to the Category Manager.

To add a category description:

1. Open the Category Manager.

2. Select the checkbox next to the Extensions subcategory.

3. On the toolbar, click Edit.

   The Extensions category has a brief description of this category. You can set category descriptions to show or hide in the front end of the web site.

   The description box is currently using the TinyMCE editor that comes with Joomla and looks similar to a word processing application **D**.

   You can click the buttons in the editor to style your text content without knowing any HTML code.

4. In the administrator toolbar, click View Site.

5. In the About Joomla menu, choose Using Joomla, and then choose Using Extensions.

   Using Extensions is the menu item name for the Extensions category. Notice the category description at the top of the page **E**.

6. Return to the Extensions category details screen in the back end.

7. In the first sentence of the description, select the word "Joomla!" and click the B (bold) button in the description editor window **F**.

continues on next page

8. Click Save.

9. Return to the front end of the site and click your browser's refresh button.

Without knowing any code, you applied the bold tag to the word "Joomla!" **G**.

10. Return to the back-end Extensions category description.

11. Near the bottom of the editor window, click the Toggle Editor button.

If you are comfortable coding in HTML, you can toggle the editor window and type HTML code directly **H**.

A category description can contain text, links, another article, an embedded image, or nothing at all. A category does not require a description.

12. Click Save & Close.

To edit category publishing options:

1. Open the Category Manager.

2. Click the Components category title.

You can click a category's title to open and edit the category.

3. Click the arrow next to the title, Publishing Options.

Publishing options tell you who created the category, the date it was created, the person who last modified the category, and the date it was modified **I**.

You cannot change the created, modified by, or modified dates for a category.

4. Click Select User to open a window that lists all the users created for the site **J**.

G The word "Joomla!" in the category description is now bolded.

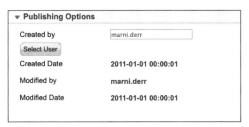

H The editor window displaying pure HTML code

I The category Publishing Options

J The Select User window lists every user who has an account on the site.

Publishing Options

Created by	Tanya Symes
Select User	
Created Date	2011-01-01 00:00:01
Modified by	**marni.derr**
Modified Date	2011-01-01 00:00:01

🅚 The new author is assigned as the creator of this category.

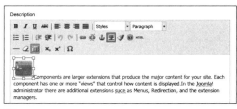

🅛 The category editor with the image highlighted. Clicking the image button opens the image details.

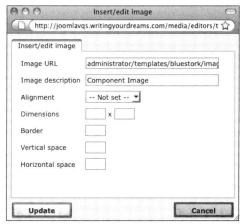

🅜 The image details editor window. Here you can set the image properties for any image embedded in the description.

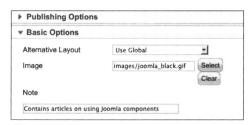

🅝 The basic options for a category

5. Select another user from the list.

As soon as you select another author's name, it is immediately applied 🅚.

6. Click Save & Close.

To set category basic options:

1. Open the Category Manager.

2. Select the Components category title.

You have two ways to add an image to a category:

▸ An image added to description text will display in the category description.

▸ An image added using the basic options will display an image next to or above the category title.

3. Click the image in the category description, and then in the editor, click the image button 🅛.

An image added to the category description is considered an embedded image. You can set this image to display above or to the left or right of the category description.

The image details window opens 🅜.

4. Click Cancel to exit the window.

5. Click the arrow next to Basic Options to open the category basic options.

Here you can choose an alternate layout for this category, select an image, and add a note that describes this category to your back-end users 🅝.

6. Leave Alternative Layout set to Use Global, the default value.

continues on next page

7. Next to the Image field, click the Select button.

   All images available to your categories and articles are contained in the Joomla Media Manager **O**. You can upload media via the Media Manager, or when you are editing a category or article.

8. In the Media Manager, select joomla_black.gif, and then click Insert.

9. On the toolbar, click Save & Close.

10. Click View Site.

11. In the About Joomla menu, choose Using Joomla > Using Extensions > Components.

    If you installed the sample data and have not modified any category options, you will see only the category description and its embedded image. This is because the global options currently are set to hide the parent category title and image.

12. Return to the Category Manager.

13. On the toolbar, click Options to open the global layout options window.

    These settings control the global layout options for all your content. Each of these global settings can be set globally, individually at the article level, or at the menu item level. These options will be discussed later. For now, you simply want to display the image that you attached to the Components category **P**.

14. Select the Category tab.

15. Set the Category Image to Show.

16. Click Save & Close.

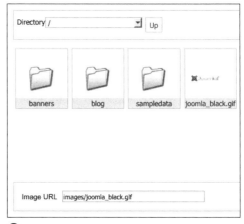

O The Media Manager stores all images to be used in your site content.

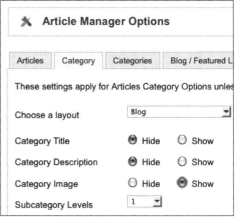

P The global content options. Setting the Category Image to Show displays the image attached to the category in the front end of the site.

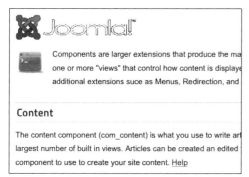

Components are larger extensions that produce the ma
one or more "views" that control how content is displaye
additional extensions suce as Menus, Redirection, and

Content

The content component (com_content) is what you use to write ar
largest number of built in views. Articles can be created an edited
component to use to create your site content. Help

Q An image attached to a category displays above the category description.

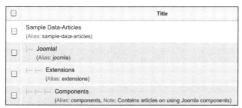

R Notes can be added to categories to inform administrators and content creators about the types of content a category can contain, or any other information you want to attach to this category.

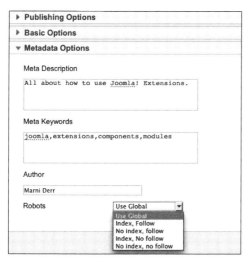

S In the category Metadata Options, you can set metadata information for this category.

17. Return to the front end of the site and refresh your browser window.

The Components category image is displayed above the category description **Q**.

18. Return to the back-end Components category detail page.

19. In Basic Options, click Clear to remove the current image attached to this category.

20. In the Note field, type an administrator description for this category.

21. Click Save & Close.

The note you entered is displayed next to the category's alias. Notes can help alert administrators to the types of articles this category should contain **R**.

To set category metadata options:

1. Open the Category Manager.

2. Select the Extensions category to open it.

3. Click the arrow next to Metadata Options.

Search engines use metadata to index your site content. Having descriptive and accurate metadata can improve your site's search engine results **S**.

4. In the Meta Description field, type a short but descriptive sentence describing this category.

5. In the Meta Keywords field, enter keywords that accurately describe this category and its articles.

6. In the Author field, enter the name of the author you want associated with this category.

7. In the Robots menu, choose the appropriate search engine robot setting.

8. Click Save & Close.

Removing Categories

In the Category Manager you can unpublish, archive, or completely delete any categories. However, these actions affect all subcategories beneath a parent category. Deleting a parent category will remove subcategories and their associated articles.

For example, if you had a parent category of Joomla that contained extensions and modules as subcategories, and these subcategories contained more subcategories, everything below the Joomla category would become unpublished. Likewise, if you delete a parent category, subcategories will also be deleted.

Archiving a category does not remove it from appearing on the site, but you would need to create a new menu item that links to those archived categories to display them on the site.

To unpublish a category:

1. Log in to the back end and open the Category Manager.

2. In the Joomla category's Published column, select the checkmark circled in green.

   To unpublish a category, you can select the checkmark or the checkbox next to a category and then click the Unpublish icon on the toolbar. Both options will unpublish the category and all subcategories beneath the parent category .

3. Click View Site.

   The site now displays no content on the Home page because you unpublished the category that contained those articles .

A The Category Manager lists all the unpublished categories and their subcategories.

B Unpublished categories and their associated articles no longer display on the web site.

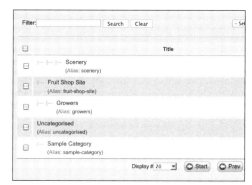

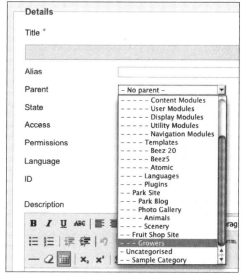

C The Recipes category, after it's set to an archived state, will no longer be listed in the Category Manager with published and unpublished categories.

D An archived category will not appear as a selection when creating new categories.

4. Return to the Category Manager and publish the Joomla category.

   When you begin site development, or even when you are creating new content for a live site, there will be times that you don't want to provide access to content until it is complete or approved by other administrators. Using the unpublish feature ensures that no one on the front end has access to content that is not approved for display on the site.

To archive a category:

1. Open the Category Manager.

2. Select the checkbox next to the Recipes category.

3. In the toolbar, click Archive.

   Recipes is no longer listed as a category in the Category Manager **C**.

4. In the Category Manager, click New to open the "Add new category" page.

5. Open the Parent drop-down menu.

   The Recipes category can no longer be selected as a parent category. This is because you cannot assign categories to an archived category. You also will not be able to assign articles to this category **D**.

   Any subcategories or articles assigned to Recipes have been archived. The only way to view them is to create a menu item to display archived content. The only way to add content to an archived category is to return its status to Published.

6. Return to the Category Manager.

continues on next page

7. From the State drop-down list, choose Archived **E**.

   An Archived category does not display with the Published and Unpublished categories, but you can still access archived items using the Select State sort options.

   Notice the archive icon in the Published column for Recipes. You can publish or unpublish a category by clicking the Publish or Unpublished button in the Published column. You cannot, however, archive a category by clicking this button. When you click the archive icon in the Publish column, it will only unpublish the archived category.

8. Select the checkbox next to the archived Recipes category, and then click Publish on the toolbar.

   The Recipes category and any articles or subcategories assigned to it are returned to a published state.

To delete a category:

1. Open the Category Manager.

2. Select the checkbox next to the Fruit Shop Site category.

3. In the toolbar, click Trash.

   The Fruit Shop Site category and all its subcategories are sent to the trash.

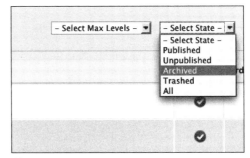

E To view archived categories, sort the Category Manager to view any categories in an archived state.

F Categories displayed with a trash icon in the Published column

4. From the State drop-down list, choose Trashed.

The categories display with a trash icon in the Published column to show that they are no longer viewable on the site but are in the trash **F**.

You now have two options: to return the category to a published or unpublished state, or to remove it completely from the database.

Generally, Joomla will not allow you to accidentally delete a category that contains articles, but do not rely on this safety measure. Anything can happen and when you click the Empty Trash button it cannot be undone.

If you receive a warning and still want to delete a category that contains articles, you will first need to delete the articles in the Article Manager and then delete the category.

5. To completely remove the category, select the checkbox next to its title, and then click the Empty Trash button on the toolbar.

To recover a trashed category:

1. Open the Category Manager.

2. From the State drop-down list, choose Trashed.

3. Select the checkbox next to any categories you want restored, and on the toolbar, click Publish.

Linking to a Category Page Using Menus Items

The most important thing to understand when using a content management system is that content will not appear on a site until a menu item is created to call that content from the database and display it.

Categories contain article content, but it is not necessary to have articles in your categories to display them. There are also two ways to control what and how your category content will display, through the category global options, and in the actual menu item itself.

You can create three types of menu items for categories: A list that displays all categories and their descriptions; a blog that displays categories, their descriptions and articles; and a category list that displays all categories in a table.

To create a category menu item:

1. Log in to the back end.

2. Choose Menus > About Joomla.

   Menus are modules that contain menu items (links). Choosing the About Joomla menu opens the Menu Item Manager displaying all menu items assigned to the About Joomla menu module .

3. Choose Using Extensions to open the Menu Manager: Edit Menu Item window.

   The Menu Item Type field shows that this menu item is a List All Categories type. The Menu Title is Using Extensions .

Ⓐ The Menu Item Manager for the About Joomla menu module

Ⓑ The Menu Item Type is List All Categories.

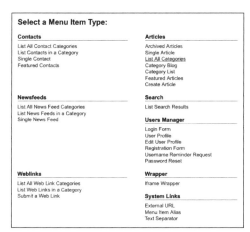

Select a Menu Item Type:

Contacts
List All Contact Categories
List Contacts in a Category
Single Contact
Featured Contacts

Newsfeeds
List All News Feed Categories
List News Feeds in a Category
Single News Feed

Weblinks
List All Web Link Categories
List Web Links in a Category
Submit a Web Link

Articles
Archived Articles
Single Article
List All Categories
Category Blog
Category List
Featured Articles
Create Article

Search
List Search Results

Users Manager
Login Form
User Profile
Edit User Profile
Registration Form
Username Reminder Request
Password Reset

Wrapper
Iframe Wrapper

System Links
External URL
Menu Item Alias
Text Separator

C The menu item selection pop-up window allows you to choose the menu item type. This window changes as you add or extend Joomla using extensions.

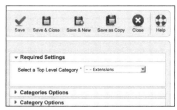

D When selecting a menu item type of List All Categories, you are required to select the top level category.

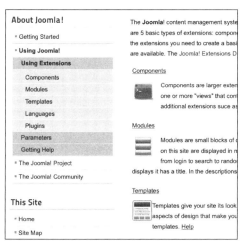

E An example of a List All Categories menu item type on the web site

4. Click the Select button.

When creating a new menu item or editing an existing menu item, clicking Select opens all available menu item types **C**.

TIP When you install extensions, any menu item type associated with the extension is added to the menu item list.

5. Close the pop-up window and return to the Using Extensions menu item.

Under Required Settings, the "Select a Top Level Category" menu is set to Extensions. This is the category name and the parent category for the list **D**.

When creating a list of all category menu items, you can select only the parent category for the categories you want displayed. Notice, however, that while the category name is "Extensions," the menu item name is "Using Extensions." You can assign any name to a menu item. Joomla does not automatically use the category name, although it is best practice to maintain some similarity between the category title and its menu item title.

6. Click View Site.

7. In the About Joomla menu, choose Using Joomla > Using Extensions.

This is an example of a List All Categories menu item and shows how the page displays. With Extensions set as the top level category, any subcategory beneath Extensions appears in the list **E**.

The parent category of Extensions is Using Joomla, but because Extensions is set by the menu item as the top level to display, Using Joomla does not appear in the list. Because the menu item type is a list of categories, articles assigned to these categories also do not display on the page.

continues on next page

8. Return to the Menu Item Manager and open the Components menu item.

The Components menu item type is a Category Blog layout **F**. In a category blog layout, you are required to select only a single parent category or subcategory. However, only articles assigned to the selected category and its subcategories will display **G**.

9. Click View Site.

10. In the About Joomla menu, choose Using Joomla > Using Extensions > Components.

A category blog menu item displays the top category description or title at the top of the page and a specified number of articles assigned to this category **H**.

11. Return to the Menu Item Manager.

F An example of the Components Category Blog menu item details

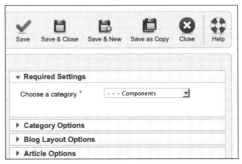

G To create a category blog menu item, you need to link to only one category, and it can be any level, root, parent, or subcategory.

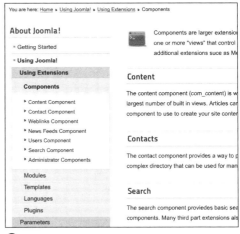

H An example of a category blog layout on the site

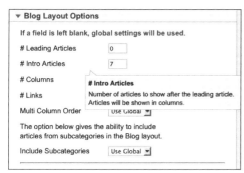

I Category blog layouts require you to define how many articles will appear on the page.

J When creating a category list layout, you define what column data to display.

K An example of a category list menu item type on the web site

12. Click the arrow next to Blog Layout Options.

The Components menu item, and therefore the page, is set to display seven intro articles **I**.

The settings for each menu item allow you total control over the category and articles that will appear on a page and how they will display.

13. Close the Components Menu Item edit page and open the Article Category List menu item.

A category list menu item does not have blog layout options because list layouts present your categories or articles in a tabular list format. The list layout options are directly related to the columns of data you want displayed **J**.

14. Click View Site.

15. In the About Joomla menu, choose Using Joomla > Using Extensions > Components > Content Component > Article Category List **K**.

Putting It All Together

1. **Map out your category structure.** You can start adding categories and subcategories immediately using the Category Manager. However, it is best to map out your main content categories before you begin.

2. **Create your categories.** Use the Category Manager to create parent categories and subcategories. Remember, you can move categories around using the Batch Process feature.

3. **Create menu items for your categories.** If your content is to display on the web site, you need to create menu items that link to your categories.

Adding Articles

Articles make up 90 percent of your site content. While site content is usually thought of as text and images, articles can also contain forms, video, entire photo galleries, links, modules, and even custom scripts such as Google or Facebook widgets. Any type of web medium can be placed into an article and placed on your site.

In this chapter, you'll learn how to create articles and assign them to categories, how to add media using the Media Manager and your editor, and how to control the display of articles using article menus.

Using the Article Managers

The Article Manager is directly connected to your Category and Featured Article Managers and allows you to navigate between them while developing content for your site.

The one requirement when creating articles is that all articles must be assigned to a category, so you first need to create your categories. Without categories, you will not be able to save an article. If you haven't chosen your categories, you can assign articles to the uncategorised category.

To use the Article Manager:

1. Log in to the back end.

2. Choose Content > Article Manager, or click the Article Manager icon on the Control Panel page.

   The Article Manager: Articles opens with links to Articles, Categories, and Featured Articles Managers **A**.

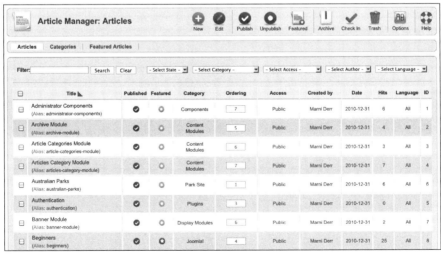

A The Article Manager: Articles with links to the Categories and Featured Article Managers

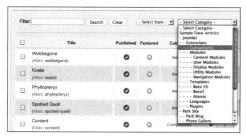

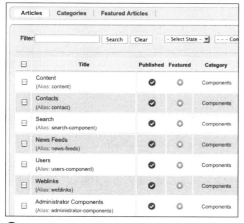

B Selecting a category from the Select Category sort field will sort the Article Manager to display only those articles directly assigned to a single category.

C The Article Manager displaying only articles assigned to the Components category

In the Article Manager you can create, edit, publish, unpublish, archive, check in, or delete any article created for the site.

Featured articles are simply articles you have marked as featured. A featured article is listed in both the Article Manager and the Featured Article Manager.

To sort, filter, or search articles:

1. Open the Article Manager.

   Because a site generally contains numerous articles, you'll usually want to apply the sort and filter options in the Article Manager. Like all managers, you can use either the sort fields or the column headings to do so, and sort the article lists by State, Category, Access Level, Author, or Language.

2. From the Select Category drop-down list, choose Components **B**.

   The Article Manager now displays only those articles assigned to the Components category **C**.

   One thing the sort fields don't do, at the time of this writing, is display articles assigned to subcategories of a selected category.

3. From the Select Category drop-down list, choose Modules.

   No articles are displayed in the Article Manager because no articles are directly assigned to the Modules category. Articles can be assigned to only a single category regardless of whether the category is a parent, child, or grandchild category.

   continues on next page

4. From the Select Category drop-down list, choose Content Modules.

No articles are directly assigned to the parent category Modules, but Content Modules—the subcategory or *child category* of Modules—does have articles assigned. Those articles appear in the list only when the Content Modules category is directly selected.

5. Reset the Select Category drop-down list to Select Category.

6. In the Title column, click the word "Title."

If you are looking for an article and know its category, state, or author, you can click the column headings to sort the list by ascending or descending order. By clicking Title, the articles are now listed alphabetically **D**.

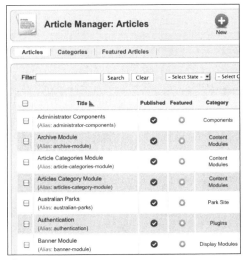

D Click the column headings to sort the articles in ascending or descending order.

Article Manager Columns

- **Title:** The article title.
- **Published:** Shows whether an article is published or unpublished.
- **Featured:** Shows when an article is marked as a featured article.
- **Category:** The category to which an article is assigned.
- **Ordering:** The order of the article relative to its category.
- **Access:** The access level users need to view an article.
- **Created by:** The author of an article.
- **Date:** The date this article was created.
- **Hits:** The number of times an article has been viewed.
- **Language:** The language selected for an article.
- **ID:** The database ID number for an article.

E Using the Filter search field, you can search for one or more words in the title of an article.

F The Featured Article Manager displays only those articles marked as featured.

G Using the pagination feature at the bottom of a manager allows you to choose the number of articles displayed.

7. In the Filter field, type **Article** and then click Search.

   If you know any part of an article's title, you can use the Filter field to search for the article **E**.

8. Click Clear to display all articles again.

9. Click the Featured Articles link to open Article Manager: Featured Articles **F**.

   The Featured Article Manager displays only articles marked as featured. However, all featured articles are also displayed in the Article Manager.

10. Scroll to the bottom of the Article Manager screen.

11. From the Display # drop-down list, choose 10.

   Using the pagination at the bottom of the manager can also help sort article lists for a more manageable display **G**.

Choosing an Editor

In the Article Manager, you can create new articles using a what-you-see-is-what-you-get (WYSIWIG) editor. However, the editors that come with Joomla aren't very good at representing how an article will look on your site. This is because all the styles available in your templates are not fully represented in the standard editors.

Editors are plug-ins, and Joomla comes with three of them. The Code Mirror and No Editor editors are best for hand coding content in HTML. The TinyMCE editor is similar to a word processor, but it's very simplified and limited in its features. More robust third-party editors are available at no cost, and we strongly recommend you try one of them (see "Popular Joomla Editors").

TIP You can install and use more than one editor. However, you should avoid using multiple third-party editors at the same time because you may encounter script conflicts.

To use the Joomla editors:

1. Log in to the back end.

2. Choose Content Article Manager, and open the article titled "Editor."

   TinyMCE editor is the default editor for the site. Wherever you can enter content, this is the editor that is used Ⓐ.

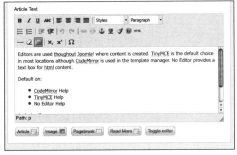

Ⓐ The TinyMCE default editor window

Popular Joomla Editors

- JCE Editor
  (www.joomlacontenteditor.net)

- JCK Editor
  (www.joomlackeditor.com)

- Artof Editor
  (www.theartofjoomla.com)

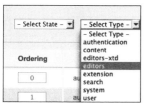

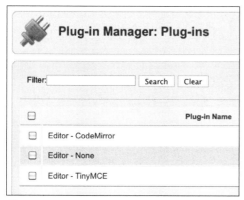

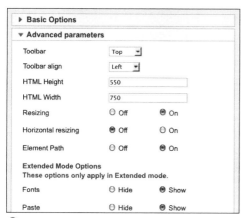

B Sorting the Plug-in Manager to display only Editor plug-ins

C The three editor plug-ins installed with Joomla

D Editor plug-ins have parameter settings you can customize.

3. Close the article, and choose Extensions > Plug-in Manager.

   The Plug-in Manager displays all plug-ins installed on the site. Plug-ins are like mini-applications, such as editors, that work with Joomla features.

4. From the Select Type drop-down list, choose editors **B**.

   This list offers two editor-related choices: editors, which includes all the editors in use by Joomla; and editors-xtd, which are additional features for those editors such as the add image, read more, and page break buttons.

   All three Joomla editors are currently enabled **C**:

   ▸ **Code Mirror:** A pure coding editor. It displays code with tabs, line numbers, and color-highlighted coding.

   ▸ **None:** A plain text editor.

   ▸ **TinyMCE:** The Joomla WYSIWYG editor.

5. Click the Editor-TinyMCE title.

   Editor plug-ins have parameter settings to completely customize the editor for your workflow and level of expertise **D**.

6. Close the TinyMCE editor plug-in.

To install a third-party editor:

1. Download the editor plug-in you want to install.

2. Choose Extensions > Extension Manager.

   The Extension Manager is where you install or uninstall all Joomla components, modules, plug-ins, and templates .

3. Click Browse and locate the editor plug-in on your computer.

4. Click Upload & Install.

   If the plug-in installs successfully, you will see a success message and information about the plug-in .

   Now that you have successfully installed the plug-in, make sure it is enabled.

5. Choose Extension > Plug-in Manager.

6. Sort the list to display only editor plug-ins, by choosing Type > editors.

   Some extensions are enabled during installation; however, you should always verify that a newly installed extension is enabled.

   The Artof Editor is installed and now appears in the Plug-in Manager .

7. In the Enabled column, click the circle to enable the Artof Editor plug-in for use on the site.

   When the Enabled column displays a red and white circle, the plug-in is not enabled.

E In the Extension Manager, you can install or uninstall all Joomla components, modules, plug-ins, and templates.

F Successful installation of the Artof Editor plug-in

G The circle in the Enabled column indicates that the Artof Editor is not enabled.

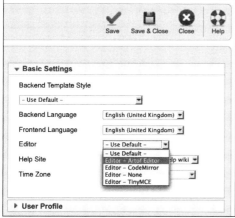

① The My Profile details screen

① Selecting an editor in your My Profile settings

To assign an editor to a user:

1. Log in to the back end as a Super User.

2. Choose Site > My Profile to open your profile details.

    The My Profile link is associated with the user logged in to the back end of the site. To manage other users, you would use the User Manager **①**.

3. Under Basic Settings, choose an editor from the Editor drop-down menu **①**.

    If you do not see the desired editor in the list, it may not be enabled. Enable the editor in the Plug-in Manager.

    You can select an editor on a per user basis, or use the editor that is set as the site default in Global Configuration. By identifying a specific editor in your profile, you change only the editor that *you* use. All other users will still use the default site editor.

4. On the toolbar, click Save & Close.

continues on next page

5. If you want to assign the new editor as the default for both the front and back ends of the entire site, choose it under Site > Global Configuration > Site .

6. Choose Content > Article Manager.

7. Open the article titled "Editors."

The new editor plug-in is installed, enabled, and selected for your profile. Whenever you edit any content on the site—front or back end—this editor will be used Ⓚ.

Ⓙ Selecting the site's default editor

Ⓚ The new, more fully featured Artof editor

L The Template Manager: Customize Template screen

M The default beez_20.css files

N Pointing to the .css file, which contains styles specific to the default template

O The Extended option turns on more features in the TinyMCE editor.

To link an editor to your template styles:

1. Choose Extensions > Template Manager.

2. Choose Templates to open Template Manager: Templates **L**.

3. Scroll down and select the title beez_20 details to list all the index.php and .css files used by the selected template **M**.

   Some editors, but not all, allow you to choose styles from your template so you can apply specific styles directly to your content in the editor. The default file used by the system is editor.css, but most template providers store typography styles in the template.css or typography.css files.

   By examining the .css files, you can find where your template stores the typography styles.

4. Close the Template Manager.

5. Choose Extensions > Plug-in Manager.

6. Choose and open the TinyMCE editor plug-in.

7. Under Basic Options in the Custom CSS classes, type the full path to the .css file used by your template **N**.

8. Under Basic Options in the Functionality drop-down menu, choose Extended.

   We will be using the extended TinyMCE editor for the remainder of this book **O**.

Adding Articles

It is not possible in this book to show every type of content you can create or to discuss every possible layout. The best way to learn how your content will appear and how to lay out your pages is through examples, practice, and a little trial and error. By installing and viewing the sample data in Joomla, you will see the many, many ways you can use and display article content.

Article content displays as long as a category or article menu item links to that content. You can also use modules to link to article content. You control how and what displays on the page by combining article, menu item, and global options.

To create a new article:

1. Log in to the back end.

2. Choose Content > Article Manager > Add New Article to open Article Manager: Add New Article.

   Articles include publishing options, article options that control content display, and metadata options. An article can be saved and published to the site as long as it includes a title, a category, and an image or text **Ⓐ**.

3. Under New Article, in the Title field, type **My New Article**.

4. Leave the Alias field empty. Joomla will use the title to create the alias for you. However, you can enter your own alias if you choose.

5. From the Category drop-down menu, choose Uncategorised.

   An article can be assigned to any category at any time. If you assign article content to the Uncategorised category, you can later assign it to a specific category.

Ⓐ The Article Manager: Add New Article screen

Ⓑ Choosing Heading 3 from the paragraph styles changes the highlighted text to an HTML h3 style.

C You can toggle the editor to HTML mode to fix or modify HTML styles used in your content.

D Finding the newly created article using menu items and links

My New Article

Category: Uncategorised
Published on Friday, 01 April 2011 20:09
Written by Marni Derr
Hits: 0

My new article example.

E The article displayed on the front end of the site

6. In the Article Text area, type **My new article example**.

7. Highlight the text you typed and then from the paragraph styles, choose Heading 3.

   You can set text styles using any of the editor buttons, as you would when using a basic word processor **B**.

8. Below the Article Text area, click the "Toggle editor" button.

   You can view the HTML code output at any time by toggling the editor to HTML mode **C**. The HTML tags for a Heading 3 are coded for you.

9. Click the "Toggle editor" button again to exit HTML mode.

10. On the toolbar, click Save & Close.

    Because this article was assigned to the Uncategorised category, it will display only if a link or menu item is present for this category.

11. Click View Site.

12. In the This Site menu, choose Site Map.

13. Click the Articles link **D**.

14. Scroll to the bottom of the page, and click the Uncategorised link.

    The sample data includes a link to all articles in every category. Clicking the Uncategorised category title displays the article that you created **E**.

    If no menu item was linked to the parent or any subcategories, this article will not display anywhere on the site.

    To make it easier to work with your article, you'll display it on the Home page.

To create a featured article:

1. Log in to the back end.

2. Choose Content > Article Manager.

3. From the Select Category drop-down list, choose Uncategorised to set the Article Manager to display only articles created and assigned to the Uncategorised category.

4. Select the checkbox next to My New Article, and on the toolbar, click Featured.

   The article is now marked by a star in the Featured column **F**.

5. Click the Featured Articles link.

   All featured articles now appear in the Featured Article Manager and in the Article Manager.

6. Choose Menus > Main Menu.

7. Select the Home menu item title to open Menu Manager: Edit Menu Item.

   The Home menu item is a Featured Articles menu item type, which means all featured articles will display on the default Home page **G**.

F The star icon in the Featured column indicates that My New Article is marked as a featured article.

G The Main Menu Home menu item is a Featured Articles menu item type.

Featured Article Menu Item Layout Options

- **# Leading Articles:** Set the number of leading articles displayed across the width of the page at the top of the page.

- **# Intro Articles:** Set the number of articles displayed after the leading articles.

- **# Columns:** Set the number of articles used to display the intro articles.

- **# Links:** Set the number of articles shown as links.

- **Multi Column Order:** Set column order.

- **Category Order:** Set the order of categories.

- **Article Order:** Set the article order.

- **Date for Ordering:** Set the date used for ordering when date ordering is selected.

- **Pagination:** Show or hide the pagination.

- **Pagination Results:** Show or hide the pagination results.

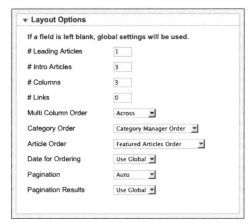

H The menu item Layout Options define how many articles are displayed, and in what order.

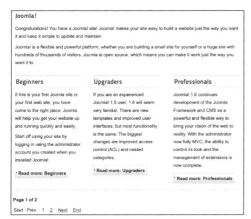

I The Home page displays one leading article, three intro articles, and pagination to indicate that more articles are available.

8. Look at the setting under Layout Options.

Your menu item options control what content is displayed on the web site, in combination with the global and individual article options **H**.

9. Click View Site.

The menu item layout options define how content will display and how it will appear on the Home Featured Article page. In this example, one leading article, Joomla, spans the width of the main body. Three intro articles occupy three columns below the leading article.

Because pagination is turned on, and because you have limited the display to display only three intro articles after the leading article, the fifth featured article currently can be accessed only by using the pagination **I**.

10. Return to the back end and open the Home menu item by choosing Menus > Main Menu > Home.

11. Under Layout Options, set # Intro Articles to 4.

12. On the toolbar, click Save.

continues on next page

13. Click View Site.

Changing the # Intro Articles value adds My New Article to the page .

14. Return to the back end, and open the Home menu item.

15. Under Layout Options return the # Intro Articles value to 3.

16. In the # Links field, enter 3.

17. Click View Site.

The page now displays the original articles, and it links to the fourth article .

To set article publishing options:

1. Log in to the back end.

2. Choose Content > Featured Articles to open the Article Manager: Featured Articles. Only articles marked as featured appear in this list.

3. Open My New Article by clicking its title.

Joomla automatically fills in the Publishing Options when an article is saved. You can change any of these options except for Modified By, Modified Date, and Revision .

J The Home page set to display intro articles

K The Home page set to display one leading article, three intro articles, and a link to more articles.

L Article Publishing Options

In the User Manager pop-up window, you can choose a new author for this article.

The Article Options can be set to use the global options, or override the global options by setting individual items to Show or Hide when the full article is displayed.

4. To change the article author, click the Select User button.

   The User Manager opens in a pop-up window listing all the users on your site. You can sort or filter users and then select a username as the author of the article .

5. Close the pop-up window.

6. Make any desired changes, and then click Save & Close.

To set article options:

1. Open the Featured Article Manager.

2. Open the article titled "Joomla!".

3. Click the arrow next to Article Options to open a list of all available article content display options .

   The "Joomla!" article is currently set to use all the global content settings.

4. On the toolbar, click Close.

5. On the Article Manager: Featured Articles toolbar, click the Options button.

continues on next page

Article Publishing Options

- **Created by alias:** Display a different name for the article's author.

- **Created Date:** Manually set the creation date for an article. Use this if you are planning to publish an article in the future.

- **Start Publishing:** Set a date and time to start publishing the article.

- **Finish Publishing:** Set the date and time to stop the article from displaying on the site. If you do not select a date in this field, the article stays on the site until you remove it.

Modified By, Modified Date, and Revision are tracked by the system and cannot be changed.

6. Click the Articles tab.

   Global article options affect all articles on the site and are the same settings available in the Article Options for individual articles. Use these options to set the common items that you want to display with the majority of your article content. Then, as desired, you can override these global settings on a per-article basis at the article level **O**.

7. Look through the available global options. Then, close the Article Manager Options and click View Site.

8. Click the title of the "Joomla!" article.

   Article global options and individual article options control what displays when you are viewing the full article **P**.

O Global article options are the same as article options. Use these options for the most common content items you want to display in the majority of your articles.

P The "Joomla!" article using the default global article options

Article Options

Article options control which article content displays when a user views the full article. All items can be shown or hidden. Article options set within the edit article screen will always override global content options.

- **Show Title:** Show or hide the article title.
- **Linked Titles:** If the title is set to Show, this option turns the article title into a link to the full article.
- **Show Intro Text:** Show or hide the intro text for the article. Intro text does not affect the full article view. This option is used for category or article pages displaying more than one article.
- **Show Category:** Show or hide the category title to which this article is assigned.
- **Link Category:** When set to Show, the category title becomes an active link to the article's assigned category.
- **Show Parent:** Show or hide the Parent category's title. If this article is assigned to a subcategory, this option will display the parent category of the subcategory.
- **Link Parent:** Makes the parent category an active link when Show Parent is set to Show.
- **Show Author:** Show or hide the author's name.
- **Link Author:** Make the author's name an active link to his profile details.
- **Show Create Date:** Show or hide the date and time the article was created.
- **Show Modify Date:** Show or hide the date and time the article was last modified.
- **Show Publish Date:** Show or hide the date set in the Publish Date field.
- **Show Navigation:** Display Prev and Next buttons at the bottom of an article.
- **Show Icons:** Show or hide the print and email icons, if they are set to show in the Global Options.
- **Show Print Icon:** Show or hide the Print icon next to the article.
- **Show Email Icon:** Show or hide the Email icon next to the article.
- **Show Voting:** Show or hide a voting bar for this article. Users can select 1- through 5-star ratings.
- **Show Hits:** Show or hide the number of hits for each article.
- **Show Unauthorised Links:** Show or hide links to content to which the reader does not ordinarily have access. The content will not be available but the title will be.
- **Read More Text:** Enter custom text to appear on the Read More button or link at the end of the intro section of an article.
- **Alternative Layout:** Select the default layout or custom layouts for your articles.

To set article metadata options:

1. Open the Article Manager.

2. Select the "Joomla!" article to open it in the article editing screen.

3. Click the arrow next to Metadata Options.

   Search engines use metadata to index your site's content. Having descriptive and accurate metadata can improve search engine results 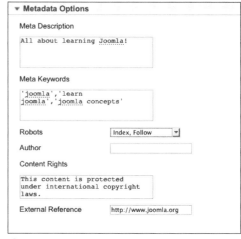.

4. In the Meta Description field, type a short but descriptive sentence describing this article.

5. In the Meta Keywords field, enter keywords that accurately describe this article's content.

6. In the Author field, enter the author name you want to associate with this category.

7. From the Robots drop-down menu, choose the appropriate search engine robot.

8. In the Content Rights field, enter a copyright statement regarding this content, if necessary.

9. In the External Reference field, enter a link to any reference, quoted, or bibliographical source for this article.

10. Click Save & Close.

Q The article Metadata Options

A Creating a link using text and the link button in the editor

Doing More with Articles

The term *article* is Joomla's way of classifying *any* type of web content displayed in the main body of your web pages, including images, video, Flash files, photo galleries, tables, links, and even modules.

In this section, you'll add several types of elements as article content.

To add links to an article:

1. Log in to the back end.

2. Choose Content > Article Manager.

3. Select the checkbox next to the article My New Article, and then on the toolbar, click Edit.

   The sample data has a complex article titled Site Map that uses an advanced way of linking to other content by loading a module into the article. In this example, you are going to create a direct link to the Site Map article.

   You can place links to other content into an article by using any of the following methods:

   ▸ Enter a link by typing it in.

   ▸ Link directly to an article title using the Article button in the editor.

   ▸ Load a module into the article.

4. In the Article Text editor, type **View the Site Map article, click here.**

5. Highlight an entire line of text, and click the Link button in the editor **A**.

continues on next page

The TinyMCE editor does not display a list of all your articles. When creating a link from highlighted text, you must know the full path to the article. All Joomla editors have advanced features to create dynamic links and interaction such as adding JavaScript functions and pop-up windows 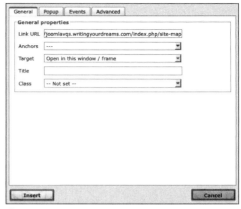.

Other third-party editors have plug-ins that allow you select another category, article, and so on.

6. Enter the full URL into the Link URL field linking to the Site Map article.

7. Click Insert.

   When you return to the article editor, the text you selected is now a link to the Site Map article .

8. On the toolbar, click Save.

9. Click View Site.

   If you followed the previous steps in this chapter, you will still see a link on the home page to My New Article.

10. Click My New Article .

11. In this article, click the link "View the Site Map article, click here."

   The Site Map article opens.

B The insert/edit link pop-up window

C The text is now a link to the Site Map article.

D The My New Article link on the home page

E Sort the Article Manager to display only articles assigned to Sample Data–Articles.

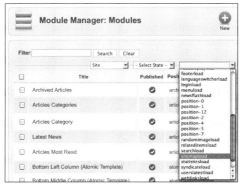

F The Site Map article is using a function called `loadposition`, which allows you to load a module into article content.

G Sorting the Module Manager by the sitemapload position reveals the module using the position created in the Site Map article.

To add a module to an article:

1. Log in to the back end.

2. Choose Content > Article Manager.

3. From the Select Category drop-down list, choose Sample Data–Articles.

The only article assigned to this category is Site Map **E**.

You can add links to other articles or even add an entire module in an article that links to other content.

4. Click the title Site Map to open the article editor screen.

In the Site Map article text editor, you'll see the following:

`{loadposition sitemapload}` **F**.

This is code that Joomla uses to place a module into a position that you create so the module will load inside the article. This position is not used by or defined by your template. You create the name and then use the Module Manager to create the position.

5. On the toolbar, click Close.

6. Choose Extensions > Module Manager.

7. From the Select Position drop-down list, choose sitemapload **G**.

The only module using this position is a menu module titled Site Map.

continues on next page

8. Click the Site Map module title to open it for editing.

   Under Basic Options, the Select Menu drop-down menu is set to Main Menu because this module is a menu module.

   Notice the Start and End Levels for the menu items.

   In the Position field, the sitemapload position is entered. You can create any position name you want and then use the **loadposition** function to assign a position inside an article .

   The **loadposition** function creates a position in the article, and sitemapload is the name of that position. Joomla recognizes the position, finds the module using that position, and loads it.

9. On the toolbar, click Close.

10. Click View Site.

11. From the This Site menu, choose Site Map.

    The three links—Articles, Weblinks, and Contacts—are actually menu items assigned to the Main Menu Module 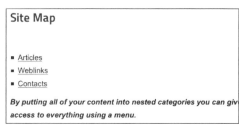.

    Because the Site Map menu module is set to display only level 2 to 3 submenus, only three links are listed.

    This shows how incredibly flexible Joomla can be when creating content and dynamic navigation. Any module can be loaded into article content.

H The Site Map menu module edit screen showing the details for this menu module that will be loaded into the Site Map article.

Site Map

- Articles
- Weblinks
- Contacts

By putting all of your content into nested categories you can giv access to everything using a menu.

I The Site Map article displayed on the web site with the links contained in the Site Map module

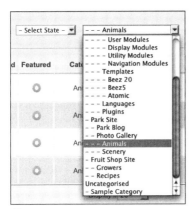

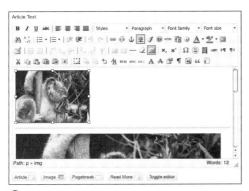

J Sorting the Article Manager by the Animals category

K An article that contains a small image above a Read More link (indicated by the line), and a larger image below it

To add an image to an article:

1. Log in to the back end.

2. Choose Content > Article Manager.

3. From the Select Category drop-down list, choose Animals **J**.

4. Open the Koala article.

   The Koala article contains two images. The first image is above a Read More link. The Read More link defines the content above it as intro text and the content below it as the remainder of the text for an article **K**.

   Both images were inserted by clicking the Image button at the bottom of the Article Text editor.

   Clicking Image opens a pop-up window to the Media Manager, where all the images used in your site content are catalogued **L**. When you select an image in the Media Manager, it loads that image into the article.

continues on next page

L The Media Manager catalogues all the images and media files to be used in your site content.

5. Close the Media Manager.

6. Close the Koala article.

7. Click View Site.

8. In the This Site menu, choose Sample Sites.

9. In the Australian Parks menu, choose Image Gallery > Animals.

   This is an example of one way to use images or create a gallery of image articles 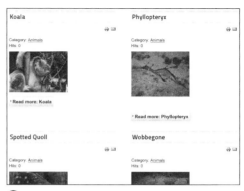.

10. Click the "Read more: Koala" button.

   The smaller image was embedded in the article's intro text. The larger image was embedded in the article below the Read More link.

   Your content can include any type of file that is allowed by the System Global Configuration settings. Videos, Flash files, PDFs, and documents are all catalogued in the Media Manager and can be inserted into an article.

TIP Web sites that use images stand out. Where appropriate, try to include images with your content.

TIP You can use images on your site in an infinite number of ways. A popular way to create stunning image galleries using Joomla is to install a third-party gallery or image extension.

M A sample way to create an image gallery using articles

Creating Article Menu Items

Joomla has four individual menu item types that you can use to create direct links to articles. However, most of your menu items will be category links that display articles below the links. The types of links you can create for articles are:

- **Archived Articles:** A link to a list of archived articles.

- **Single Article:** A link to a single article.

- **Featured Articles:** A link to articles marked as featured. A Featured Article menu item can display as many or as few featured articles as you define in the menu item settings.

- **Create Article:** A link to a location where users can submit article content to the web site. Article submission can be set to publish immediately or be moderated and published after submission by a back-end administrator.

Putting It All Together

1. **Choose an editor in your user profile.** Download and install an editor or choose one of the Joomla editors to use when adding your article content.

2. **Configure the editor.** Use the Plug-in Manager to configure the editor settings.

3. **Add articles to your site.** Remember to first create the categories to which you will be assigning articles.

4. **Add images, other media, or links to your articles.** Articles are for more than just text. Create articles using images, lists, video, links, or even modules.

5. **Set your article options.** Set individual article options, or leave article options at their default values to inherit the global article or menu item options.

6. **Create menu items.** Use your category menu items to display articles or create menu items that link to specific articles.

5

Managing Menus

Menus display content and, as a result, are the most important parts of a Joomla web site. They also control navigation and literally *define* how the content is laid out and presented to the user. Content cannot appear on the site without being linked to a menu item. Because your visitors access and view all information through their menu clicks, it's vitally important to get menus right.

Menu modules control the placement (position) of menu items on the site, and in turn those menu items help control the presentation and layout of the displayed content. The good news is that you can freely edit and change menus as you develop your site.

Creating menus is a three-step process:

1. Create a menu type.
2. Create the menu module.
3. Add menu items to the menu module.

In This Chapter

Using the Menu Manager

Menus are *modules* that contain menu *items* (links). Menu modules can be placed in almost any position supported by your template: top, left, right, or bottom. The only place you cannot directly position a menu module is in the main body of a page.

Menus *types* are created and managed in the Menu Manager, and then placed into positions using the Module Manager. Prior to Joomla 1.6, the menu module was automatically created for you. However, with the current versions you must create the module after you create the menu type. This workflow increases functionality and allows for greater control of individual menus and styling.

During the installation process, Joomla automatically creates the first menu module: the Main Menu.

> **TIP** There is a trick to using modules in the main body of the page, including adding menus. By creating a module and then adding the {loadmodule} function in an article or category description, you can load a module in the content area.

To use the Menu Manager:

1. Log in to the back end.
2. Choose Menus > Menu Manager.

   Each menu type created for the site will display in the Menus menu **A**.

A The Menus menu displaying all the menu module types created on the site

The Menu Manager Columns

- **Title:** The menu title that appears above the menu when Show Title is set to Show.
- **Menu Type:** The menu type you defined for this menu.
- **# Published:** The number of published menu items in this menu.
- **# Unpublished:** The number of unpublished menu items in this menu.
- **# Trashed:** The number of menu items in the trash for this menu. Deleted menu items are held in the trash until permanently deleted. If you delete a menu module, it is deleted immediately along with all its menu items.
- **Modules Linked to the Menu:** Displays other menu modules associated with this menu, their positions, and access level. Selecting the module name in this column will open the menu module settings screen. Menu modules can be contained in other menus.
- **ID:** The database ID number for this menu module.

By choosing Menu Manager, you open the Menu Manager: Menus, which lists all menu types created on the site **B**.

3. Select the User Menu title to open the Menu Manager: Menu Items. By selecting the title of a menu type, you open the Menu Items Manager, which lists all menu items assigned to this menu type.

4. To return to the Menu Manager: Menus, select the Menus link.

TIP Menu types are simply names that you assign to a menu so Joomla can identify what menu to use when creating the module in the Module Manager. This allows you to style individual menus using CSS.

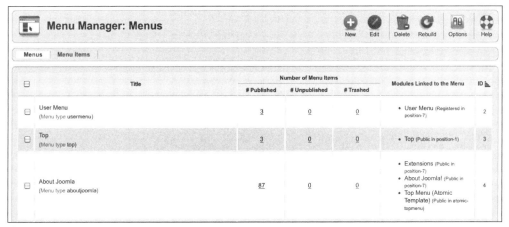

B The Menu Manager: Menus displays each menu type created for the site.

To view or edit menu type details:

1. Log in to the back end.

2. Choose Menus > Menu Manager.

   The Menu Manager toolbar contains the following options **C**:

   ▸ **New:** Create a new menu module.

   ▸ **Edit:** Edit an existing menu module.

   ▸ **Delete:** Permanently delete a menu module and all its associated menu items.

   ▸ **Rebuild:** Reconstruct or refresh the menu table. This is used if the *database* menu tables are corrupted. Choosing Rebuild will not rebuild deleted items.

   ▸ **Options:** Assign permissions to the menu module.

   ▸ **Help:** Open the Joomla help documentation associated with the Menu Manager.

3. Select the checkbox next to User Menu **D**.

   You cannot click the title of the menu to open the menu details. Selecting the title will open the Menu Item Manager for this menu.

4. On the toolbar, click Edit to open the Menu Manager: Edit Menu **E**.

   This menu contains the following menu details:

   ▸ **Title:** The menu title used to identify the menu in the Menu Manager and on the site if the menu module title is set to Show.

   ▸ **Menu Type:** Used by Joomla to identify the menu type name. The type name must be all lowercase and contain no spaces. You can create any type of menu, but the type name

C The toolbar gives you access to the Menu Manager functions.

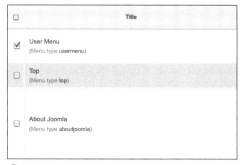

D You must select the menu by selecting its checkbox. You can then click the Edit button to modify the menu type details.

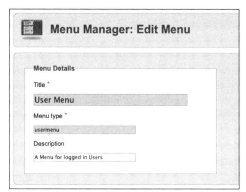

E The Menu Manager: Edit Menu details screen

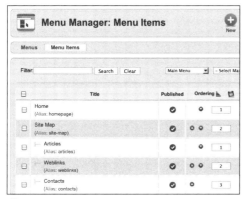

F The Menu Manager: Menu Items displaying the User Menu's menu items. Use the Sort field to change to the proper menu items list.

G The Menu Items Manager displaying the Main Menu's menu items

should be descriptive of the menu contents. When creating the menu module, this is the name to identify which menu the module is using.

▸ **Description:** A brief description of the menu for administrators.

5. Click Close to exit the Menu Manager.

Remember that if the menu type and its name are changed at any time, those changes also need to be updated in the Module Manager.

To view the menu items assigned to a menu module:

1. Log in to the back end.

2. Open the Menu Manager.

3. Select the Menu Items link.

When selecting the Menu Items link from the Menu Manager: Menus, the list of menu items displayed will be the most recently viewed menu items. It does not display every menu item created for every menu type. This may be a bug and could be changed in later releases **F**.

To find the menu items for a specific menu type, or to view all menu items, you will need to use the Sort or Filter fields.

There is a better way to access the specific menu items you are looking for until this is either fixed or changed.

4. Click the Menus link to return to the Menu Manager.

5. Click the menu title Main Menu.

The Menu Items Manager opens display-ing all menu items assigned to the Main Menu only **G**. (You can also open the Menu Item Manager by choosing the menu directly from the Menus menu.)

continues on next page

6. Choose Menus > Main Menu.

The Menu Manager: Menu Items opens displaying all the menu items assigned to this menu.

As you can see, you can navigate through Joomla's managers in multiple ways. As you work with Joomla, you will develop your own workflow and navigation methods.

To access menu module settings from the Menu Manager: Menus:

1. Log in to the back end.

2. Open the Menu Manager: Menus.

3. In the "Modules Linked to the Menu" column, select "User Menu (Registered in position-7)" **H**.

This opens the menu module details screen for this menu type **I**.

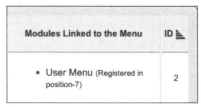

Modules Linked to the Menu	ID ≣
• User Menu (Registered in position-7)	2

H Other menu module(s), if any, linked to this menu type showing access levels and positions

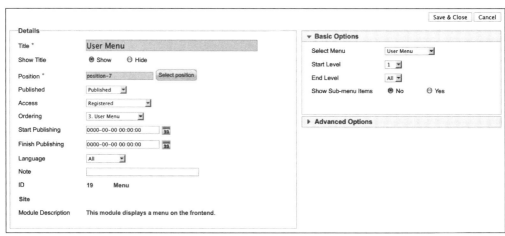

I The menu module details screen

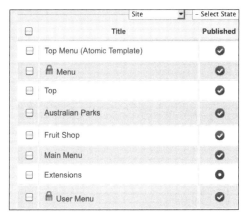

J The Module Manager is where you set the details for all modules created on the site.

K The Select Type drop-down list with Menu selected

L Sort the Module Manager to display only menu modules by using the Select Type sorting drop-down list.

Using this method is a fine way to access the menu module settings to make a quick edit or view settings. When creating a menu module or making major changes, it is best practice to use the Module Manager.

You first need to set up the menu in the Module Manager.

4. Click Cancel to exit the module details screen.

To access menu module settings using the Module Manager

1. Choose Extensions > Module Manager.

The Module Manager opens displaying all published and unpublished modules **J**.

2. From the Select Type drop-down list, choose Menu **K**.

This will sort the list to display only modules of the type Menu.

Menu modules with a lock icon next to their names are still checked out by the system or another administrator. This can occur when another administrator is making changes to the module, or when the module was opened and not saved **L**.

If you need to work in an item that is locked, you must check it in.

3. Click the checkbox next to each of the locked modules.

4. On the toolbar, click Check In to check in all locked items and enable them for editing.

continues on next page

5. In the Module Manager, select the Main Menu title to open the Main Menu module details.

The Module Manager: Module Menu edit details screen opens containing all available settings and parameters for this module. Installing plug-ins or extensions that work with menus can add to these settings.

6. Click Close to exit the Module Manager: Module Menu.

TIP You can create menu modules and assign them to another menu module. However, this is an advanced practice and not covered here. To create a menu this way, you would not create a menu type in the Menu Manager. You would create the menu type using the Module Manager and then assign it to another menu module. As a result, the menu appears in the Module Manager, but not as an actual menu type in the Menu Manager. To see how this works, view the sample data This Site menu, which is assigned to the Main Menu type.

To delete a menu type:

Deleting a menu type will permanently delete the menu, and all menu items assigned to the menu, from the database! Only delete a menu type if you are sure you are not going to use it.

1. Log in to the back end.

2. Choose Menus > Menu Manager.

3. Select the checkbox next to the menu you want to delete.

4. On the toolbar, click Delete.

A warning dialog explains that you are about to delete a menu and all of its menu items 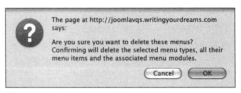.

Click Cancel if you do not want to delete the menu.

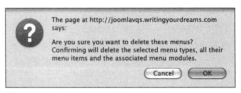

M Warning dialog that indicates you are about to completely delete a menu module and all its menu items from the database

A The Menu Manager: Add Menu details screen

Creating a New Menu

Creating menus and their menu items are the most time consuming tasks you will perform on the site. A menu type must be created, a menu module must be created, and menu items must be assigned to the new menu. Then you begin the process of controlling your content layouts through the menu item options. This process can become fairly overwhelming in the beginning, and that is why we stress developing a site map and web design plan before you begin to create the site.

Know the type of menus your site will need before you create them. Create your categories and as many articles as you can before you begin adding menu items.

To create a new menu type:

1. Log in to the back end.

2. Choose Menus > Menu Manager.

3. On the Menu Manager toolbar, click New.

   The Menu Manager: Add Menu details screen opens **A**.

4. Enter a Title for the new menu.

   The title is the name for the menu in the Menu Manager.

5. Enter a Menu type.

   The Menu type is used by the system to identify this menu when creating the menu module. The type should be descriptive of what the menu is but doesn't have to match the title. The type must be all lowercase and contain no spaces.

   continues on next page

6. Enter a description for the menu module.

   The description helps site administrators identify the menu's intended use.

7. On the toolbar, click Save & Close to return to the Menu Manager.

   All new menu modules appear as the last item in the list, by default.

8. At the top of the Title column, click the Title link to sort the list by alphabetical ascending or descending order **B**.

   The new Sample Menu type appears in the menu list but contains no menu items. Before you can place this menu on the site, you need to create and publish it as a menu module.

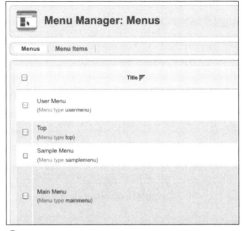

B The Menu Manager sorted by the title

Menu Module Detail Settings

- **Title:** Enter a title for the menu. It should be a close or exact match of the title you created for the menu type. This title will display on the web site if you choose Yes for Show Title.

- **Show Title:** Choose Show to show the title when displaying the menu, or Hide to hide the menu title.

- **Position:** Select the position for this menu. To view the available positions in your template, click the Select position button.

- **Published:** Choose Publish to publish the menu, or Unpublished to retain the menu in the database but not display it on the site.

- **Access:** Select the access level to identify which users can view this menu in the front end of the site.

- **Ordering:** Select the order in which this menu is to appear relative to all other modules published in this position.

- **Start Publishing:** Set a specific date to begin publishing this menu, or leave the field blank to publish the menu immediately.

- **Finish Publishing:** Set a date to stop publishing this menu.

- **Language:** If you have multiple languages installed, choose the default language for this menu.

- **Note:** Add any additional notes about this menu for administrators.

- **Menu:** This setting tells you that the menu is a Site (front-end) menu, not an Admin (back-end) menu.

- **Module Description:** A system-generated message about this module.

- Archived Articles
- Articles Categories
- Articles Category
- Articles - Newsflash
- Articles - Related Articles
- Banners
- Breadcrumbs
- Custom HTML
- Feed display
- Footer
- JA Comment Latest comments
- Language Switcher
- Latest News
- Latest Users
- Login
- Menu
- Most Read Content
- Random Image
- Search
- Statistics
- Syndication Feeds
- Weblinks
- Who's Online
- Wrapper

C A list of all the module types you can create for your site

D The Menu Module Details

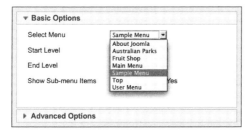

E The Basic Options with Sample Menu selected

TIP You can create multiple modules for the same menu type. For example, if the main menu contains submenus and you want the submenus to display in the main menu and also in the right column of a page, you would create a second menu module and assign it to the right column positions. This is very common.

To create the menu module:

1. Choose Extension > Module Manager.

    In early versions of Joomla, the menu module was created automatically by the system as soon as you created a new menu. Because Joomla now offers finer control over styling and menu type creation, you need to create and define the menu module settings before the menu can be displayed on the site.

2. On the Module Manager toolbar, click New to open a list of all the module types you can create for your site **C**.

3. From the list, select Menu to open the Module Manager: Module Menu, where you can configure the details for this menu module.

4. Enter the Menu Module Details **D**.

5. On the toolbar, click Save.

    If you did not select a position for this menu module, an error message will appear. For a menu module to be saved, it must have at least a title and position.

6. From the Basic Options Select Menu, choose the name of the menu type you created in the Menu Manager.

    This module is now associated with the menu in the Menu Manager.

    Make sure to select the right menu. If you don't this menu module will be saved as the first menu type in the list causing a duplicate menu module to be created **E**.

7. On the toolbar, click Save & Close.

8. Open the Menu Manager.

    You can now access this menu's module settings via the Menu Manager or the Module Manager.

To set menu module basic options:

1. Open the Module Manager.

2. Select the menu module you want to edit.

3. Set the following basic options **F**:

   ▸ **Select Menu:** Select the menu type for this menu module, the one you created in the Menu Manager.

   ▸ **Start Level:** Select the menu item level display as the top or starting level for the module. For example, a parent menu item starts at 1, while submenus or secondary menu items beneath the parent would be 2.

   ▸ **End Level:** Set the ending menu level. For example, to show only the parent or first level with no submenus, you would choose 1. To show the next level of menus, you would choose 2.

   ▸ **Show Submenu Items:** Set this to Yes to display the submenus, based on your Start and End Level settings. Choosing No will display only the Start Level menu items regardless of the End level setting.

4. On the toolbar, click Save & Close.

To set menu module advanced options:

1. Open the Module Manager.

2. Select the menu module you want to edit.

3. Click the arrow next to Advanced Options.

   The following advanced options help style the menu module **G**:

   These settings work with your template's styles. If you do not know how to use the CSS classes of your template, leave these fields blank, or consult your template's documentation for styling modules.

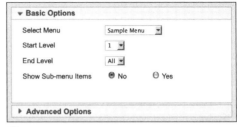

F Menu Module Basic Options

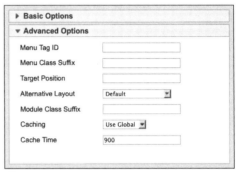

G Menu Module Advanced Options

H The Menu Assignment fields

▸ **Menu Tag ID:** Enter the menu ID to use special styling for the menu module.

▸ **Menu Class Suffix:** Enter the menu CSS class to use specific styling for the menu items.

▸ **Target Position:** Enter JavaScript values to position the menu module.

▸ **Alternative Layout:** Select an alternative layout for this menu module when alternative layouts are available.

▸ **Module Class Suffix:** Enter the module CSS class to use specific styling for the menu module.

▸ **Caching:** Select to cache the menu using the system's global cache settings, or not to cache this menu.

▸ **Cache Time:** If the menu is set to cache, set the length of time (in seconds) the menu should be cached.

4. On the toolbar, click Save & Close.

To assign a menu module to specific pages:

1. Open the Menu Manager.

2. Select the Menu Module.

Scroll down to view the Menu Assignment fields. This box lists all the menus and menu items created for your site. The menu modules are listed on the tabs, and the menu items can be selected by clicking the Menu's tab **H**.

By selecting specific menus or menu items, you control on which pages this menu module will display and which pages it will not display.

continues on next page

3. Click the Module Assignment drop-down list.

You can choose from the following options when selecting pages :

> **On all pages:** Display this menu on all pages selected.

> **No Pages:** Do not display this menu on any pages.

> **Only on the pages selected:** Clear the selected items so you can choose individual menu items.

> **On all pages except those selected:** Select all pages and then choose only those pages where you don't want the module to display.

4. Click the Toggle Selection button.

This button toggles selected items—click to select all, click again to select none.

5. Make your selections and then click Save.

To make the new menu appear on the site, you need to add menu items. Menu items tell Joomla what content to display 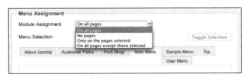.

I The Module Assignment field, which enables you to select on what pages the menu appears

J The Menu Assignment page showing the module being assigned to the Home menu

A The Menu Manager: Menu Items displaying only those menu items assigned to the Top menu module

Menu Item Toolbar

- **New:** Add a new menu item.
- **Edit:** Edit an existing menu item.
- **Publish:** Publish a menu item.
- **Unpublish:** Unpublish a menu item.
- **Check In:** Check in any locked menu items.
- **Trash:** Send menu items to the trash.
- **Home:** Make a single menu item the default home page. You must have at least one menu item set as your default home page.
- **Rebuild:** Rebuild a broken menu item database table.
- **Help:** Open Joomla help documentation.

Adding Menu Items

Menu modules are containers to hold your menu items and control the position in which they will appear on your site. Menu items are the links through which you navigate a site, and they help define how the content is displayed.

Joomla contains numerous menu item types. Adding third-party extensions further increases the number of menu types you can use.

In this section, you will learn how to add menu items to your menu modules while getting a brief overview of the most common menu items used. Because the menu items grow and change as you add extensions to your site, we do not cover every menu item in this chapter.

To create a new menu item:

1. Choose Menus > Top.

   This opens the Menu Manager: Menu Items and displays all menu items assigned to the Top menu module **A**.

   continues on next page

2. Click View Site.

The Top menu module is assigned to the Beez20 template's position-1 and is the main navigation found at the top of the home page **B**.

3. Return to the back end. If you are no longer in the Menu Manager, choose Menus > Top > Add New Menu Item.

The Menu Manager: Menu Items page opens. From the toolbar you can add, edit, publish, unpublish, check in, and delete menu items **C**.

4. On the toolbar, click New.

The first screen that opens is the New Menu Item edit screen **D**.

You must first select the menu type. The available settings vary depending upon the menu item type that you are creating. Notice the options to the right of the screen **E**.

B The main navigation for the Top module in the Beez20 template is located at the top of the home page.

C The Menu Item Manager toolbar

D The Menu Manager New Menu Item edit screen

E Link Type Options

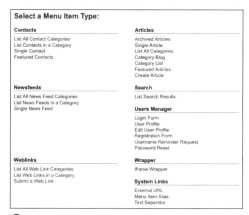

Select a Menu Item Type:

Contacts
List All Contact Categories
List Contacts in a Category
Single Contact
Featured Contacts

Articles
Archived Articles
Single Article
List All Categories
Category Blog
Category List
Featured Articles
Create Article

Newsfeeds
List All News Feed Categories
List News Feeds in a Category
Single News Feed

Search
List Search Results

Users Manager
Login Form
User Profile
Edit User Profile
Registration Form
Username Reminder Request
Password Reset

Weblinks
List All Web Link Categories
List Web Links in a Category
Submit a Web Link

Wrapper
Iframe Wrapper

System Links
External URL
Menu Item Alias
Text Separator

F The "Select a Menu Item Type" screen

G The options to the right will change based on the menu item type.

H The menu item displayed in the Menu Item Manager list

I The new menu item added to the Top module

5. At the end of the Menu Item Type field under Details, click the Select button.

A pop-up window opens listing every available menu item type. Because you have not installed any third-party extensions, you currently see only those types provided by the Joomla core **F**.

6. From the System Links list, choose External URL.

Notice that the Details fields to the left and right of the screen have changed. Each menu type has its own specific settings **G**.

Menu items require a type and a title.

7. In the Menu Title field, enter `Back to Writing Your Dreams`.

8. In the Link field, enter `http:// writingyourdreams.com`.

Because you selected external URL as the menu type, you need to provide the destination URL for this link. For internal links, Joomla will automatically fill in the necessary link information.

The menu item type, menu title, and link fields are required. All other fields are optional and can remain at their default settings.

9. On the toolbar, click Save & Close.

The menu item is created and now appears in the Menu Manager: Menu Items list **H**.

10. Click View Site.

The menu item has been added to the Top menu module **I**.

To change the order of a menu item:

1. Open the Menu Item Manager for the Top menu module.

2. Click the Ordering column title to change between ascending and descending order.

   A Save icon appears next to Ordering .

   If the numbers beneath Ordering are greyed out, click Ordering again.

   You can now alter the order of the menu items as they appear in the menu module.

3. Click the blue up arrow next to the "Back to Writing Your Dreams" menu item to move the menu item up one position.

4. Click the Save icon.

5. Click View Site.

   The new menu item is now placed before the last menu item.

J The menu items screen

Menu Item Details

- **Alias:** When you have turned on SEF URLs, this alias is used in the browser URL.
- **Note:** A note to help administrators identify the purpose of this link.
- **State:** Published or unpublished. A menu item that is unpublished does not display in the menu module.
- **Access:** Set the front-end access level that a user needs to view this menu item on the front end.
- **Menu Location:** The menu module in which this menu item will be placed.
- **Parent Item:** If this menu item is a submenu, assign it to the appropriate parent menu item.
- **Target Window:** Open the link in the same browser window, a new window, or a new window without navigation.
- **Language:** Set the default language for this menu item.
- **Template Style:** Set this menu to use a specific template.
- **ID:** Assigned by Joomla to identify this menu item to the database.

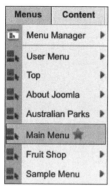

Menus	Content
Menu Manager ▶	
User Menu ▶	
Top ▶	
About Joomla ▶	
Australian Parks ▶	
Main Menu ★	
Fruit Shop ▶	
Sample Menu ▶	

Ⓐ The star beside the Main Menu indicates that the home page for your site is contained in the Main Menu.

The Default Menu Item (Home)

Joomla sets the home page of the site to the Featured Articles menu item type, by default. This means that all articles marked as featured will display on your home page.

You can set any type of content as your home page, and changing the default is very easy to do. You don't even need to use the title of "Home." The home page of your site can have any title, and can use any menu type; but your site must have an assigned default menu item.

To change the default Home menu item:

1. Open the Menus menu.

   Notice the star next to the menu title. This indicates that the default home page for your site is contained in the Main Menu Ⓐ.

2. Choose Main Menu.

   The first item in the Menu Item Manager is Home. It is first in the menu order, has an access level of Public, and a menu item type of Articles » Featured Articles Ⓑ. There is also a star in the Home column marking it as the default home page.

continues on next page

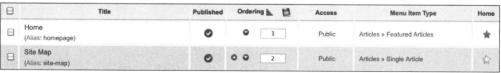

	Title	Published	Ordering ⬇ 🗂	Access	Menu Item Type	Home
☐	Home (Alias: homepage)	✔	● ⬤ 1	Public	Articles » Featured Articles	★
☐	Site Map (Alias: site-map)	✔	● ● 2	Public	Articles » Single Article	☆

Ⓑ The first item in the Menu Item Manager is Home.

3. Select the checkbox next to Articles.

4. On the toolbar, click Home (an orange star).

The home page of the site is now set to Articles.

5. Click View Site, and refresh the browser window.

The default page now displays the content being called by the Articles menu item **C**.

This is all that the default Home menu item does—it displays the content called from the menu item that you set as the default.

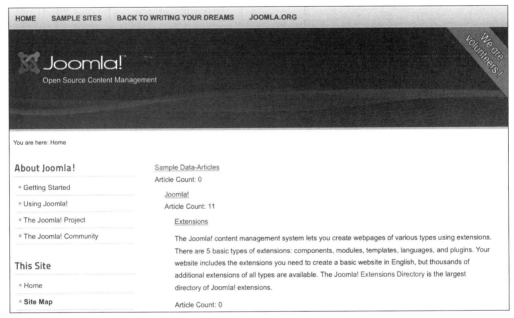

C The Articles menu item is the first page that appears to a user and links to all the content contained in this menu item type.

6. In the front end of the site, click the Home link.

The original home page is still there because you simply set the Article menu as the first page a user sees when she arrives on your site.

The Joomla sample data is a little weird. Normally you would create one of the following as a default home page:

- A featured article page on which you control what displays on the home page by setting articles to featured.

- A top level or root category page.

- A single article page.

- A third-party extension page.

7. Return to the back end and reset Home to the default.

Joomla 1.5 and earlier used the term "default," which is far more descriptive of what the default menu item is doing. Starting with Joomla 1.6, this is renamed to Home. Don't let the name fool you. Whatever page you set as the Home page will be the first page displayed.

Putting It All Together

1. **Create a menu.** Menu modules contain menu items and can be assigned to any position available by your template. Common menus are Main Menu, Top menu, Legal menu, User menu, and so on.

2. **Create the menu module.** Once you have created a new menu, configure the menu by creating it through the Module Manager.

3. **Assign menu modules to specific pages.** With the exception of the main menu and footer menus, most menus are specific to only certain areas on the site. Use the menu assignment to assign menu modules to those pages.

4. **Add menu items to the menu module.** Menu modules left empty do not display on the web site; they need to have menu items telling Joomla what to display.

5. **Create a few different types of menu items.** There are many different ways to present your content. Try creating and using different menu items to see how the pages are laid out when using each type.

6. **Choose a home page.** Think about the content you want displayed on the home page of your site. Create the menu item and set it as the default.

Controlling Content Layouts

Since the days of static web sites, we have been trained to think of web sites as collections of individual pages. You start with a design, create single html pages, link them, and then insert content. The problem is that content management systems don't really create individual, hand-tooled pages. The CMS-created pages are generated dynamically using links and content *options*.

So compared to the traditional design-to-content process, a CMS works somewhat in reverse. You start with the content, choose the options that determine how that content will display on any given page, and then the CMS creates the final page design. Confusing? A little, perhaps, but this chapter will show you how to control your CMS-based page layouts.

You can control the display of your site's content in three places: Global content options, menu item options, and individual article options.

TIP Menu item options will override global and individual content options.

Setting Article Layout Options

Article global options are set from within the Article Manager. They affect all articles on your site by controlling the information that displays when a user clicks an article's title and opens the full-length article.

Global options tell Joomla to display items such as the author's name, the date the article was written, the article's content category, user votes and ratings, number of hits, and so on. These options apply to the entire site, but any global option can be overridden at the individual article level and menu item level.

Ⓐ The article global options window

To access the global layout options:

1. Log in to the back end.

2. Open the Article Manager.

3. On the toolbar, click the Options button.

   A pop-up window opens with the global option settings. The tabs across the top of the manager show the range of available options Ⓐ.

   You have access to all global content settings in this one window. No matter which manager you are using—Article, Category, or Featured Articles—these options affect all category and article content.

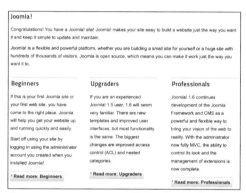

The category-level settings for articles

The front page showing the article titles, intro text, and read more links

The full Beginners article displaying more article options

To set global article options:

1. Log in to the back end.

2. Open the Article Manager.

3. On the toolbar, click the Options button.

4. In the pop-up window, select the Articles tab.

   The first set of options show or hide details when articles display with their assigned categories .

5. Close the Options window.

6. Click View Site.

7. From the main menu, choose Home.

   The Joomla sample data home page is an example of a featured article menu item. Articles marked as featured are set to display on this page.

   As determined by the first set of article options, the article titles are set to show and to link to the full article. The intro text is also set to show. The Read More link is set to show with a limit of 100 words .

8. Click the Beginners title to link to the full Beginners article and observe how the next group of article options appear.

   The category, Joomla, and the published date are set to show. The author name is set to show, but the author title is not linkable. Also set to show are the hits, the print and email icons, and the navigation buttons .

Global Article Option Settings

- **Choose a layout:** If you have specific layout overrides for your articles, you can select them from this list. This is an advanced technique.
- **Show Title:** Hide or show an article's title.
- **Linked Titles:** If the title is set to show, selecting Yes makes the title a direct link to the full article. Selecting No prevents the title from being a link to the full article.
- **Show Intro Text:** Select Show to display the article's intro text on the category page. Selecting Hide will not show any article text on the category page.
- **Show Category:** Hide or show the category to which this article is assigned.
- **Link Category:** If the category is set to show, select Yes to make the category title linkable.
- **Show Parent:** Hide or show the parent or root category of the article.
- **Link Parent:** If the parent is set to show, select Yes to make the parent category linkable.

The following set of options apply directly to the article content and affect the display of the full article **E**:

E The article-level settings for articles

- **Show Author:** Hide or show the user name of the article's author.
- **Link Author:** Select Yes to make the author's user name a link to the author's profile details.
- **Show Create Date:** Hide or show the date the article was created.
- **Show Modify Date:** Hide or show the date this article was last modified and saved.
- **Show Publish Date:** Hide or show the date the article was published.
- **Show Navigation:** Hide or show navigation buttons at the bottom of the article so the user can go to the next or the previous article in this category.
- **Show Voting:** Hide or show a rating system for this article. A user can select a 1- to 5-star rating for the article.
- **Show "Read More":** Hide or show the Read More button below the article's intro text.
- **Show Title with Read More:** Hide or show the article's title on the Read More button.
- **Read More Limit:** Set the number of words to display as intro text to the article.
- **Show Icons:** Hide or show the print or email icons above the article. You must also set the print and/or email icon to show.
- **Show Print Icon:** Hide or show a print icon that enables a user to print the article.
- **Show Email Icon:** Hide or show an email icon that enables a user to email a link to the article.
- **Show Hits:** Hide or show the number of times an individual article has been viewed.
- **Show Unauthorized Links:** If you have content on your site that is restricted to a specific user group, this setting will hide or show links to articles that the user may not have permission to view. Restricted users will not be able to access an article, but its title will appear to show the user that more articles are available.

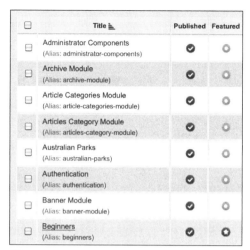

	Title ▲	Published	Featured
☐	Administrator Components (Alias: administrator-components)	✓	○
☐	Archive Module (Alias: archive-module)	✓	○
☐	Article Categories Module (Alias: article-categories-module)	✓	○
☐	Articles Category Module (Alias: articles-category-module)	✓	○
☐	Australian Parks (Alias: australian-parks)	✓	○
☐	Authentication (Alias: authentication)	✓	○
☐	Banner Module (Alias: banner-module)	✓	○
☐	Beginners (Alias: beginners)	✓	✪

F The Beginners article in the Article Manager that shows which article is featured. By selecting the title, you will open this article where you can modify its layout settings.

G The Article Options settings for the actual article. These options are the same as in the global and menu item options, but override those options for this specific article.

To set individual article options:

1. Log in to the back end.

2. Open the Article Manager.

3. Open the Beginners article by selecting its title from the Article Manager **F**.

   The Edit Article details open. To override the global article settings, set the options for this specific article under the Article Options **G**. If you leave these settings at Use Global, the article will continue to reflect the global options.

   One additional field is present among the individual article options:

   ▸ **Read More Text:** Enter the text you want to display on the Read More button. For example, you could change "Read More" to "Find Out More," "Join Now," and so on.

   ▸ In the Read More Text field, enter **Learn More About**. Be sure to add a space, or a colon, after the word "About."

   ▸ Click View Site and select the Home page.

continues on next page

The Beginners article now has a Read More link that contains the text you set in the individual article options. The other articles' Read More links are not affected **H**.

To set article menu options:

1. Log in to the back end.

2. Choose Menus > Main Menu to open the Menu Manager: Menu Items for the main menu. The manager lists each menu item assigned to the main menu **I**.

3. Select the Home menu item to open the Menu Manager: Edit Menu Item. You will be modifying the settings for the Home menu item, which is a Featured Article menu item type **J**.

   Each menu item type has its own options settings relative to the type of content you can display.

   Menu item settings control what and how much of the content displays when a user clicks this link. You then have the option to override the global and individual options set for articles and categories.

   Menu Item options affect only the content that displays immediately when a user clicks this menu item. Individual settings for articles and categories are still used if a user navigates away from the page by selecting the category or article titles. Any fields left blank or set to Use Global will use the article and/or category global settings.

Beginners

If this is your first Joomla site or your first web site, you have your website up and running quickly and easily.

Start off using your site by logging in using the administrator

> **Learn More About Beginners**

H The same Beginners article with the Read More button text changed

I The Menu Manager: Menu Items

J The Menu Manager: Edit Menu Item screen with Featured Articles as the menu item type

 The menu item layout options. These options override any global options set for the Blog / Featured Layouts.

4. Select Layout Options to open the Layout Option fields.

Here you can define what content is placed on this page, how much of it will appear, and how it is ordered in the layout .

continues on next page

Menu Layout Options for Articles and Featured Articles

- **# Leading Articles:** Leading articles display an article's intro text or its full text across the main body of a page based on your article settings. Leading articles cannot be split into columns. In this field, enter the number of articles to display at the top of the page. If you don't want any articles to span the full width of the page, enter 0.

- **# Intro Articles:** Intro articles can be divided into columns. Enter the number of articles you want displayed beneath the leading articles. If you do not have any leading articles, intro articles will appear across the top of the page in single or multiple columns based upon the # Columns setting.

- **# Columns:** Enter the number of columns used to display intro articles. Entering 1 will display the full width (a single column), 2 will divide the content into two equal columns, and so on.

- **# Links:** At times you will have more featured articles—or articles under a specific category—than you have set to display using the Leading and Intro fields. Use this field to set how many of those articles' titles will appear as links below the intro articles.

- **Multi Column Order:** If you have entered more than one column in the # Columns field, this option sets the order of the articles. Choose Across to display the articles horizontally in order. Choose Down to display the articles vertically in order. Choose Use Global to display the articles according to the global option settings.

- **Category Order:** Display all articles in the order set by the Category Manager. For example, if you have three categories, each with articles, the articles will display in category order, not in their article order. This option is often useful for complex layouts with large amounts of content 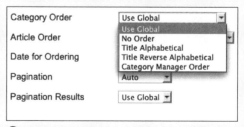.

 The category order selection options

5. Click View Site.

You can see that the featured article menu item Home is set to one leading article, followed by three intro articles. The intro articles are set to span three columns. No article links appear and pagination buttons are hidden because the articles on these pages are the only articles assigned to Featured on the site **Ⓜ**.

You could further refine this page using the remaining options for a Featured Article menu item type.

You are here: Home

About Joomla!

- Getting Started
- Using Joomla!
- The Joomla! Project
- The Joomla! Community

This Site

- **Home**
- Site Map
- Login
- Sample Sites

Beginners

If this is your first Joomla site or your first web site, you have come to the right place. Joomla will help you get your website up and running quickly and easily.

Start off using your site by logging in using the administrator account you created when you installed Joomla!.

› **Read more: Beginners**

Joomla!

Congratulations! You have a Joomla! site! Joomla! makes your site easy to build a website just the way you want it and keep it simple to update and maintain.

Upgraders

If you are an experienced Joomla! 1.5 user, 1.6 will seem very familiar. There are new templates and improved user interfaces, but most functionality

Professionals

Joomla! 1.6 continues development of the Joomla Framework and CMS as a powerful and flexible way to bring your vision of the web to

Ⓜ The featured articles home page displaying one leading article and three intro articles in a three-column layout

TIP For simple layouts, you can generally set global options and leave all the other options at their defaults. When creating complex or specific layouts, there is no shortcut to understanding and becoming familiar with where these options are and how they affect your pages.

TIP Controlling page layouts is one of the more difficult skills to learn when using a content management system. A bit of repetition, practice, and trial and error will eventually make controlling your page layouts much easier.

TIP The most important concept is that global options are used by the system first, followed by menu item settings, followed by the individual article and category options that override those global and menu settings.

Setting Category Layout Options

The best argument for using Joomla 1.6 and above is the new category structure. Nested categories have been desired by the Joomla community for a long time. By implementing this structure, controlling layout in Joomla is easier than ever, yet it can also become complicated.

Global options may change with future releases, but for now the ability to create and control complex layouts means that the system includes many new options. You may never need to use all these options, so don't struggle or worry over them in the beginning. Remember that category global options are the highest level of management and can be controlled at the menu level. The general layout of your site is all you need to worry about at the global level.

To set global category options:

1. Log in to the back end.
2. Open the Category Manager.
3. On the toolbar, click the Options button.
4. In the pop-up window, select the Category tab.

   Category options affect category display. These are the default settings for root, single, and parent categories **A**.

5. Close the options window.
6. Click View Site.
7. From the About Joomla menu, choose Using Joomla.

   This is an example of a link to a single article. This article is contained in a category, but no category options are shown **B**.

A The Category global option settings

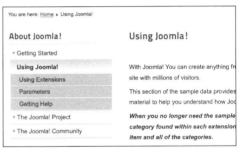

B An example of a link to a single article with no category information displayed

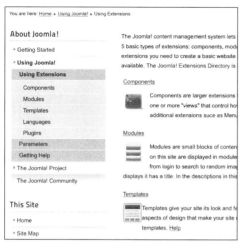

You are here: Home ▸ Using Joomla! ▸ Using Extensions

About Joomla!
- Getting Started
- Using Joomla!
  - **Using Extensions**
    - Components
    - Modules
    - Templates
    - Languages
    - Plugins
  - Parameters
  - Getting Help
- The Joomla! Project
  - The Joomla! Community

This Site
- Home
- Site Map

The Joomla! content management system lets
5 basic types of extensions: components, mod
extensions you need to create a basic website
available. The Joomla! Extensions Directory is

Components

Components are larger extensions
one or more "views" that control ho
additional extensions suce as Men

Modules

Modules are small blocks of conten
on this site are displayed in module
from login to search to random ima
displays it has a title. In the descriptions in this

Templates

Templates give your site its look and fe
aspects of design that make your site
templates. Help

ⓒ An example of a category page displaying the category, subcategories, descriptions, and images

8. Under Using Joomla in the About Joomla menu, choose Using Extensions.

Even though the category layout option is set to Blog, Using Extensions is a List All Categories menu item type. The category descriptions and images are displayed on this page, with no articles. Components, modules, and templates are all categories. Each of those categories has subcategories, which don't display because the subcategory level is set to 1 **ⓒ**.

continues on next page

Global Category Option Settings

- **Choose a Layout:** Categories have two display types: Blog or List. Because you can individually control both types through their own options and menu items, the choice you make here simply identifies the majority of content types on your site. How do you choose? In general, blogs are major sources of article content. In contrast, an e-commerce, catalogue, or reference site may more often present its content in the form of lists.

- **Category Title:** Hide or show the category title. Category titles display as a subheading below the page title.

- **Category Description:** Hide or show the category descriptions.

- **Category Image:** Hide or show the category image. This is the image assigned to the category, not images embedded in the category description or articles.

- **Subcategory Levels:** Set the number of subcategory levels to display if the category has subcategories.

- **Empty Categories:** Hide or show categories that have no articles or subcategories assigned to them.

- **No Articles Message:** Hide or show a "There are no articles in this category" message when no articles are assigned to a category.

- **Subcategories Descriptions:** Hide or show the subcategory descriptions.

- **# Articles in Category:** Hide or show the number of articles assigned to the category.

9. Click the category title, Components.

The category Components has seven subcategories, each with its own subcategories, but only the first level is displayed (along with the category description and image, if any.) The Components menu item type is a Category Blog layout. So you can see that once global options are set, your content will display consistently, unless the global options are overridden at the individual category or menu item level **D**.

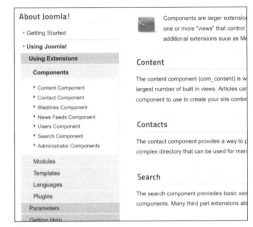

> **TIP** Global category options define layout defaults at a category level, whether that category is a stand-alone category, root category, parent, or subcategory. Global categories options define how items are laid out within a nested category structure.

> **TIP** All category options can be overridden by your menu item options. Unlike articles, categories do not have individual layout options because the only content they contain are subcategories and articles (aside from a short description and image.) To override a category page's layout, you need to set those options at the menu item level.

To set global categories options:

1. Log in to the back end.

2. Open the Category Manager.

3. On the toolbar, click the Options button.

4. From the pop-up window, select the Categories tab.

The Categories options (listed on the following page) let you set the default display behavior when a category has subcategories **E**.

D A choice of Blog or List from the category global options can be overridden at the menu level. This page displays a top-level category and its first-level subcategories.

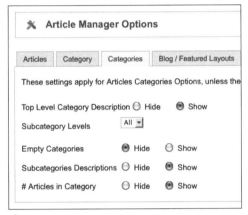

E The Categories global options settings

You are here: Home ▸ Site Map ▸ Articles

About Joomla!

⁕ Getting Started

⁕ Using Joomla!

⁕ The Joomla! Project

⁕ The Joomla! Community

This Site

⁕ Home

⁕ **Site Map**

⁕ Login

⁕ Sample Sites

⁕ Site Administrator

⁕ Example Pages

Sample Data-Articles
Article Count: 1

Joomla!
Article Count: 11

Extensions

The Joomla! content mana
There are 5 basic types of
website includes the exten
additional extensions of all
directory of Joomla! extens

Article Count: 0

Components

Components
component h
administrator
extension managers.

Article Count: 7

 An example page of categories with the article counts set to show

Global Categories Option Settings

- **Top Level Category Description:** Hide or show the parent category description.

- **Subcategory levels:** Select the number of nested categories to display.

- **Empty Categories:** Hide or show the nested categories, even if they are empty with no articles or subcategories assigned to them.

- **Subcategories Descriptions:** Hide or show the nested category descriptions. Depending on the level of subcategories you have set to show, only those will display.

- **# Articles in Category:** Hide or show the number of articles a category contains.

5. Click View Site.

6. From the This Site menu, choose Site Map.

7. Click the Articles link.

This is an example of the category options, and also the behaviour of a category with subcategories. All subcategories are displayed, and the number of articles in each category is set to show **F**.

To set category menu options:

1. Log in to the back end.

2. Open the Menu Manager.

3. Choose the About Joomla menu item to open the Menu Manager: Edit Menu Item screen **G**.

   When you select Category Blog, Category List, or List All Categories as a menu item type, the ability to override all the category options is available.

Menu Layout Options for Categories

- **Required Settings:** You must select the top level, or highest, parent category for this category link.

- **Categories Options, Category Options, Blog Layout Options,** and **List Layouts:** These contain the same options as in the global level options. Here you can override the global defaults to create a custom layout for this page.

- **Article Options:** This contains the same options as individual articles and global article settings. Here you can override those settings for only this category page.

- **Integration Options, Link Type Options, Page Display Options, Metadata Options,** and **Module Assignments** are covered later in the book.

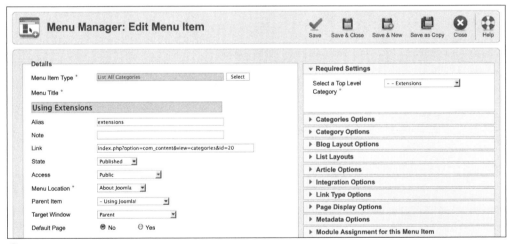

G The menu item options are the same as the global option settings. Here you override the global settings at the menu item level for complete control over the individual page layouts.

Article Manager Options

| Articles | Category | Categories | Blog / Featured Layouts | List Layouts | Integration |

These settings apply for blog or featured layouts unless they are changed for a specific menu i

Leading Articles `1`
Intro Articles `4`
Columns `2`
Links `4`
Multi Column Order ⦿ Down ◯ Across

The option below gives the ability to include articles from subcategories in the Blog layout.
Include Subcategories `None ▾`

Category Order `Category Manager Order ▾`
Article Order `Most recent first ▾`
Date for Ordering `Published ▾`

Ⓐ The Blog/Featured Layouts global option settings

Setting Blog and Featured Article Layout Options

Blog and featured layouts control the default behavior of your category blog and featured article menu item types. These options are the same as the menu item options for Blog Layout and Featured Article options. They can be set once globally and then overridden at the menu item level.

If you have a simple site in which your content should look consistent from page to page, these global options allow you to create menu items quickly and leave these settings at their defaults.

To set global blog / featured article layouts:

1. Log in to the back end.
2. Open the Category Manager.
3. On the toolbar, click the Options button.
4. Select the Blog / Featured Layouts tab Ⓐ to set the options.

TIP When you create a category, you can select Use Global, Blog, or List from the Alternative Layout basic options. Selecting Use Global will use these options by default at the category level.

Global Blog/Featured Article Option Settings

- **# Leading Articles:** Leading articles display an article's intro text or full text across the main body of a page based on your article settings. Leading articles cannot be split into columns. In this field, enter the number of articles to display at the top of the page. If you don't want any articles to span the full width of the page, enter 0.

- **# Intro Articles:** Intro articles can be divided into columns. Enter the number of articles you want displayed beneath the leading articles. If you do not have any leading articles, intro articles will appear across the top of the page in single or multiple columns based on the # Columns setting.

- **# Columns:** Enter the number of columns used to display your intro articles. Enter 1 to display in the full page width (one column.) Enter 2 to divide the content into two equal columns, and so on.

- **# Links:** At times you will have more featured articles—or articles under a specific category—than you have set to display using the Leading and Intro fields. Use this field to set how many of those articles' titles will appear as links below the intro articles.

- **Multi Column Order:** When you have entered more than one column in the # Columns field, set the order of the articles. Choose Across to display the articles horizontally in order. Choose Down to display the articles vertically in order.

- **Include Subcategories:** Display articles that are assigned to subcategories for the parent category.

- **Category Order:** Select the order in which the categories appear on your pages: Category Manager Order, Title Alphabetical A to Z or Z to A, or using No Order.

- **Article Order:** Set the default order of the articles that will appear on your blog or featured article pages.

- **Date for Ordering:** If you set the Article Order to Most Recent or Oldest, set the date to use here.

A The List Layout global options

Setting List Layout Options

Category list options are the default global settings used to present your content in lists. A list is displayed in table format and includes the columns and fields you select. Individual list options can be overridden at the menu item level under List Layout options.

These list options should not be confused with category list layouts. These global settings control tabular data used by the contacts, web links, author, and news feeds lists.

One additional option appears for your menu item list layout: the ability to include articles.

To set global list layout options:

1. Log in to the back end.
2. Open the Category Manager.
3. On the toolbar, click the Options button.
4. Select the List Layouts tab **A** to view the options.

continues on next page

Global List Layout Option Settings

- **Display Select:** Hide or show the Display field, allowing a user to select how many items should appear in the table list.
- **Filter Field:** Hide or show the Filter field, allowing a user to filter the table data.
- **Table Headings:** Hide or show the table column headings.
- **Show Date:** Hide the Date column, or set the type of date you want displayed in the Date column.
- **Date Format:** Enter a code string that displays the date in a certain format. This must be in PHP format.
- **Show Hits in List:** If the data is a list of articles, hide or show the Number Of Hits column.
- **Show Author in List:** If the data is a list of articles, hide or show the Author name column.
- **Pagination:** Display the Next and Previous buttons below the table.
- **Pagination Results:** Display the total number of pages (1, 2, 3, and so on) between the Previous and Next buttons.

5. Click View Site.

6. Choose Using Joomla > Using Extensions > Components > Content Component > Article Category List.

This is an example of an Article Category List layout **B**.

7. From the same menu, choose Contact Component.

8. Under Contact Component, choose Featured Contacts.

This is an example of a Contact List layout **C**.

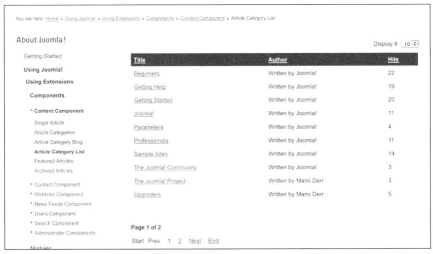

B An example of an article category list table

C An example of a contact list table

Global Integration Option Settings

- **Show Feed Link:** Hide or show a button that enables the user to subscribe to this category feed.

- **For each feed item show:** Select Intro Text to display only the article intro text in the user's feed reader. Select Full Text to display the full article text in the user's feed reader.

Using Integration Options

Integration options are designed to allow article components with other extensions. The available options will change depending on which extensions and Joomla core updates you use on your site.

The default integration options allow you to create a feed link in your content. You set this at the global level for your site content, and then turn it on or off at the menu item level for content that you do not want to provide in an RSS feed.

To set integration options:

1. Log in to the back end.
2. Open the Category Manager.
3. On the toolbar, click the Options button.
4. Select the Integration tab **A** to view the options.

Articles	Category	Categories	Blog / Featured Layouts	List Layouts	Integration

These settings determine how the Article Component will integrate with other extensions.

Show Feed Link   ◯ Hide   ⦿ Show

For each feed item show   ⦿ Intro Text ◯ Full Text

A The Integration tab global options

Putting It All Together

1. **Set the article manager options.** These options are the default global options that affect the display of all content across the site.

2. **Set individual article options.** Individual article options set at the article level will override the global article manager options.

3. **Set Menu Item Options.** When creating menu items, you control the display of categories and articles through the menu item layout options. Menu item options will override global and individual article options.

Working with
Templates

Joomla's template system is one of the main reasons Joomla is so convenient to use. The template system is contained in its own folder structure, named *templates*, which completely separates the site design from the content management. This structure makes it easy to modify the look and feel of your site by installing a new template, or if you are comfortable with CSS, by directly editing the CSS files. Popular third-party template developers use template *frameworks*, which allow you to change colors, styles, and layouts without modifying any HTML or CSS code.

In addition to styling content, templates also contain *positions* that define where your modules and components display on your site.

You can install and use multiple templates on a single Joomla site. You can assign different templates to different pages on your site. You can even install and customize the back-end (administrator) templates.

Using the Template Manager

Joomla installs with three site templates and two administrator templates, but adding new templates is as easy as clicking the Install button.

To view installed templates:

1. Log in to the back end.

2. Choose Extensions > Template Manager.

   The Template Manager lists each template that is installed and available for use on the site, in both front and back ends **A**.

   Note that an administrator template cannot be assigned to the front end of a site, and a site template cannot be applied to the back end.

   The Template Manager provides access to:

   ▸ Setting the default template.

   ▸ Editing template parameters.

   ▸ Editing template styles.

   ▸ Duplicating templates.

   ▸ Deleting templates.

Template Warning!

Be very careful while using the Template Manager. In Joomla versions before 1.6, the site and administrator templates were kept in separate managers. With Joomla 1.6, you can access both template types on a single screen.

You do not want to accidentally delete an administrator template! The back end of Joomla is a web site just like the front end. Deleting an administrator template can cause you to lose your back-end interface. Fortunately, you will receive a warning should you try to delete a template set as the default.

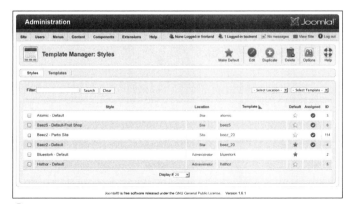

A The Template Manager displays site and administrator templates available on the site.

Understanding Joomla Template Positions

Templates use *positions* to display site content on a page. Joomla contains two types of content: components and modules.

Remember that categories and articles are components. Components display in the main body of the page, and all templates contain a main body, sometimes called the content or component position.

Even though the main body of your template is a position, it is not a position that you can select in the same way you would select positions for your modules. The system automatically uses the main body template position to display your categories, articles, and other components.

Modules—such as your menus, logo, recent comments, login forms, and so on— must be assigned to a specific template position in order to display them on a page.

Module positions surround the main body of the page. For example, your logo is a module that uses the logo position. A footer is a module that uses the footer position. Menus and other modules that appear to the left or right of your articles use positions.

Unfortunately, each template developer uses personal position naming conventions. To understand and use the correct positions in your template, you need to know the names of the positions and where they are located.

To view template positions:

1. Log in to the back end.
2. Choose Extensions > Template Manager.

   All site and administrator templates are listed. To view the template positions, you need to configure Joomla to display them because template positions are hidden by default.

3. On the Template Manager toolbar, click Options **A**.

   A pop-up window displays the Template Manager Options in two tabs: a Templates tab, which allows you to display or hide (enable or disable) template positions, and the Permissions tab, in which you can assign user permissions for your template **B**.

4. Set Preview Module Positions to Enabled.

5. Click Save & Close.

   You can now view all positions contained in any template installed on the site.

6. In the Template Manager, click the Templates link.

   The Template Manager: Styles allows you to manage your templates, including setting default templates and accessing the template parameters **C**.

   The Template Manager: Templates displays information about each template, lets you preview the positions contained in that template, and permits you to edit the template's HTML and CSS files **D**.

A The Template Manager toolbar

B Template Manager Options. Selecting Enabled for Preview Module Positions displays the positions and position names used in your template.

C The Template Manager: Styles link provides access to template parameters.

D The Template Manager: Templates link provides access to the template HTML and CSS source files and the position preview.

7. Scroll down to the beez_20 template.

This is a thumbnail preview of the full template; in this case, it's the default home page template used when Joomla is first installed **E**.

8. Click the Preview link beneath the beez_20 Details link to open the home page of your web site.

Your content and the template's positions are outlined to identify where the positions are located. Notice that article and category content fills the main body of the page while the positions surround the component (main body) area of the page **F**.

The main body of the page does not have a position name or a position outline because it is not an assignable position.

E Clicking the Preview link beneath the template name will open the front end of the web site and display all positions available to the template.

F The positions displayed in the template

To assign a module to a template position:

1. Log in to the back end.

2. Choose Extensions > Module Manager.

   This is your first view of the Module Manager. Like the other managers in Joomla, this one helps you manage every module created for your site .

   The Position column identifies the position to which this module is assigned and where it will appear in the front end of the site.

3. From the Select Type drop-down list, choose Menu **H**.

   Choosing Menu as the sort type filters the list to show only menu modules **I**.

G The Module Manager screen displays both published and unpublished modules.

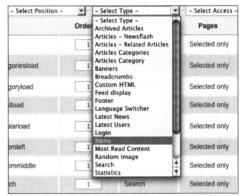

H The Select Type drop-down list in the Module Manager

I If you choose Menu as the Module Manager sort type, the manager will list only menu modules, which makes it much easier to locate the module you are working with.

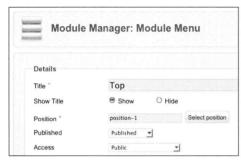

Module Manager: Module Menu

Details

Title *	Top
Show Title	● Show ○ Hide
Position *	position-1 Select position
Published	Published
Access	Public

J The Position field tells Joomla where to display the module on the web page.

Filter: [   ]   Search   Clear

Title ⬆

archiveload
articlescategoriesload
articlescategoryload
articleslatestload
articlespopularload
atomic-bottomleft   • atomic (Bottom left)
atomic-bottommiddle   • atomic (Bottom middle)
atomic-search   • atomic (Search)
atomic-sidebar   • atomic (Sidebar)
atomic-topmenu   • atomic (Top Menu)

K The Position screen displays every position available from all templates installed on the site.

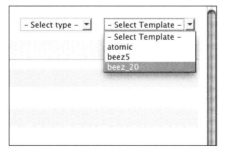

– Select type –   – Select Template –
– Select Template –
atomic
beez5
beez_20

L Sort the position list to display only those positions available in a specific template.

4. Choose Top to open the Top menu modules details screen.

   You assign a module to a position using the Position field. Note that the Top menu module is currently assigned to position-1 **J**.

5. Click the "Select position" button to open a pop-up window in which you can select from *all* the positions available for *all* the templates on the site **K**.

   The Top menu appears on all pages, but you are concerned only with the default template at this point so you need to isolate the positions to only those available to the beez_20 template.

6. From the Select Template drop-down list, choose beez_20 **L**.

continues on next page

The module positions displayed are only the available positions contained in the beez_20 template. Use the pagination at the bottom to see all the positions available for this template. The positions are listed in alphabetical order **M**.

The Top menu module is currently assigned to position-1, which is at the top of the page. In the front end of the site, it is the menu at the top of the page containing Home, Sample Sites, and Joomla.org.

7. Select Position-7. You may need to click the Prev and Next buttons to locate this position in the list.

You cannot save your selection here. As soon as you click on a position name, the position is assigned and you are returned to the Module Manager.

8. From the Module Manager: Module Menu toolbar, click Save to save all your changes, including the new module position assignment. Leave the details screen open.

9. Click View Site.

The Top menu module is no longer at the top of the page in the position-1 position. It is now positioned to the left of the page in the position-7 position **N**.

M The positions available have been isolated to the beez_20 template.

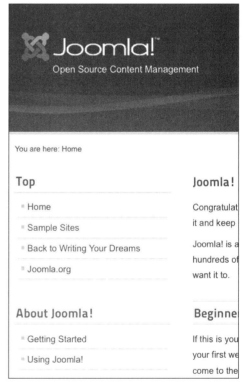

N The Top menu module displayed in position-7

0 More than one module can be assigned to the same positions. Modules assigned to the same position will display according to the Ordering drop-down list.

10. Return to the back end. Make sure you are still in the Top menu module's edit screen.

When you viewed the front page, the Top menu was in its new position and displayed first above two menus. When you assign a module to a position, it will default to the top of the ordering.

The Ordering drop-down list controls the order in which modules appear when assigned to the same position **0**.

11. Set the Top menu module position back to position-1.

12. Click Save & Close, and then view the front page again.

The top menu is once again displayed at the top of the page in the position-1 position.

Changing where the information appears on the page is as easy as switching the module position.

TIP You can assign multiple modules to the same position. When the positions are styled horizontally, they will display side by side according to the ordering selected. When the positions are styled vertically, as in this menu example, they will display vertically according to the ordering selected.

TIP Most template developers use common terms for positions. For example, the main navigation position is usually called *mainnav* or *horznav*. Left and right columns are generally called *left* and *right*, and so on.

Using Site Templates

So far you've learned the following facts about templates:

- Joomla templates contain positions for modules, and a main body position for displaying component content (categories, articles, banners, and so on).

- Templates have unique position names. By enabling the Preview Module Positions feature, you can easily identify the position names for any template.

- Joomla templates comprise HTML/ XHTML, PHP, JavaScript, and CSS stylesheets, but you need not know any coding to use a Joomla template.

- You have thousands of free and commercial Joomla templates to choose from.

In this section, you'll learn how to use the Template Manager, install a new template, set a template as the default for your site, assign a new template to a page, and delete a template entirely.

To view site templates:

1. Log in to the back end.

2. Choose Extensions > Template Manager.

3. From the Select Location drop-down list, choose Site.

   The Template Manager now displays only the site templates **Ⓐ**.

   When working on your site templates, it's strongly recommended that you filter the Template Manager to display only the site templates. By filtering, you can avoid accidentally deleting or modifying the administrator templates.

Ⓐ Filtering the Template Manager to display only site templates prevents you from accidentally modifying or deleting an administrator template.

B An orange star in the Default template column identifies the default template for the site. This template is used on all pages unless another template is assigned to a page using the Menu Assignment feature.

C The Beez2 - Default template applied as the default template is used for the home page of the site.

If you did not install the sample data, Joomla includes three site templates. If you did install the sample data, you'll have four site templates:

▸ **Atomic - Default:** A basic template with very little styling or graphics.

▸ **Beez5 - Default-Fruit Shop:** A cutting edge, HTML 5 template that takes advantage of all the new HTML 5 and CSS3 template features.

▸ **Beez2 - Parks Site:** A duplicate of the Beez2 original template, styled specifically for the Parks Site portion of the web site sample data.

▸ **Beez2 - Default:** The default template for the sample data site.

To set or change the default site template:

1. Open the Template Manager.

2. Set the Select Location filter to Site.

   Notice that the orange star is highlighted in the Default column for the Beez2 - Default template. This indicates that this template is set as the default template for the web site **B**.

   Only one template can be assigned as the default template for a site. This template is the default template used for the entire site. You can then assign any other template to a specific menu item (page).

3. Click View Site to display the default Beez2 template **C**.

4. Return to the Template Manager.

continues on next page

5. Select the checkbox next to the Atomic - Default template. On the toolbar, click the Make Default button.

An orange star appears in the default column for the Atomic template to indicate that it is now the default template.

The term *default* in the title of the templates does not mean these are the default templates applied to the site. It means only that these are the "original" templates installed. Notice that the Beez2 - Parks template does not have *default* in its title, which indicates that it is a copy of the original template. Only a template with the orange star in the Default column signifies the site's default template.

6. Click View Site.

The Atomic template is applied as the default template **D**.

Notice that the menu modules no longer display on the site. This is because the Atomic template contains different positions than the Beez2 template.

The category and article content still displays because all templates share one common position, the main body.

Applying a new template is as simple as setting that template as the default; however, you will need to assign modules to positions supported by the new template.

7. Return to the Template Manager and reset the Beez2 - Default template as the default.

Joomla VQS

Joomla!

Congratulations! You have a Joomla! site! Joomla! makes your site easy to build a we and keep it simple to update and maintain.

Joomla! is a flexible and powerful platform, whether you are building a small site hundreds of thousands of visitors. Joomla is open source, which means you can mak it to.

Beginners

If this is your first Joomla site or your first web site, you have come to the right place. website up and running quickly and easily.

Start off using your site by logging in using the administrator account you create
Read more: Beginners

Upgraders

If you are an experienced Joomla! 1.5 user, 1.6 will seem very familiar. There are new interfaces, but most functionality is the same. The biggest changes are improved acc categories.
Read more: Upgraders

Professionals

Joomla! 1.6 continues development of the Joomla Framework and CMS as a powerf vision of the web to reality. With the administrator now fully MVC, the ability to contro extensions is now complete.
Read more: Professionals

©2011 Joomla VQS

D The Atomic template assigned as the default template. The positions in the Atomic template are different from the Beez2 template; therefore, modules assigned to positions that don't exist in the current template can't display. The content, however, does display because the main body position is consistent from template to template.

Template Manager: Edit Style

Details

Style Name *

Beez2 – Parks Site

Template   beez_20

Site

Default   No

ID   114

Template description   Accessible template for Joomla 1.6

E You can assign the default template here, or by clicking the Make Default button in the Template Manager toolbar.

Menus assignment

Menu Selection: Toggle Selection

About Joomla   **Australian Parks**

☐ - Getting Started   ☑ - Parks Home
☐ - Using Joomla!   ☑ - Park Blog
☐ - - Using Extensions   ☑ - Write a Blog Post
☐ - - - Components   ☑ - Image Gallery
☐ - - - - Content Component   ☑ - - Animals
☐ - - - - - Single Article   ☑ - - Scenery
☐ - - - - - Article Categories   ☑ - Park Links
☐ - - - - - Article Category Blog
☐ - - - - - Article Category List **Fruit Shop**
☐ - - - - - Featured Articles   ☐ - Welcome
☐ - - - - - Archived Articles   ☐ - Fruit Encyclopedia
☐ - - - - - Submit Article   ☐ - Growers
☐ - - - - Contact Component   ☐ - Contact Us

F This area details every menu item created on the site. From here you can assign a template to specific menu items (pages).

This Site

▪ **Home**

▪ Site Map

▪ Login

　Sample Sites

▪ Site Administrator

▪ Example Pages

G The This Site menu with the Sample Sites menu item

To assign a template to a specific page:

1. Open the Template Manager.

2. Select the Beez2 - Parks Site template by clicking its title, or selecting the checkbox next to the title and then clicking the Edit button on the toolbar.

   The Template Manager: Edit Style opens. Here you can set the template to default view and change any template parameters, and assign this template to specific pages **E**.

3. Scroll down to view the "Menus assignment" area **F**.

   Here you assign specific templates to specific menu items. Templates assigned to menu items will override the default template.

4. Click View Site.

5. From the home page, choose Sample Sites from the This Site menu module **G**.

continues on next page

6. Under Australian Parks, choose the Parks Home link.

You are still on the same Joomla site, but the menu items for the Australian Parks content do not use the site's default template .

The main navigation is still available so the user can return to the main portion of the site.

By assigning a template to specific menu items, you can create a very diverse and graphically creative site.

TIP Another option, when using multiple templates on a single site, is to duplicate a template and change only a few color styles or graphics. Using this method, pages look similar and contain the same positions but have different color schemes.

To install a new template:

1. Download a commercial or free template from the Internet to your computer.

Make sure the template is a Joomla-compatible template and is created for your current version of Joomla. For example, a template that says it is compatible with Joomla version 1.5 is not compatible with Joomla versions 1.6 and above.

2. Log in to the back end.

3. Choose Extensions > Extension Manager.

Templates are extensions, and all extensions are installed through the Extension Manager .

You can update and delete extensions here or in their respective managers.

H The Australian Parks menu items are not assigned to the default template. Assigning a template to specific menu items overrides the default template assignment for those pages.

I The Extension Manager, in which all extensions are installed, including third-party extensions and templates

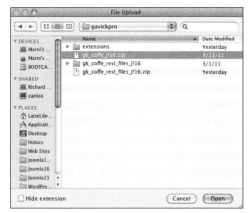

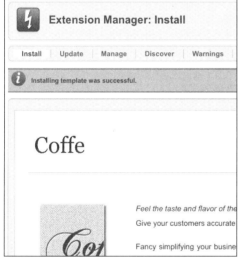

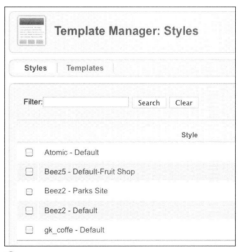

J Locate the downloaded template file on your computer by clicking the Extension Manager Browse button.

K The Extension Manager reports a successful installation of the template and displays information about the template.

4. In the Upload Package File area, click the Browse button.

5. Navigate to the template's .zip file on your computer. Select it and click Open **J**.

All templates and other extensions are installed using compressed files. If you experience permission issues when installing extensions, check with your hosting provider.

You can also install an extension from a directory on your server or an external site using the Install Directory and Install URL fields.

6. Click Upload & Install.

If the template installs successfully, you will see a successful installation message and information about the new template will display **K**.

7. Open the Template Manager.

The template is installed and ready for use on your site **L**.

continues on next page

L The Template Manager displays the newly installed template.

The template name followed by - *Default* shows that it is the original template and not a duplicate.

This template can now be assigned as the default template or assigned to specific site pages.

8. Select the template you just installed and make it the default template.

9. Click View Site.

The new template styles and design are applied immediately. The only issue you have now is to assign modules to the positions supported in this template .

To delete a site template:

1. Open the Template Manager.

2. Select the checkbox next to the template that you installed in the previous section.

Do not uninstall any of the core templates unless you want to remove them completely from the database.

3. Click Delete.

If you receive a warning "Cannot delete last style of a template" or "Cannot delete the default template," the template is set as the default for the site and Joomla will not allow you to delete it as a safety measure 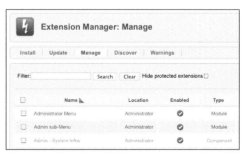.

If you really intend to delete this template, assign another template as the default and then try deleting the template again.

You can also delete a template from the Extension Manager.

4. Open the Extension Manager.

5. Click the Manage link to open the Extension Manager: Manage screen.

From here you can access every component, module, plug-in, and template installed on the site .

M The newly installed template applied to the web site as the default

N A template set as default for the site cannot be uninstalled. You will receive an error warning.

O You can delete templates using the Template Manager; or delete templates, components, modules, and plug-ins via the Manage link in the Extension Manager.

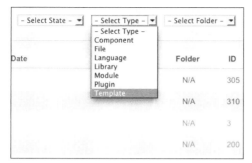

P Filtering the Extension Manager to display only templates

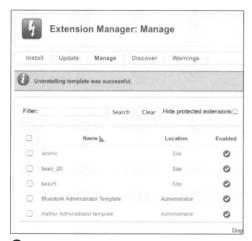

Q An error message will display if you try to uninstall a default template, which protects you from accidentally removing a template required for Joomla to work correctly.

R A successful uninstall message in the Extension Manager. The template has been completely removed from the site and database.

6. From the Select Type drop-down list, choose Template **P**.

   This filters the Extension Manager to display only template extensions.

7. Select the template you want to uninstall, and on the toolbar click the Uninstall button.

   Again, if you accidentally try to uninstall a template set as default, you will receive an error message **Q**.

   If the template successfully uninstalls, you will receive a confirmation message and the template will be removed from the list **R**.

   The template is also completely removed from the database. The only way to recover the template is to reinstall it.

Editing and Modifying Templates

All templates have parameters that you can modify. However, like positions, each template will have different parameter settings. Simple templates, such as the default templates that come with Joomla, have a limited number of parameters, including setting the width of your site, using an image or text for your logo, and adjusting font sizes. More advanced templates can have complete frameworks that allow you to adjust module positions, colors, font types, and so on.

There is a difference between parameters and actually modifying the template core files, but you access them in the same place. If you are going to modify any template files—for example the CSS or HTML—we strongly recommend that you create a duplicate of the template, so you can always return to the original styles.

To create a duplicate template:

1. Log in to the back end.
2. Open the Template Manager.
3. Select a template to duplicate by selecting the checkbox next to the template's title. On the toolbar, click Duplicate.

   A complete and full copy of the template and all its files is created in the database. The duplicated template appears in the list **A**.

   You will want to change the template name so you can clearly distinguish the copy from the original.

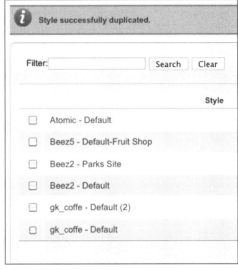

A Creating a copy of an installed template

In the Template Manager: Edit Style screen, you can modify template details and parameters.

The template copy with a new name assigned to identify it as a modified template

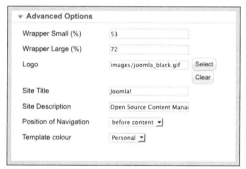

The template parameters for the Beez2 - Default template

4. Click the duplicate template's title to open the template's Template Manager: Edit Style screen ⓑ.

   This screen displays all the template's information along with the parameters that can be modified.

5. In the Style Name field, leave the template name, but replace **Default (2)** with something like **modified**.

6. Click Save & Close.

   The duplicate template can now quickly be identified as a duplicate or modified template ⓒ, and you can make any desired changes to the template's source files.

To modify template parameters:

1. Open the Template Manager.

2. Select the Beez2 - Default template, and then in the toolbar, click Edit.

   The Template Manager: Edit Style screen opens. The Beez2 template has only a few advanced options ⓓ.

continues on next page

3. On the toolbar, click Close to return to the Template Manager.

Every template has a set of parameters that you can modify. Some will have advanced frameworks; others will have very few.

In this figure is a template built by Gavick Pro (www.gavickpro.com), which uses a framework called Gavern. The Gavern template parameters allow extensive customization **E**. They even allow you to automatically create a handheld or iPhone-friendly version of your site **F**.

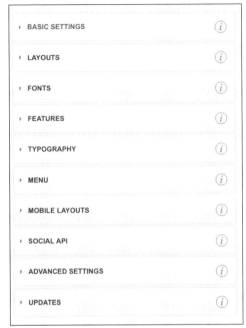

E The template parameters for the Coffe template produced by Gavick Pro. Each template contains its own parameters to let you further customize styles.

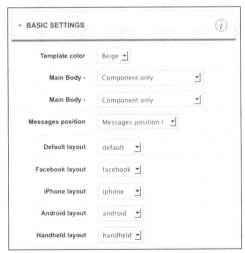

F Basic settings for Gavick Pro's Coffe template. Advanced templates can provide multiple layouts to support mobile devices and social media integration.

G The Template Manager: Templates screen links to all template HTML and CSS source files in which you can edit template coding.

H In the Template Manager: Customize Template screen you can edit the template's HTML/XHTML code files.

To modify template source files:

1. Open the Template Manager.

   The Template Manager: Styles screen is open by default. You need to switch to the Template Manager: Templates screen.

2. Select Templates to open the Template Manager: Templates screen.

   This screen provides access to the templates' source files and position previews **G**.

   You should modify these files only if you know HTML/XHTML and/or CSS programming. After you modify and save a file, you cannot undo those changes.

3. In the Template column, click the beez20 Details link to open the Template Manager: Customise Template screen. In this screen, you can access the "Master files: The index.php" page, the error page, and the print view page **H**. You also have access to all the CSS stylesheets associated with this template **I**.

continues on next page

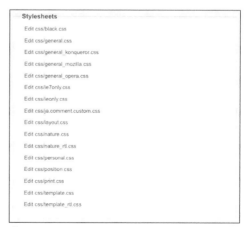

I All the template's CSS source files may be edited.

4. From the Template Master Files area, click "Edit main page template."

The Joomla internal editor opens the index.php page for the beez20 template. Here you can modify and save changes to the code 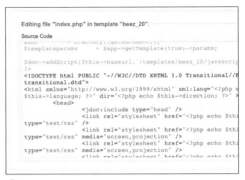.

5. Close the editor window without saving.

To change a template logo:

1. Open the Template Manager.

2. Select the Beez2 - Default template. On the toolbar, click Edit.

3. Click View Site and look at the Joomla logo on the home page, and then return to the back-end template editor .

4. Under Advanced Options, click the Clear button to clear the link to the logo .

J The editor window for the template's index.php source file

K The logo image styled by the Beez20-Default template

L The Beez20-Default template parameters in which you can change the default widths of the template, link to a new logo image, or use plain text as the site logo

You are here: Home

 The new logo set as plain text without using an image

 The Media Manager contains all media files used on the site. Some templates can use an image file linked to the site media files; others contain a logo image in the template's image folder.

You are here: Home

 A new logo image linked using the Media Manager as displayed on the site

5. Click Save, and then click View Site.

The logo image has been replaced by the site title and description set in the template's parameters .

6. Return to the Advanced Options and click the Select button next to the Logo field.

7. In the Media Manager, select the joomla_logo_black.jpg image, and then click Insert .

8. Click Save, and then click View Site.

The image you selected is now used for the site's new logo . This is one of the quickest methods for changing a site logo.

For most sites you will need to identify the full path to the logo image file of your template and then upload your logo image to the appropriate template's image folder using the same name as the template developer. Because every template has a different template folder structure, this exercise doesn't specifically describe how to do this for each template.

Using Administrator Templates

Among the most underused features of Joomla is the ability to modify or change the administrative back end. Joomla's back end has templates and module positions just like its front end that can be modified to fit a specific workflow by providing individualized access to features and functions. You can also install various administrator templates.

Avoid changing the administrative back end until you are an experienced Joomla user. However, in this section, you'll explore these back-end capabilities that are often overlooked. You'll learn how to install a new administrative back-end template. You'll also see that Joomla's menus and interface can change with new revisions or templates, but this does not change the core functionality.

To change the default administrator template:

1. Log in to the back end.

2. Choose Extensions > Template Manager.

3. From the Select Location drop-down list, choose Administrator to filter the templates to display only the administrator template .

   Joomla has two administrator templates: Bluestork (the default template) and Hathor (a high-contrast template).

A The Template Manager can be filtered to display only the available administrator templates on the site. The Bluestork template is currently the back-end default template.

4. Select the checkbox next to the Hathor - Default template. On the toolbar, click Make Default.

The administrative back-end styles have changed according to the styles and positions of the new template. The Template Manager links are now tabs, and the menus and quick icons are in different positions **B**.

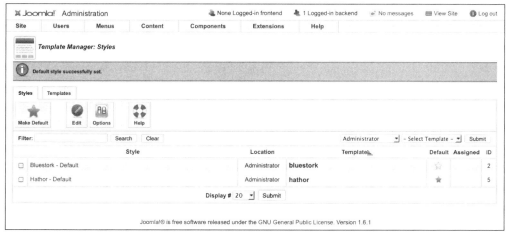

B The back-end interface after changing the template to the Hathor administrator template

To modify administrator template settings:

1. Open the Template Manager.

2. Make the Hathor - Default template the default administrator template.

3. Select the Hathor - Default template. On the toolbar, click Edit.

4. Under Basic Options, choose High Contrast for the color .

5. Click Save.

   Notice the change to a high-contrast, color-accessible template .

   Administrator templates contain options and parameters just as front-end templates do.

6. Return the default template to Bluestork.

7. Choose Extensions > Module Manager.

8. From the Site drop-down list, choose Administrator.

   The Module Manager now displays the administrative back-end modules, along with their positions, ordering, type, pages, access, language, and ID information . These constitute all the modules used in the administrative interface. You can move them to different positions within the administrator template.

   By modifying the Joomla back end, you can completely customize the administrative experience of a site.

To use a third-party administrator template:

1. Log in to the back end.

2. Choose Extensions > Extension Manager.

C Selecting the High Contrast option for the Hathor administrator template

D The high-contrast settings for the Hathor administrator template change the entire look of the Joomla back end.

E Just like the front end of a Joomla site, the back end comprises modules and positions. In this image, the Module Manager displays all back-end modules for the Joomla site.

3. Install the administrator template using the Upload Package File.

   Admin Praise (www.adminpraise.com) is one of the primary providers of administrator templates. In this example, you will apply their Admin Lite template (available at no cost to Joomla users).

4. Open the Template Manager and assign the Admin Lite template as the default.

   You can see the versatility of customizing the administrative interface in Joomla . One of the huge benefits of using a custom administrative template is that most of them have handheld, iPhone, and iPad versions that allow you to access and manage your site on the go.

   The most important point, however, is that regardless of your workflow or back-end interface, Joomla core concepts and functionality remain the same. Once you've mastered the concepts, you'll be able to use and customize Joomla to your processes and workflows.

Ⓕ Like the front end, the back end of Joomla can be styled to suit your workflow and design preferences.

Putting It All Together

1. **Install a new site template.** Thousands of free and commercial templates are available for Joomla. Find a template that reflects your site branding and design choice and install it.

2. **Change the default site template.** Only one template can be assigned as a default template. All other templates can be used or assigned to individual pages using menu assignments. Try various combinations of default and page-specific templates.

3. **Create a duplicate template.** Make a copy of a template and customize it independently of the original.

4. **Enable the template Preview Module Positions options.** Modules are assigned to positions used by your template. View positions and assign modules so they will display where you want them on the site. Learn the positions used by various templates.

5. **Upload a site logo.** Open a new site logo from the Joomla Media Manager or the template's images folder.

6. **Change the template logo.** Change the default template logos by modifying template parameters or directly editing the source files.

7. **Change the administrator template.** Modify the look and feel of the back end of Joomla by installing a new template or modifying an existing template.

8

Working with Modules

Modules add interactive elements to your Joomla site, such as login forms, menus, search bars, comments, and links to content. While components display in the main body of a web page, modules are positioned around the main body of the page. For example, the Login module is usually positioned to the top, left, or right of the page, and a footer module is at the bottom.

Modules work in combination with your content, components, and other elements on your site. While you can create many module types within Joomla, adding extensions will further increase the number of modules available to you.

In this chapter, you'll create and configure basic modules, assign modules to positions, and display modules on your site.

In This Chapter

Using the Module Manager

You use the Module Manager to create, edit, and manage all modules created for your site. The Module Manager contains modules for both the front and back ends of your site.

Joomla groups modules into the following types:

- **Content modules:** Display information from your content.
- **User modules:** Interact with the user system.
- **Display modules:** Work with components other than content.
- **Utility modules:** Provide functional interaction.
- **Navigation modules:** Create menu modules and breadcrumbs for navigation.

To use the Module Manager:

1. Log in to the back end.

2. Choose Extensions > Module Manager, or on the Control Panel screen, click the Module Manager quick icon.

The Module Manager displays all modules created for your site **Ⓐ**.

If you have installed the sample data and/or third-party extensions, some modules in this list may appear as unpublished. Unpublished modules do not appear on the front end of the site.

continues on next page

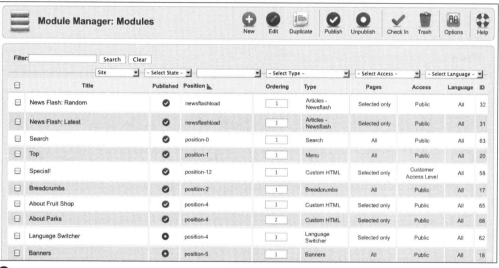

Ⓐ The Module Manager

3. On the toolbar, click New to open a pop-up window in which you can select the type of module you will create 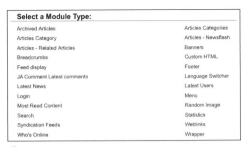.

All module types available to the site appear in this list. If you have added third-party extensions that contain module types, they also appear in this list.

4. Select Archived Articles.

The Module Manager: Module Archived Articles edit screen opens **C**.

Module details are the same for every module type, but different Basic Options will be available for each module **D**.

Modules can be assigned to specific menu items and appear only on those pages you select **E**.

5. On the toolbar, click Cancel.

When creating or editing a module you can:

- ▸ **Save:** Save and leave the current screen open.
- ▸ **Save & Close:** Save and exit to the Module Manager.
- ▸ **Save & New:** Save the current module settings and create a new module.
- ▸ **Cancel:** Close the module window without saving and return to the Module Manager.
- ▸ **Save as Copy:** Modules that have been created and saved have this additional option. It allows you to save the current module and create an exact copy.

6. On the toolbar, click Close.

B Module type selection screen

C The module's details screen

D Basic options vary depending on the module type.

E Modules can be assigned to all menu items or only those items you select.

F The Module Manager filter and sort fields

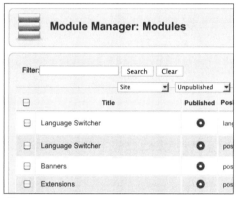

G The Module Manager displays only unpublished items when Unpublished is chosen in the Select State sort drop-down list.

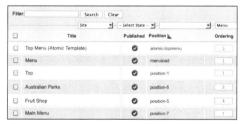

H Sorting the Module Manager by Type displays only modules of the type selected in the Select Type drop-down list.

To sort, filter, or search modules:

1. Open the Module Manager.

   The Module Manager has several fields that allow you to sort module types in ascending or descending order. Doing so allows you to limit the list to display only items that match the search criteria and enable you to more easily find the module you are working with **F**.

   You can search for a specific module title by using the Filter field, or sort modules by using the following drop-down list choices:

   ▸ Site or Admin

   ▸ Select State

   ▸ Select Position

   ▸ Select Type

   ▸ Select Access

   ▸ Select Language

2. In the Select State drop-down list, choose Unpublished.

   The Module Manager now displays only modules with an Unpublished status **G**.

3. Return the drop-down list to Select State.

4. From the Select Type drop-down list, choose Menu.

   The Module Manager displays only modules of the type Menu **H**.

continues on next page

5. Reset the drop-down list to Select Type.

6. Click the Title column heading.

The modules are sorted in ascending alphabetical order. Click the column heading again to toggle the sort between ascending and descending order **Ⓘ**.

TIP Only one column can be sorted at a time. For example, if you sorted the modules by Title, and then sorted them by Type, the Title column would no longer be sorted alphabetically.

TIP If a module has a lock icon next to its title, the module is in a checked-out state, which indicates that someone else is modifying the module. If the module is locked and no one is editing it, you can unlock the module by selecting the checkbox next to the module's title and then clicking Check In on the toolbar.

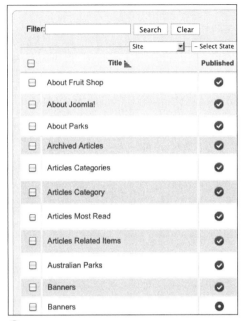

Ⓘ Clicking the Module Manager column headings will toggle the sort between ascending or descending order.

Module Details

All modules require a title and a position to be created. All other details are optional.

- **Title:** The title of this module.
- **Show Title:** Show or hide the module title on the front end of the site. Module titles use h3 HTML/CSS styling.
- **Position:** Select the position to display this module.
- **Published:** Publish or unpublish this module.
- **Access:** Set the access level for viewing this module on the front end of the site.
- **Ordering:** Set the ordering for this module based on any other modules that are assigned to the same position.
- **Start Publishing:** Set the date that this module should be published to the site.
- **Finish Publishing:** Set the date that this module should be unpublished on the site. Leave this field blank if the module should always be published.
- **Language:** Select the language to use for this module.
- **Note:** Enter a descriptive note about this module. This note is for back end use only and will not appear on the front end.
- **ID:** This field is automatically filled in by the system.
- **Site:** This field identifies the module as a site module and cannot be changed.
- **Module Description:** The system description for this module type.

Using Content Modules

Content modules are used to retrieve and display small pieces of your articles or categories. Joomla has eight standard content module types:

- **Archived Articles:** Displays a calendar that links to archived articles by month.
- **Articles Categories:** Displays a list of subcategories from a single parent category.
- **Articles Category:** Lists a user-defined number of articles for one or more categories.
- **Articles – Related Articles:** Displays a user-defined number of articles related to the current article. Articles are related through keywords and metadata information.
- **Articles – Newsflash:** Displays a specific number of articles from a specific category.
- **Latest News:** Lists the most recent articles.
- **Most Read Content:** Lists articles based on their hit counts.
- **Random Image:** Displays a random image from a directory of images selected in the Media Manager.

To create a newsflash content module:

1. Choose Extension > Module Manager to open the Module Manager.

2. On the toolbar, click New.

3. Click Articles Newsflash to open the Module Manager: Module Articles – Newsflash details .

   A Newsflash module can display articles from a single category or multiple categories. The number of articles to display is set in the Basic Options.

4. In the Title field, type **Newsflash**.

5. In the Position field, type **position-8**.

6. Leave the menu assignment set to On all pages.

7. Click the arrow next to Basic Options.

   The basic options define one or more categories from which to pull articles and the article content to display .

8. In the Category list, choose Content Modules.

9. For Show Article Title, choose Yes.

10. In the Linked Titles drop-down menu, choose Yes.

11. In the Number of Articles field, type **3**.

12. Click Save, and then click View Site.

   Click through the Newsflash articles by clicking their titles 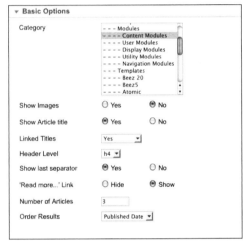.

   TIP With long articles that do not have a Read More link, the Newsflash module will span the entire length of the article. It is best practice for newsflashes to consist of short, descriptive content, or for longer content, to attach a Read More link to the full article.

Ⓐ Newsflash module detail settings

Ⓑ The Newsflash module Basic Options

Ⓒ Example of a Newsflash module on the site

Newsflash Module Basic Options

- **Category:** Display only items from the category selected in this field.

- **Show Images:** Choose Yes to show images in the article, and No to hide them.

- **Show Article title:** Choose Yes to show the title, and No to hide it.

- **Linked Title:** Choose Yes to make the article title linkable. Choose No to display the article title without a link. Or choose Use Global to apply the article's global setting.

- **Show last separator:** Choose Yes to include an article separator after the last article. Choose No to omit a separator after the last article.

- **"Read more..." Link:** Display a Read More link in the Newsflash module.

- **# of Articles:** Set the number of articles to display.

- **Order Results:** Select the order of articles in the module.

Using User Modules

User modules create user accounts and display user information, such as user profiles and user settings.

Joomla's standard User modules are:

- **Login:** Enables users to create an account, log in to the site, and then displays a user menu.

- **Latest Users:** Displays the most recent user accounts created on the site.

- **Who's Online:** Displays the total number of users viewing the site.

To create a Who's Online module:

1. Choose Extension > Module Manager to open the Module Manager.

2. On the toolbar, click New.

3. Click Who's Online.

4. In the Title field, type **Who's Online**.

5. In the Position field, type **position-3**.

   The Position field controls where the module appears on the page **A**.

6. Set Menu Assignment to "Only on the pages selected."

continues on next page

7. Set Menu Selections to Using Joomla.

This module will now appear only on the Using Joomla page.

8. Under Basic Options, choose Both from the Display drop-down menu.

The number of guests/members will now appear in addition to the names of the members .

9. Click Save, and then click View Site **C**.

B The Who's Online Basic Options

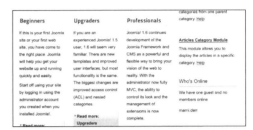

C The Who's Online module as it appears on the site

Who's Online Options

- **Display:** Determine what will display for the Who's Online module, such as the number of guests and users online.

- **Link:** Select whether or not to link to the user's information.

- **Information:** Select the type of user information to display.

- **Alternative Layout:** Apply a layout other than the standard module template.

- **Module Class Suffix:** Use a CSS class from the template to customize the appearance of this module.

- **Caching:** Select to cache or not cache the module content.

Ⓐ The Footer module details

Ⓑ The Footer module added to the site

Footer Options

- **Alternative Layout:** Use a layout other than the standard module template.

- **Module Class Suffix:** Use a CSS class from the template to customize the appearance of this module.

- **Caching:** Select to cache or not cache the module content.

- **Cache Time:** Select how much time passes before the module is cached.

TIP The Footer module is not the same as a Footer menu. Most web sites contain a footer area for such links as privacy notices, webmaster information, legal notices, and so on. The Footer module in Joomla displays copyright information.

Using Display Modules

Display modules can display information about your site or component information, such as banners, feeds, and web links.

Joomla has four standard display modules:

- **Feed Display:** Creates a single RSS feed from another web site into your web site.

- **Banners:** Displays banners on your site.

- **Weblinks:** Displays a list of weblinks.

- **Footer:** Displays copyright and Joomla information from a .php include file. To modify this information, you must edit the include file. To create your own footer information, create a Footer module.

To create a Footer module:

1. Choose Extension > Module Manager to open the Module Manager.

2. On the toolbar, click New.

3. From the list of module types, choose Footer.

4. In the Title field, type `Footer`.

5. For Show Title, choose Hide.

6. In the Position field, type `Position-10`.

   Leave all other settings at their default settings including the All selection from the Menu Assignment details. Doing so ensures that the footer is displayed on all pages of the site Ⓐ.

7. Click Save, and then click View Site.

   The footer appears at the bottom of the web site Ⓑ.

Using Utility Modules

Utility modules provide functionality on the front end of your site, such as a search box in which users can enter search terms and locate matching articles.

Joomla has five standard Utility modules:

- **Search:** Creates a search box for items on your site.

- **Syndication Feeds:** Creates a feed for the page to which this module is assigned.

- **Language Switcher:** Allows a user to select the content language when language packs are installed.

- **Statistics:** Provides statistical data about your site such as server information, the number of web links, and the number of articles in the database.

- **Wrapper:** Creates an iFrame window in the position selected for the module.

To create a Search module:

1. Open the Module Manager.
2. On the toolbar, click New.
3. Click Search.
4. In the Title field, type **Search**.
5. In the Position field, type **Position-6**.
6. From Menu Assignment, choose "On all pages."

    Because a search box searches everything on your site, it is best to make a search box available on all pages .

Ⓐ The Search module details

Search Module Options

- **Box Label:** Set the label for the Search box.

- **Box Width:** Set the width of the Search box.

- **Box Text:** Enter the text to display in the Search box.

- **Search Button:** Show or hide the Search button.

- **Button Position:** Set the position of the Search button.

- **Search Button Image:** Use an image for the Search button.

- **Button Text:** Enter the text that will appear on the Search button.

- **Set ItemID:** Set the ItemID used to display the search results.

- **Alternative Layout:** Use a layout other than the standard module template.

- **Module Class Suffix:** Apply a CSS class from the template to customize the module appearance.

- **Caching:** Choose whether or not to cache the module content.

- **Cache Time:** Selects how much time passes before the module is cached.

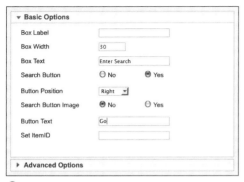

B The Search module options

C The search box displayed on the site

7. Under Basic Options, in the Box Width field, type **30**.

   This field sets the number of characters allowed in the search box.

8. In the Box Text field, type **Enter Search**.

   This text displays in the search box.

9. For Search Button, choose Yes.

   When you choose Yes, a clickable search button is displayed. When you choose No, the user starts a search by pressing Enter.

10. From the Button Position drop-down menu, choose Right.

    This option determines where the search button will appear in relation to the search box.

11. Leave Search Button Image set to No.

    If you have enabled a search button, choosing No will place a radio button near the search field. Choose Yes to use an image as the search button. That image must be named searchButton.gif and located in the images/M_images folder.

12. In the Button Text field, type **Go**.

    This is the text that appears on the search button **B**.

13. Click Save, and then click View Site.

    A search box appears on the web site in which users can search the entire site **C**.

TIP The search module is styled by your template. If the Go button is displayed below the search field, rather than to the right, your template position does not have enough room to display the module correctly. To fix this, shorten its length by changing the value in the Box Width field.

Using Navigation Modules

Navigation modules create navigational menus for your users. Joomla has two navigational modules:

- **Menu:** Creates a module to contain a menu type created through the Menu Manager.
- **Breadcrumbs:** Provides a pathway or breadcrumb trail.

To create a Breadcrumbs module:

1. Open the Module Manager.
2. On the toolbar, click New.
3. Click the Breadcrumbs link.

   The Module Breadcrumbs page opens in which you can set the details and options for the Breadcrumbs module.

4. In the Title field, type `Breadcrumbs`.

Breadcrumbs Module Options

- **Show "You are here":** Show or hide the text "You are here" in the breadcrumbs.
- **Show Home:** Show or hide Home in the breadcrumbs.
- **Text for Home Entry:** The text for Home. Allows you to assign a custom name for your home page.
- **Show Last:** Show or hide the last selection in the breadcrumbs.
- **Text Separator:** Select a text separator.
- **Alternative Layout:** Use a layout other than the standard module template.
- **Module Class Suffix:** Use a CSS class from the template to customize the module appearance.
- **Caching:** Select whether or not to cache the module content.
- **Cache Time:** Select how much time passes before the module is cached.

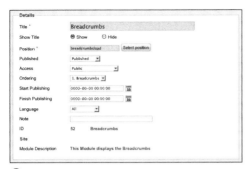

A The Breadcrumb module details

B The breadcrumb module Basic Options

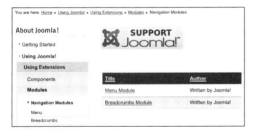

C The Breadcrumb module as it appears on the site

5. In the Position field, type **Position-6**.

Most Joomla templates have a position and styling for breadcrumbs/pathways. The Position field controls where the module displays on the page. The placement of the positions is controlled by the template.

See Chapter 7, "Working with Templates," to view template positions.

6. Leave the rest of the Details and Menu Assignment options at their default settings.

Breadcrumbs are generally configured to display on all pages of a web site, making it easier for users to navigate the site **A**.

7. Leave the Text Separator field empty.

Leaving this field blank places a greater-than sign (>) between each link **B**.

8. Click Save, and then click View Site.

Click through the menus to see the breadcrumbs trail **C**.

Putting It All Together

1. **Create user modules.** For a site that allows registered users, you should create a log in module for the front end.

2. **Create your navigation modules.** Common modules are menus, breadcrumbs, category links, and so on. Create multiple ways for your users to move through your web site.

3. **Create a search utility module.** Provide a search box on your site pages to help users find specific content.

4. **Create content modules.** Include Content modules that display snippets of site content or teaser articles. These modules are a great way to lead site visitors toward content that they may otherwise miss, or to find recently added or updated content.

5. **Create a footer display module.** Include a foot module—the most common display module—that contains the copyright information for your web site.

6. **Assign your modules to menu items.** Use the menu assignment to display your modules on all pages or just those pages you specify.

Utilizing
Components

Components are extensions that contain the largest pieces of content on your site and display in the main body of your web pages.

Large third-party extensions such as the K2 or Zoo content construction kits are components, as are social media extensions such as JomSocial, Community Builder, and EasyBlog. These will display in the Component menu when installed. Just like categories and articles, components can be tied to modules and must have a module or menu item associated with them if they are to display on the site.

Because components are large pieces of content, they follow the same rules as content categories and articles. All components have global options, individual options, and menu item options that control how they display on pages.

Adding Advertising Banners

Components usually display in the main body of your web pages, but banners are one of the exceptions to this rule. Since the Banner component is used primarily to create and manage advertising banners on your web site, banners display using a banner module. As a result, you can place banners in any module position allowed by your template.

Banners can be set to cycle through multiple images or display a single image or piece of content. Banners are organized using categories and client lists. Like articles, you cannot create a banner without assigning it to a category.

Banner categories are created using the Banner Category Manager and are completely separate from your content categories.

Banners contain a tracking system to track clicks and impressions, and a client list to store client information and contact details.

TIP Like any feature in Joomla, the banner component can also serve other purposes. For example, a real estate site could use banners to display its hottest properties. A family site could use banners to display pictures from various family members.

To create a banner category:

1. Log in to the back end.

2. Choose Components > Banner > Categories.

   The Category Manager: Banners opens. You can access any of the Banner Managers using the links at the top: Banners, Categories, Clients, or Tracks **A**.

Using Component Types

Joomla includes seven predefined components: four that display content on the front end and three that are used by the back end:

- **Banners:** Manages and displays advertising.

- **Contacts:** Creates a single contact form or a list of contacts that link to a contact form.

- **News Feeds:** Pulls feeds from other web sites into your Joomla site.

- **Web Links:** Creates a list of web links.

- **Messaging:** (Back end only) Provides an administrator private messaging system.

- **Redirects:** (Back end only) Manages expired or outdated links by redirecting them to working web pages.

- **Search:** (Back end only) Monitors and tracks search terms entered by users visiting your site.

A The Banner Category Manager

B The Category Manager: Add A New Banners Category details screen

3. On the toolbar, click New.

   The Category Manager: Add A New Banners Category screen opens **B**.

4. In the Title field, type **Banner Examples**.

   The banners created for the sample data use advanced features. You are going to create a simple banner and display it on the Home page.

5. Leave all other Details fields at their default values.

continues on next page

Banner Category Details

- **Title:** Enter a descriptive title for this category.

- **Alias:** Enter an alias for this category or leave the field blank and Joomla will create an alias for you based on the Title field. If you enter an alias, make sure to use all lowercase with no spaces.

- **Parent:** For a parent or level 1 category, leave this set to No Parent. If this is to be a subcategory or child category, choose its parent from the drop-down menu.

- **State:** Choose Published to publish this category immediately, or choose Unpublished to create the category but leave it in an unpublished state.

- **Access:** Choose the group that has access to view this category on the front end of the web site.

- **Permissions:** Click this button to open the Category Permissions box and set the access-level permissions for the category.

- **Language:** If you have multiple languages installed, select which language this category appears in on the front end of the site.

- **ID:** When the category is saved, the Joomla database assigns an ID number.

6. Enter a brief description for this banner category.

Banner categories contain Publishing, Basic, and Metadata options:

Publishing options define who created the category, the date it was created and modified, and who last modified the category **C**.

Basic Options control the category display options **D**.

Metadata Options contain any metadata information you want associated with this banner category **E**.

The only requirement for a banner category to work is the title.

7. On the toolbar, click Save & Close.

The new banner category is created and can be used to create and assign banners and clients.

To create a banner:

1. Choose Components > Banner > Banners to open the Banner Manager: New Banner screen **F**.

2. In the Name field, type **Support Joomla!**.

3. Leave the Alias field blank.

4. From the Category drop-down menu, choose Banner Examples.

5. From the State drop-down menu, choose Published.

To use a banner, only a name and category are required; however, most advertising and affiliate banners have images and a URL link.

6. Set the Type field to Image.

C Banner category publishing options

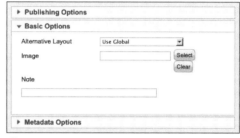

D Banner category basic options

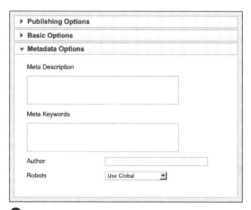

E Banner category metadata options

F The New Banner details screen

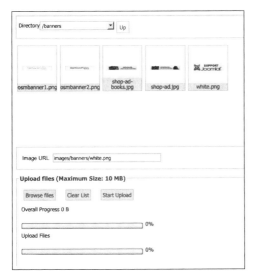

G The Media Manager banners folder containing images to be used in your banners

7. Next to the Image field, click Select.

Images used in advertising banners are stored in the Media Manager. By clicking Select, you can choose an existing image or upload a new image to use for this banner.

The Media Manager banner image path is set to open the Banner folder automatically. All advertising or affiliate banner images should be stored in this folder.

8. In the Media Manager pop-up window, select the white.png image, and then click Insert **G**.

9. Leave the Width and Height fields blank.

You can set the size of the banner image using the width and height fields. However, it is best practice to create an image with the correct dimensions. Setting a width and height forces the system to resize the image, which can slow your site page load time if a page includes a lot of advertising.

10. In the Alternative Text field, type **Support Joomla**.

Alternative text is used by screen readers. This text appears when a user hovers over the banner image with the mouse.

11. In the Click URL field, type **http://www.joomla.org/about-joomla/the-project/sponsorship.html**.

This is the link for the image. This URL is also used to track clicks and impressions.

12. In the Description field, type **A link to the Joomla donation page**.

The Description field describes the purpose of this banner.

13. Leave Language set to All.

14. Click Save & Close.

Before you can see this banner on the site, you must create a banner module.

To create and display the banner module:

1. Choose Extension > Module Manager to open the Module Manager.

2. On the toolbar, click New.

   The New Module pop-up window opens, displaying all available module types that you can use on your site.

3. Choose Banners.

   The Module Manager: Module Banners screen opens. Here you can enter the banner module details, select menu assignment, and choose Publishing and Metadata Options for this banner ad .

4. In the Title field, type **Support Joomla Ad**.

5. Set Show Title to Hide.

   Normally a title would not appear above a single banner ad, so we are going to hide the title.

6. In the Position field, type **position-12**, or select a position by clicking the Select Position button.

   The title and a position are the only requirements to display the banner module.

7. Leave all other Details options at their default values.

8. Click the arrow next to Basic Options to open its parameter settings 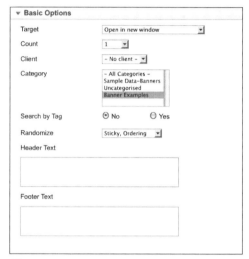.

H The banner module details

I The banner module basic options

You are here: Home

About Joomla!

* Getting Started
* Using Joomla!
* The Joomla! Project
* The Joomla! Community

This Site

* Home
* Site Map

SUPPORT
Joomla!™

Joomla!

Congratulations! You have a Joomla! site! Joo
and keep it simple to update and maintain.

Joomla! is a flexible and powerful platform, wh
hundreds of thousands of visitors. Joomla! is o
want it to.

J The banner is displayed using the banner module.

9. From the Target drop-down menu, choose "Open in a new window."

   When a user clicks this ad, a new window will open in the browser, while leaving your site open in a separate tab.

10. From the Count drop-down menu, choose 1.

    This tells Joomla how many banner images to display. You can create a rotating banner using more than one image if you assign multiple banners to a single category.

11. Leave Client set to "No client."

    You are not tracking or assigning this link to a particular client. If you needed to generate reports for clients or track specific affiliate advertising, you would choose that client in this field.

12. From the Category list, select Banner Examples.

    This isolates the banner module to display only the banner images assigned to this category. If you chose All Categories, all banners would display based on the Count field, or cycle through images based on the Randomize field.

13. Leave all other fields at their default values.

14. Click Save, and then click View Site.

    The Support Joomla banner image is now displayed in the banner module. The module is set to the Beez_20 template position-12 **J**.

    Because you did not define the menu assignment to limit the pages this banner displays on, it will display on all pages of the site that contain this position.

To create a banner client:

1. Choose Components > Banner > Clients to open the Banner Client Manager.

2. Click the Joomla client title to open the Banner Manager: Edit Client details **K**.

   Client details are used to manage your advertising or affiliate details. These fields are also used with the banner tracking feature to track clicks and impressions and payment details.

3. On the toolbar, click Close.

K The Banner Client edit page

Client Details

- **Client Name:** The name of the client, business, or affiliate.
- **Contact Name:** A contact name for the client, business, or affiliate.
- **Contact email:** A contact email address for the client, business, or affiliate.
- **State:** A published client can be selected for a banner module; unpublished clients are not available to the system modules or tracking.
- **Purchase Type:** Clients or businesses that pay you for advertising can be tracked on an unlimited, yearly, monthly, weekly, or daily basis. This is used in conjunction with page impressions or pay-per-click billing types.
- **Track Impressions:** Choose Yes to track the page impressions of this client's banners.
- **Track Clicks:** Choose Yes to track per-clicks for this client's banners.
- **ID:** A number assigned by the Joomla system.
- **Metadata Options:** Enter any metadata options for this client.
- **Additional Information:** Enter a note to administrators about this client.

Creating Contacts

The Contacts component creates a contact form for users to email a contact associated with the web site. You can place a single contact or multiple contacts on a single web site.

You can create four types of Contact menu items:

- List of all contact categories
- List of contacts in a category
- Single contact
- Featured contacts

Contacts use categories, and you cannot create a contact without first creating at least one category to assign it to. After a contact category is created, you can create the contact information and a menu item to display it.

The contact lists and forms appear in the main body of a web page. They are styled using a combination of global contact options at the contact level, and through the menu items.

TIP Contacts can use information from the User Manager if the contact created has a user account on the site. User information does not automatically create contact information. You must create that info manually.

To create a contact category:

1. Choose Components > Contacts > Categories.

The Category Manager: Contacts screen opens with a list of all the contact categories created on the site **Ⓐ**.

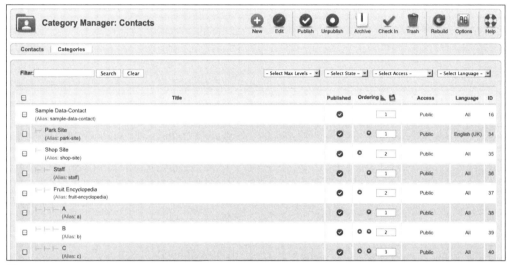

Ⓐ The Category Manager: Contacts screen

B The contact category details screen

2. On the toolbar, click New.

 The Category Manager: Add A New Contact Category screen opens **B**. Contact categories can also contain an image and description.

3. In the Title field, type **Administrators**.

4. Leave all other fields at their default values.

 Only a title is required to create a contact category.

5. In the Description field, type **A contact list for administrators for this web site**.

6. Under Publishing Options, select a user.

7. Under Basic Options, you can select an alternative layout, add an image to this category, and add a note about this contact category for back-end users.

 You can elect to use the Global contact layout provided by the system and the default template, or select an alternative layout if your template provides one.

8. Under Metadata Options, enter any metadata information you want to associate with this contact category.

9. Click Save & Close.

 Your category is created, and you can now use it for menu items and to assign specific contacts.

To create a contact:

1. Choose Components > Contacts > Contacts.

   The Contact Manager opens with a list of all contacts from all categories .

2. On the toolbar, click New to create a new contact 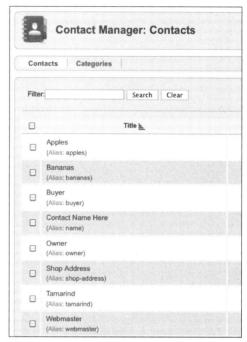.

3. In the Name field, type your name.

4. Leave the Alias field blank.

5. Click the Select User button and select your name from the list of users.

   You can select a user from the User Manager to associate this contact information with that user. The only information required to create a contact and display a contact form is a name, category, and an email address for this user.

6. From the State drop-down menu, choose Published.

   If you choose Unpublished, this contact will not display on a contacts page.

7. From the Category drop-down menu, choose Administrators.

C The Contact Manager: Contacts screen

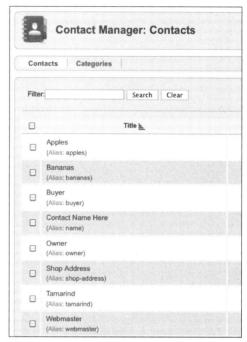

D The New Contact details

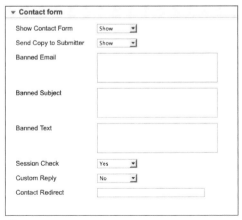

E Contact publishing options

F In the contact details, you attach a contact image, position, email, and so on.

G Contact detail display options

H The contact form details

8. Leave Public chosen in the Access drop-down menu.

   If you wanted only registered users to see certain contacts, you could choose Registered or any other restricted access user group.

9. Set the publishing options.

   Publishing options identify the user who created the contact and the publishing start and end dates **E**.

10. Set the contact details.

    There are numerous fields of contact information. Anything entered in the contact details can be hidden or shown on the front end **F**.

11. Set the display options.

    The display options control what information from the contact detail items will display on the site **G**.

12. Set the contact form options.

    The contact form options control the behavior of the contact form and its display options **H**.

13. Set any metadata options you desire.

14. Click Save & Close.

    Even though you have added contacts, you will not be able to see contact information or contact forms until you link a menu item to them.

To use contact menu item types:

1. Open a Joomla site that has the sample data installed.

2. In the About Joomla menu, choose Using Joomla > Using Extensions > Components > Contact Components > Contact Categories **①**.

    A List All Contact Categories menu item will display links to all the contact categories or subcategories you tell it to display **①**.

3. Choose Contact Single Category.

    A "List Contacts in a Category" menu item displays a table with all contacts assigned to a single category **ⓚ**.

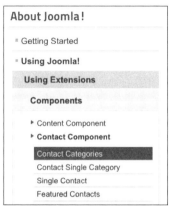

① The About Joomla menu

① An example of a List All Contacts Category menu item

Staff

Please feel free to contact our staff at any time should you need assistance.

Name	Position	Phone	Suburb	State	Country
Buyer					
Owner					

ⓚ An example of a "List Contacts in a Category" menu item

4. Choose Single Contact.

A Single Contact menu item displays a single contact's information. This will appear as a single form, or it will use tabs and sliders depending on the details and options you set at the contact level 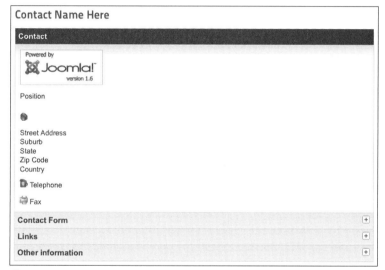.

5. Choose Featured Contacts.

A Featured Contacts menu item displays a table of all contacts marked as featured .

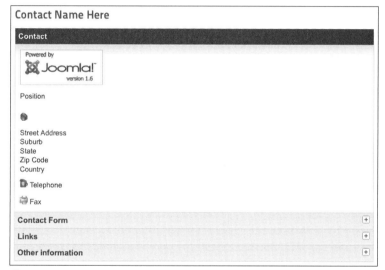

An example of a Single Contact menu item

An example of a Featured Contacts menu item

Using News Feeds

The News Feed component allows you to pull feeds from other sites into your Joomla site. Because news feeds are organized into categories, at least one category must exist before you can create a news feed. After creating your news feed categories, you can create links to the news feed and create a menu item to display them on the site.

The news feed menu item types are:

- List All News Feed Categories
- List News Feeds in a Category
- Single News Feed

News feeds can also be displayed in a news feed module.

To create a news feed category:

1. Choose Components > Newsfeeds > Categories to open the News Feeds Category Manager.

2. Open the Sample Data-Newsfeeds category by clicking its title.

   The News Feeds Category Editor opens. A news feed category requires only a title to be created **A**.

   News feed categories have standard publishing, basic, and metadata options.

3. On the toolbar, click Close.

A The News Feed category details

B News Feed Manager: News Feed screen

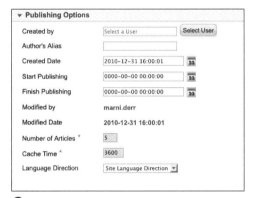

C News feed publishing options

D News feed display options

To create a news feed:

1. Choose Components > Newsfeeds > Feeds to open the News Feed Manager.

2. In the News Feed Manager, select the Joomla Announcements title to open it for editing.

   News feeds require a title, a link to the feed, and a category. They also require that you set the number of articles and the cache settings before the news feed can be created **B**.

3. Click the arrow next to Publishing Options.

   Publishing options details are similar to all other content components, including author, publishing, and modification details **C**.

4. In the Number of Articles field, enter the number of articles to be included and displayed in this feed.

5. In the Cache Time field, enter the time in seconds that the feed articles should be cached by the system.

   Some sites are constantly updating information, while other sites may refresh their content only once a day or once a week. By setting a cache time, you tell Joomla how long to wait before refreshing this news feed.

6. Click the arrow next to Display Options.

   Display options control what displays with the feed articles: an image, a description, and content can all be shown or hidden. The character count controls how many characters of the article appear on your site **D**.

7. Set any desired metadata options for this feed.

8. On the toolbar, click Close.

To use news feed menu item types:

1. View the front end of the site.

2. In the About Joomla menu, choose > Using Joomla > Using Extensions > Components > News Feeds Component **E**.

3. Choose News Feed Categories.

   The site has only two news feed categories right now. Because this menu item links to the parent, only the root category Sample Data-Newsfeeds is displayed. If you had more categories, they would display in this list as links **F**.

4. Choose Single News Feed.

   A single news feed menu item links to a single feed. This will display the total number of articles you set in the Publishing Options for this feed. The titles are links to the web site where the content resides **G**.

5. Choose News Feed Category.

   This is an example of news feed categories displayed in table format. If you have multiple feeds assigned to a single category, this list will appear so that a user can select the feed she wants to read **H**.

Sample Data-Newsfeeds	
Feed Name	**Feed Link**
Joomla! Announcements	http://www.joomla.org/announcements.feed?type=rss
Joomla! Security News	http://feeds.joomla.org/JoomlaSecurityNews
Joomla! Connect	http://feeds.joomla.org/JoomlaConnect
New Joomla! Extensions	http://feeds.joomla.org/JoomlaExtensions

H A tabular list of "List News Feeds in a Category" menu item page

E The About Joomla menu where the example News Feeds are located

---

Because this links to the root category the "uncategorised" category is displayed.

Sample Data-Newsfeeds

F The List All News Feed Categories menu item page.

JoomlaConnect

Joomla! - the dynamic portal engine and content management system

1. Solución al bug de Joomla 1.5.X con MySQL 5.5.X

   La nueva rama de MySQL 5.5.X implementa de forma definitiva el termi
   cual se encontraba marcado como obsoleto desde hace un tiempo. Este
   versiones de Joomla! 1.5.X, dado que por defecto, en el proceso de inst
   mediante el termino TYPE que Joomla! requiere el motor MyISAM. Joor

   ◆ Email this   ◆ Digg This!   ◆ Share on Facebook

2. Dominion 1.5.12 Update Released

   The Dominion Joomla 1.5 template has been updated to version **1.5.12**

   ◆ Email this   ◆ Digg This!   ◆ Share on Facebook

3. جوملا ننتهيمان Phoca Download 1.3.8 شد منتشر

   دانلود فوکا میکنیم پیشنهاد کاربرها همه به هستیم. قبل نسخه مشکلات حل شاهد نسخه این
   : گرفت صورت زیر تغییرات نسخه این در دهند. ارتقا شده منتشر نسخه آخرین به را خود

   * Fixed CSS (removed...

G A Single News Feed menu item

Creating a Web Links Page

You can use the web links component to create resource pages that link to other content or web sites. Web links are organized into categories, and you can use menu items to create web links pages. Joomla also has a web link module.

There are three types of web link menu items:

- List All Web Link Categories
- List Web Links in a Category
- Submit a Web Link

To create a web link category:

1. Choose Components > Web Links > Categories.

   The Category Manager: Weblinks opens with a list of all web link categories created for the site **Ⓐ**.

continues on next page

Ⓐ The Category Manager: Weblinks screen

2. Select the title Sample Data-Weblinks to open it for editing.

A web link category needs only a title to be created and saved .

Web link categories have standard publishing, basic, and metadata options.

3. On the toolbar, click Close.

To add web links to a web links component:

1. Choose Components > Web Links > Links to open the Web Links Manager: Web Link screen.

2. Select the title "Joomla!" to open the web link for editing.

Web links require only a title and a URL to be created and saved. Web links can contain descriptions of the link 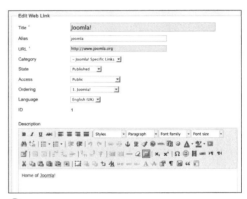.

3. Click the arrow next to Basic Options 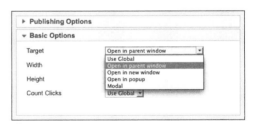.

4. In the Target field set how the link will open:

  ‣ Use Global (the default)

  ‣ Open in parent window

  ‣ Open in new window

  ‣ Open in popup

  ‣ Modal

5. If you set the link to open in a pop-up window, set the Width and Height of the pop-up window.

6. From the Count Clicks drop-down menu, choose Yes or No.

7. On the toolbar, click Save & Close.

B The web links details

C The web link edit screen

D Web link basic options

E The About Joomla menu with the Weblinks component menu items

F An example of the "List Web Links in a Category" menu item

G An example of the List All Web Link Categories menu item

To use web links menu item types:

1. In the About Joomla menu on the front of the site, choose Using Joomla > Using Extensions > Components > Weblinks Component **E**.

2. Choose Weblinks Single Category.

   Even though you are linking to a single category, multiple web links can be assigned to that category. This menu item will display all the category's links in a table. At the end of the table, the number of clicks on a link is displayed **F**.

3. Choose Weblinks Categories.

   This menu item displays a list of all web link categories **G**.

Using the Messaging Component

Joomla's back-end messaging system can be used to communicate with other back-end users and web site administrators.

TIP Do not use this feature to email all registered users on your site. Using the messaging system in this manner can cause serious system performance issues and potentially crash the site.

To view, create, or edit messages:

1. Log in to the back end.

   The top toolbar displays the total number of messages waiting in your inbox.

2. Click Messages.

   The Private Messages Manager opens **A**.

A In the Private Messages Manager, you can view messages sent to you from the back end by other administrators.

In the Write Private Message screen, you can write and send messages to other back-end users.

3. On the toolbar, click New.

The Write Private Message screen opens **B**. Select the recipient of the message, enter the subject, write the message, and then click Send. The next time the user logs in to the back end, he will have a message waiting.

4. Click Cancel to return to the Private Messages Manager.

5. On the toolbar, click the My Settings button to view the options you can set to manage your messages **C**.

6. Make any desired changes to your message settings, and then click Save & Close.

7. On the toolbar, click the Options button to display the new access control level options you will find throughout Joomla.

You can create your own groups and user levels and control access to every front- and back-end feature. These functions are covered in more detail in Chapter 10, "Managing User Access and Permissions."

TIP You can also access the internal message system by choosing Components > **Messaging.**

C A pop-up dialog box opens to modify your back-end message settings.

Putting It All Together

1. **Create a Banner component.** To create a banner, you have to create a banner category, create the banner itself, create and display a banner module, and create a banner client.

2. **Create a Contact component.** Create a contact category, the contact, and then add a contact menu item.

3. **Create a News Feed component.** Create a news feed category, add links to your favorite news feeds, and then create a menu item to display it on the site.

4. **Create a Web Link component.** Create a web links category, add a list of web links and then create a menu item to display the links on your site.

Managing User Access and Permissions

New to Joomla 1.6 is the ability to create your own user groups and assign these groups' permissions to both the front and back ends of the web site. Furthermore, you can set access control levels, or ACL.

TIP Just because Joomla now has these features does not mean that you need to use or change them. If your site does not require specific permissions or access levels, don't change the core groups and permissions. If you're not experienced with these features, it is very easy to accidentally lock yourself out of your site.

Managing Users

Joomla has three user managers from which you can add, edit, and delete users, user groups, and access levels :

- **User:** Manage all individual user accounts for the site, both front and back ends.

- **User Group:** Manage user groups.

- **Viewing Access Levels:** Manage access level control for the site.

Permissions are controlled individually through their associated managers. For example, component or module permissions are controlled in the Component and Module Managers, respectively. Similarly, user permissions are controlled in the User Manager .

A The User Manager provides access to the User Groups and Viewing Access Levels Managers.

B User group permission settings for the User Manager

Understanding Permissions and ACL

Permissions and ACL are not the same, and they do not behave the same way. For example, say you create a group called subscribers and give that group access to view subscription-based content so only that subscriber group can view that content on the front end. You might assume that a Super User logged in to the front end could also view this content because the Super User group has full permissions.

However, although a Super User has full site permissions, she does not have access to the subscriber content, because unlike permissions, groups do not inherit access levels in the same way. The Super User group must also be assigned access to this content. This is one of the most important differences you need to understand when creating groups, setting permissions, and controlling access levels.

To open the User Manager:

1. Log in to the back end of the site.

2. Choose Users > User Manager or click the User Manager quick icon on the Control Panel screen.

   The User Manager lists all registered users on your web site. Here you can add, edit, delete, activate, block, and unblock user accounts and manager user group permissions **C**.

C The User Manager

The User Manager Fields

- **Name:** The full name of the user. Click the name to open and edit that user's details.
- **User Name:** The name used to log in.
- **Enabled:** A checkmark in this field indicates that the user account is enabled.
- **Activated:** A checkmark in this field indicates that the user account is activated.
- **User Groups:** Displays the group this user belongs to.
- **Email:** Displays the user's email address. Click the address to open your email program to send this user a message.
- **Last Visit Date:** The date and time this user last logged in to the web site.
- **Registration Date:** The date and time this user registered on the web site.
- **ID:** The database ID number for this user.

  The User Manager can be searched, sorted, and filtered using the column titles.

To add a new user:

1. Log in to the back end.

2. Choose Users > User Manager.

3. On the toolbar, click New to open the User Manager: Add A New User screen.

4. Fill in the user's account details **D**:

   ▸ **Name:** The user's full name.

   ▸ **Login Name:** The username for this user, used to log the user in to the site.

   ▸ **Password** and **Confirm Password:** Enter a secure password for the user.

   The Registration Date and Last Visit Date are automatically added when the user information is saved.

5. Set "Receive System emails" to Yes if you want to send system emails to this user.

   System emails are notifications sent by the system, such as an alert that a new user has registered on the site. Normally only administrators should receive system emails.

   The Name, Login Name, Password, and Email fields are the only required fields for a new user account.

6. Set "Block this User" to No.

   A user that has been blocked from the site cannot log in to the front end.

7. Under Assigned User Groups, select the group to which this user is assigned. New user accounts default to the Registered user group **E**.

   User groups generally inherit the permissions from each group above them in their tree, unless you change the permission inheritance for a group.

   You can select a single group or multiple groups. Selecting multiple groups is generally used for access level control.

D New user account details

E Assigning a user to one or more groups

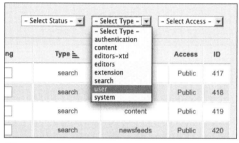

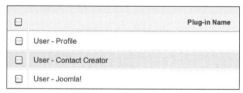

F User account basic settings

G Sort the Plug-in Manager to display only user type plug-ins.

H The three User plug-ins used by Joomla

8. Under Basic Settings, select the default preferences for this user **F**.

9. On the toolbar, click Save & Close to add this user account to the site.

To enable extended user profile field information:

1. Log in to the back end.

2. Choose Extensions > Plug-in Manager.

   Joomla has additional fields that you can add to user profiles, registration forms, and contact modules. These extra fields are enabled through the Plug-in Manager.

3. In the Plug-in Manager, sort the list by choosing user from the Select Type drop-down list **G**. Doing so sorts the Plug-in Manager list to display only user type plug-ins **H**.

continues on next page

User Basic Settings

- **Backend Template Style:** Choose the back-end template style. Different users can choose different templates while working in the back end of Joomla.

- **Backend Language:** Choose the language file for the back end. If you have language packs installed, the list of languages available for the back end will display in the drop-down menu.

- **Frontend Language:** Choose the front-end language. If you have front-end language packs installed, you can choose which language displays in the front end.

- **Editor:** Joomla installs with three editors. Select the editor you wish to use when creating content through the back and front ends of the site.

- **Help Site:** Choose which help system to use when you are logged in. This feature still has only one option. Perhaps the Joomla development team hopes to embed help at some point. For now, you are still taken to the Joomla documentation wiki.

- **Time Zone:** Choose your time zone.

Joomla has three user plug-ins:

▸ **User - Profile:** Enabling this plug-in extends the Joomla user profiles to include more fields of information that a user can add to his profile.

▸ **User - Contact Creator:** Enabling this plug-in automatically creates contact information for a user when she is added to or registered on the site. This plug-in works with the contact component.

▸ **User - Joomla:** *Do not* disable this plug-in. It is required to manage the Joomla user system.

4. Open the User - Profile plug-in.

5. From the Enabled drop-down menu, choose Enabled .

6. Under Basic Options, for each field choose one of the following 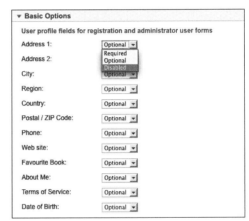:

▸ **Optional:** This field is not required when registering.

▸ **Required:** This field must be filled out before a user can register through the front end.

▸ **Disabled:** Turns off the field.

Basic Options fields are used in the back end of Joomla for user profiles and during front-end registration.

The user profile fields for the profile edit form are the same as fields used in the Basic Options. However, these fields control the information that a user can edit in her profile through the front end.

7. On the toolbar, click Save & Close.

8. Choose Site > My Profile.

9. Click the arrow next to User Profile to open it.

The fields you chose in the User - Profile Basic Options are now displayed in all user profiles 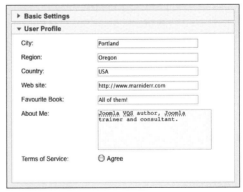.

ⓘ Enabling the User - Profile plug-in

ⓙ All additional user profile fields can be set to Optional, Required, or Disabled.

ⓚ After the User - Profile is enabled and the field options are set, those fields will display in the user profile.

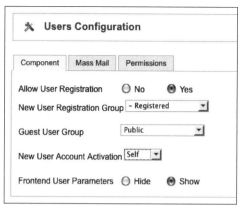

The user registration settings for the front end of the web site

To enable front-end registration:

1. Log in to the back end.

2. Choose Users > User Manager.

3. On the toolbar, click the Options button to open the registration settings for the site.

4. In the Users Configuration pop-up window, select the Component tab ❶.

5. To enable front-end user registration, set Allow User Registration to Yes.

   If you set it to No, users will not be able to register or create accounts on the web site.

6. From the New User Registration Group drop-down menu, choose the default group that all users will be assigned to automatically when creating a user account. The default group is Registered.

7. Leave Public as the default Guest User Group.

8. From the New User Account Activation drop-down menu, choose one of the following:

   ▸ **None:** A user can register and create an account automatically upon saving.

   ▸ **Self:** A user can register but will need to activate the account through a system-generated email. Once the user receives the email and clicks the activation link, the account is enabled on the site.

   ▸ **Admin:** Only an administrator can enable a user account.

9. Set Frontend User Parameters to Show.

   This allows a user to edit his profile settings and basic options through the front end.

10. Click Save & Close to close the user configuration pop-up window.

Managing User Groups

While there are only two types of users—front end and back end—you can create as many user groups as your site needs, each with its own set of permissions and access levels.

Joomla has eight predefined user groups. You can modify these user group permissions, or create your own groups. If you installed the sample data, Joomla has two additional user group examples: Shop Suppliers and Customer Group **A**.

TIP The important thing to remember when creating or modifying a user group is that permissions are inherited and access levels are not inherited.

A All user groups created for the site are in the User Manager: User Groups.

Preconfigured User Groups

Front-end users:

- **Public:** The public group provides front-end viewing access to all content, components, and modules set to public access.
- **Registered:** A registered user has a user account and can edit her user details when logged in to the front end.
- **Author:** An author can contribute content and edit that content. An author inherits the Registered group setting for editing his profile. An author cannot publish content to the site.
- **Editor:** An editor has all author and user privileges. An editor can edit her own content and the content of any author. An editor cannot publish content to the site.
- **Publisher:** A publisher has all editor privileges and can also publish content to the site.

Back-end users:

- **Manager:** A manager has the same privileges as a publisher, including back-end access to content and component managers. A manager cannot access the global configuration settings, install extensions, or modify template or user settings.
- **Administrator:** An administrator can access all front- and back-end features, except global configuration settings.
- **Super User:** A super user has unrestricted access to all front- and back-end features.

B In the user group details, you can create new user groups.

To add or edit a user group:

1. Log in to the back end.

2. Choose Users > User Groups.

   You can only create user groups in the User Group Manager. Global permissions are set in the global configuration permission settings and in individual content, component, and module option settings.

3. From the list, click the Customer Group Title list to open it.

   User groups contain a group title and a group parent **B**.

   The title identifies this user group in the permission and access level options.

   The group parent controls which permission settings are inherited for this group. All groups must have a parent.

4. On the toolbar, click Close.

Understanding Permissions

User group permissions provide access to features and functions in the front or back end of the site, even if the permission setting options are the same throughout the site.

After setting global permission options through the global configuration options, you can then set individual permission options through content, component, and module managers. Because there are infinite combinations for configuring these options, we will only describe the permission options.

Permissions control what a specific user group can *do* on a site. They do not control what a user group can *view* on the site.

Permission Actions

- **Site Login:** Permission to log in to the front end of the web site.
- **Admin Login:** Permission to log in to the back end of the site.
- **Super Admin:** Permission to log in and perform any action on the front or back ends of the site.
- **Access Component:** Permission to log in to the front or back end of the site and perform any action except modifying the global configuration settings.
- **Create:** Permission to create content.
- **Delete:** Permission to delete any content.
- **Edit:** Permission to edit any content.
- **Edit State:** Permission to publish, archive, or unpublish any content.
- **Edit Own:** Permission to edit only the user's own content.

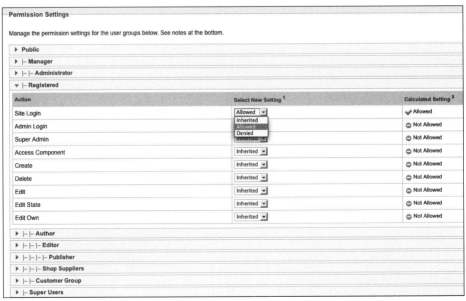

A The global configuration permission screen

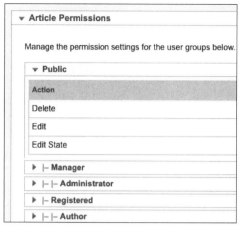

B Individual article permission options

C Individual component permission options

Permission Settings

- **Inherited:** Inherit the parent group's settings.

- **Allowed:** Permission to perform a function or use a feature.

- **Denied:** Deny permission to perform a function or use a feature.

TIP The Public group has an additional setting, Not Set. The public group is the parent of all other groups because it provides full access to the front end of the web site. Viewing access is controlled through access levels, not permissions. We recommend you never change the Public group settings because doing so can cause you to lose your administrative access.

To access and set global permissions:

1. Log in to the back end.

2. Choose Site > Global Configuration.

3. Select Permissions.

   There are nine permission options and three settings **A**.

4. On the toolbar, click Cancel.

5. Choose Content > Article Manager.

6. Open the first article in the list and scroll to the bottom of the screen.

   Articles, categories, components, modules, templates, and plug-ins all have permission options that can override the global permission options.

   For content, the only permission options are the abilities to delete, edit, or change the state of content **B**.

7. On the toolbar, click Close.

8. Choose Components > Banners.

9. On the toolbar, click Options.

10. In the pop-up window, select the Permissions tab.

    The component permission options specify what user groups can do with components **C**.

Managing Access Levels

Access control level settings share the same user groups as permission settings. However, instead of using the user group to set the access level, you create an access level type and then assign the user groups.

For example, the sample data has an access level type of Customer Access Level, which is assigned to the user groups: Manager, Author, and Customer Group.

One of the difficulties in understanding and using access levels is they do not "inherit" settings like permissions. In order for a user or user group to use an access level, the user must be assigned to the user group that is assigned to that access level, or the access level must include the group to which a user is assigned. Access levels can be very confusing, and must be seen in action to truly understand them.

To create a new access level:

1. Log in to the back end.

2. Choose Users > Access Levels to open the User Manager: Viewing Access Levels **Ⓐ**.

   Joomla installs with three access levels: Public, Registered, and Special. The sample data includes an additional access level called Customer Access Level.

3. Select the Customer Access Level group.

   Access levels require a Level Title and a user group assignment **Ⓑ**.

   The Customer Access Level is assigned to the Manager, Author, and Customer user groups.

Ⓐ The User Manager: Viewing Access Levels screen

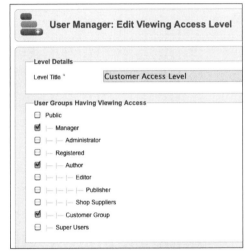

Ⓑ Assigning user groups to the access level

C The Special custom HTML module with its access level set to be viewable by user groups assigned to Customer Access Level

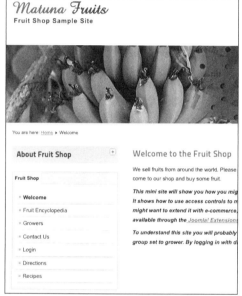

D The sample fruit shop page of the sample data site

4. On the toolbar, click Close.

Access levels require only a title and group selection.

To see the access control in action, we will look at a module with the Customer Access Level by logging into the front end of the site.

To assign access levels to user groups:

1. Choose Extensions > Module Manager.

2. Locate and open the Special custom HTML module.

3. Under the module details, the access field is set to Customer Access Level **C**.

4. Click View Site.

5. From the This Site menu, choose Sample Sites > Fruit Shop > Welcome.

   The sample fruit shop portion of the web site is displayed **D**.

6. From the Fruit Shop menu, click Login, and enter your Super User login information.

7. On the fruit shop Welcome page, refresh the page.

   Nothing has changed. Even as a Super User, you cannot see the module that should be viewable because access levels do not inherit settings in the same way that permissions do. You have permission to log in to the site, but do not have access to the Customer Access Level content.

8. Return to the back end.

9. Choose Users > Access Levels.

10. Click Customer Access Levels to open it for editing.

continues on next page

11. Under User Groups Having Viewing Access, click the checkbox next to Super Users **ⓔ**.

12. On the toolbar, click Save & Close.

13. Click View Site and return to the Welcome page. Be sure you are still logged in to the front end.

Now that you have included the Super User group as a group with access to any item assigned to the Customer Access Level, you can see the Special module displayed on the site **ⓕ**.

You can also assign access levels by selecting user groups at the user profile level.

ⓔ Assigning the Super Users group viewing access to the Customer Access Level

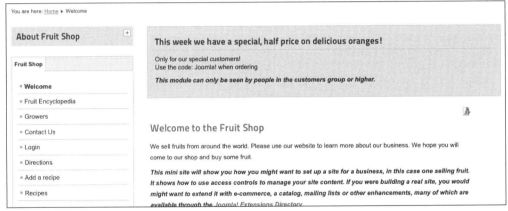

ⓕ Logged in as a Super User with Customer Access Level viewing permission, you can now see the Special module.

G Assigning individual users to user groups

To assign user groups to users:

1. Log in to the back end.

2. Choose Users > User Manager.

At the time of this writing, user group assignment is available only through the User Manager and not in user profiles.

3. Select your Super User account.

In the Assigned User Groups details, you can assign individual users to other user groups **G**.

As you can see, there are many, many ways to control access and permissions to the front and back ends of your web site.

Putting It All Together

1. **Add a user account.** Add user accounts through the back end using the User Manager.

2. **Enable user registration.** If you want users to be able to create accounts through the front end of the web site, enable this ability in the User Manager options.

3. **Enable extended user profiles.** If you want to use the extended fields, enable the user profile plug-in using the Plug-in Manager.

4. **Create a new user group.** Create a custom user group for your web site using the User Group Manager.

5. **Create a custom access level.** Create a custom access level through the Access Level Manager.

6. **Assign permissions.** Set permissions for groups under the site's global configuration settings. Remember, do not change the Public group settings.

7. **Assign user groups to access levels.** If you have custom viewing access to content on the site, assign which groups will be able to view that content.

Building Your Site Structure

By now, you should have a basic understanding of Joomla's features and functional concepts. You know how to use extensions, enable plug-ins, create categories and menus, and much more.

The remaining chapters of this book walk you through creating a real-world web site using this book's companion web site, www.writingyourdreams.com. This site incorporates the most common types of web functions:

- Portfolios—professional, personal, and services

- Media (image and video) galleries

- Blogging

- Social media integration

Planning Your Web Site

In this chapter, you will set up your web site's basic structure.

Planning a web site is paramount to a smooth development process. Without a site plan and a few simple mock-ups, you could wander aimlessly trying to create content and lay out your pages. Careful site planning takes the guesswork out of your site structure and identifies your extension needs before you begin building the site.

A well thought out site map also helps when selecting the right templates and extensions. If you are considering a third-party template, look at the design and layout of a site that already uses it. Usually a design appeals to you based not only on its colors and images but also on its functionality. The thoughtful layout and positioning of all elements are also essential to a good design. When creating sample wireframes, plan for the positions you will need in your template.

TIP For the remainder of this book, we will work with a fresh installation of Joomla with no sample data installed. When creating your own site, we highly recommend you do not install the sample data. That data may help you learn to use Joomla, but it can be hard to completely remove.

TABLE 11.1 Site Map: Main Menu

Category	Subcategories
Home Page	
Joomla Book	
	Joomla 1st Edition
	Errata
	Updates
	Downloads
	Joomla 2nd Edition
	Errata
	Updates
Our Blog	
	Joomla News
	Joomla Reviews
	Random Web Stuff
Author Portfolios	
	Tanya Symes
	Marni Derr
Resource Directories	
	Joomla Books
	Joomla Training
	Joomla Extensions
	Joomla Templates
	Joomla Documentation
Our Forum	

The Joomla Web Site Process

An orderly development process will help you create your web site in the most efficient and effective manner:

1. Create a site map.
2. Create wireframes for the main pages.
3. Install Joomla *without* the sample data.
4. Install all third-party extensions and templates.
5. Configure components, extensions, plug-ins, and templates.
6. Create the main category/subcategory structure.
7. Create the main menu.
8. Add content.
9. Create menus and menu items.
10. Customize page layouts.
11. Create user groups and assign permissions.
12. Add and customize modules.
13. Finalize the Home page and launch the site.
14. Create a site map and submit it to search engines.

To create a site map:

1. On paper or in a word processing program define the main categories of your site.

   The initial category structure will help you build the main navigation for your site (**Table 11.1**).

2. List any subcategories you anticipate needing. You can always add to them later.

   Remember, you can change or add categories as you develop the site, but without categories you cannot create your content or menus.

continues on next page

3. List any additional menus you will need for the site, such as a User menu, Top menu, Legal menu, and so on.

From our site map example, we are creating a professional web site that supports this book, its authors, and Joomla. The main pages or structure of the site will be:

- **Home page**
- **Joomla VQS**—Information about the book, and the ability to purchase the book.
- **Blog**—A blog about Joomla maintained by the authors.
- **Portfolios**—Mini-portfolios for each author.
- **Resources**—Directories of other Joomla resources on the web.
- **Forum**—A third-party extension forum.

To create basic wireframes:

1. Using a paper notebook or a graphics program, sketch out the basic page layouts.

2. Create the wireframe for your Home page.

What is the general purpose of the site? A web site's home page should reflect your site's mission and purpose, and present a quick summary of what a user will find on the site.

In our example, the main purpose of the web site is to support this book and the users that purchase it. The Home page reflects this **Ⓐ**.

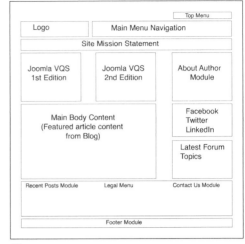

Ⓐ Sample home page wireframe

3. Create wireframes for the inner pages of your site.

   For example, for our web site, we include the following features:

   - **Blog**—Information on Joomla topics in the form of a blog page.

   - **Books**—A page for errata, corrections, and additional topics based on the book.

   - **Authors**—Links to our other Joomla endeavors by providing portfolio pages for both authors.

   - **Resources**—A resources page where users can find more information on Joomla.

   - **Forum**—A forum where users can ask questions and contribute corrections or feedback about the books.

TIP You may want to start laying out your Home page right away, but this usually doesn't work and you can end up stuck. Why? Because without content, you have nothing to display. As a general rule, first create content and lay out your inner pages. Then, at the end of site creation, lay out the Home page.

Must-Have Extensions

Joomla is a robust content management system and contains most of the functionality needed to create a stunning web site. To add more advanced applications or functionality such as tags, comments, fields, and forms, you need to code these functions yourself or install a third-party extension.

Joomla has one of the largest third-party extension development communities on the web, and if there is a feature or function you need for your site, you will find it available. You will also find a large assortment of template designs and custom template frameworks. As a result, Joomla can be used to create any type of web site you might need.

In this section, you'll install the following extensions, which we recommend for every Joomla web site:

- A more robust editor: JCE Editor

- A file manager: eXtplorer

- A site backup tool: Akeeba

- A sitemap generator: Xmap

- A site security and update tool: Akeeba

  The Akeeba security and update tool is described in Appendix A, "Updates and Maintenance."

TIP With each new release, the Joomla development team will continue to bring more advanced features into the Joomla core framework, but it is challenging to achieve a balance between functionality and ease of use. A basic Joomla installation can be used by anyone without coding experience. However, adding advanced functionality can require advanced technical expertise. To increase your personal expertise, join the Joomla groups. Joomla is community-driven software, and that community can provide a wealth of information to newcomers and experts alike.

A The Extension Manager is used to install Joomla extensions, including components, modules, plug-ins, and templates.

B Successful installation of the JCE Editor component

To install an editor:

1. Go to www.joomlacontenteditor.net.

2. Download the newest JCE Editor release for Joomla 1.6 or later.

3. Log in to the back end.

4. Choose Extensions > Extension Manager.

    The Extension Manager: Install screen opens **A**.

    There are three separate options for installing extensions; however, most of the time you will use the packaged file.

    The "Install from Directory" option allows you to upload large extensions to your temp directory that can then be installed from the server.

    The "Install from URL" option will install an extension directly from another web site.

    The Install from Directory and URL options are generally used when server upload or script memory limits are too restrictive to allow a large extension to install completely. This is rare, but it does happen.

5. Click the Browse button and select the com_jce_package.zip file that you downloaded.

6. Click the Upload & Install button.

    After an extension installs successfully, the system reports a successful install and sometimes displays information about the extension **B**.

continues on next page

7. Choose Extensions > Plug-in Manager.

The JCE Editor is a fully functional component. However, it also contains a plug-in that must be installed to use this component with Joomla. Remember that any installed extension that is a plug-in or contains plug-ins has to be enabled using the Plug-in Manager.

8. In the Select Type drop-down list, choose editors.

This tells the Plug-in Manager to display only plug-ins of the editor type, making it easier to locate an editing plug-in **C**.

You now have access to four editors, and each one should be enabled.

If an editor plug-in is not enabled, a red circle will appear next to its name in the Enabled column.

Note that the editor-xtd type plug-ins are for the article, image, pagebreak, and readmore buttons used at the bottom of all editor windows.

9. Enable the Editor - JCE plug-in by clicking the red circle in the Enabled column.

10. Choose Components > JCE Administration Component to open the JCE Administration: Control Panel screen.

Here you can configure the editor to work with your template files, turn on or off editor buttons, install JCE-specific plug-ins, and configure your file browser **D**.

If you need help configuring the editor, see the documentation on the JCE web site.

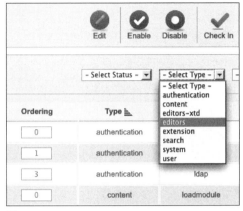

C Sorting the Plug-in Manager to display only plug-ins of the editor type

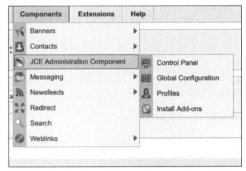

D The JCE Editor component is added to the Components menu after installation. Here you can configure the new editor.

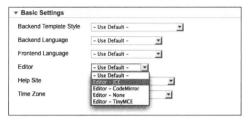

Selecting and assigning the JCE Editor to your user profile.

11. Choose Site > My Profile.

The default editor for the entire site, back and front ends, is the TinyMCE editor. You can change the default editor in the Global Configuration settings if you want the JCE Editor to be used by everyone, or isolate the editor to function with your account only.

12. In the Editor drop-down menu, choose JCE Editor.

This tells Joomla to use the JCE Editor for all content that you create and manage **Ⓔ**.

13. Click Save & Close to save the new settings.

14. Choose Content > Articles > Add New Article.

The Article text box now uses the JCE Editor when creating your content. This editor will be used for all content, including categories, articles, and modules **Ⓕ**.

> **TIP** If you have trouble seeing the new editor, clear Joomla's cache and your browser's cache, and then refresh. JCE uses JavaScript. If you encounter errors, turn off JavaScript compression.

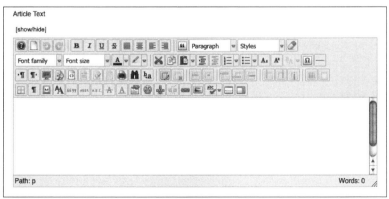

Ⓕ The full JCE Editor

To install a site backup extension:

1. Go to www.akeebabackup.com.

2. Download the most recent Akeeba Backup extension release.

   The Akeeba Backup utility comes in free and commercial versions. This extension allows you to create complete and partial backups of your web site **G**.

3. Log in to the back end of your web site.

4. Choose Extensions > Extension Manager.

5. Install the Akeeba Backup extension.

   The Akeeba Backup extension comes with a plug-in called Akeeba Lazy Scheduling. With this plug-in, you can schedule and store daily, weekly, or monthly site backups to your server that you can access through the back end of Joomla **H**.

   The only issue with using this backup scheduling is that you may run out of storage space quickly if you set the backup times too frequently. If you use this feature, make sure you configure it to delete older backups or regularly clean out the files manually to avoid server space problems.

6. Choose Components > Akeeba Backup.

   The Akeeba backup component can be customized to perform site backups manually or automatically. Read the Akeeba documentation on how to use and configure this extension for your site **I**.

   Akeeba also has a security and update extension discussed in Appendix A, "Updates and Maintenance."

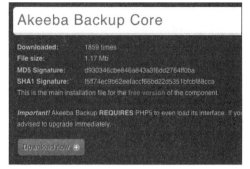

G In the Akeeba Backup Core web site, you can download this free backup extension.

H The Akeeba Backup Lazy Scheduling plug-in settings

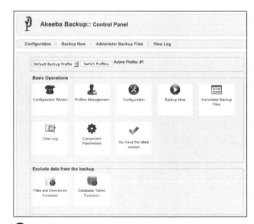

I The Akeeba Backup component control panel, where you customize and create site backups

J The eXtplorer extension for Joomla is available through the Joomla Extension Directory.

K The eXtplorer component is a complete file manager running within the Joomla back end. It provides access to your entire server and all sites installed on the server.

To install a file manager extension:

1. Go to http://extensions.joomla.org/extensions/core-enhancements/file-management/26302.

2. Download the most recent eXtplorer extension release.

    The eXtplorer extension is just one of many file managers on the Joomla Extension Directory **J**.

    The eXtplorer extension is a file management extension that allows you to access web server files through Joomla instead of using an FTP program or cPanel.

3. Log in to the back end of your web site.

4. Choose Extensions > Extension Manager.

5. Install the eXtplorer extension.

6. Choose Components > eXtplorer.

    The eXtplorer component has two modes: normal and FTP. FTP mode requires you to log in with your web server's FTP user name and password in order to access the files. Using this extension you can access all the files and directories on your server and perform any server function such as adding directories, editing files, renaming files and directories, and modifying permissions **K**.

7. To return to the Joomla administrator interface, click the "Back to Joomla" link at the top of the screen.

> **TIP** The eXtplorer component provides access to your entire web server, whether local or hosted. If you have a single server running multiple web sites, you will be able to access all the files and folders for each site.

To install a site map generator:

1. Go to http://joomla.vargas.co.cr/en/ downloads/components/xmap.

2. Download the Xmap component for your Joomla version.

3. Log in to the back end of Joomla.

4. Choose Extensions > Extension Manager.

5. Install the Xmap extension.

6. Choose Components > Xmap.

   Xmap is a site map extension you can use to create sitemaps and indexes. With Xmap you can create both HTML and XML sitemaps and submit them to search engines such as Google, Bing, and Yahoo ①.

   Xmap provides plug-ins for the most popular Joomla extensions.

① When using the Sitemaps Manager with Xmap, you can create custom site maps for your Joomla web site.

Selecting a Template

Joomla installs with three templates:

- **Atomic**—A completely clean template you can use to create custom CSS designs.

- **Beez2**—The default template that provides great examples of standard Joomla layouts, parameters, and table-less CSS layouts .

- **Beez5**—A cutting-edge template that allows you to choose between an XHTML and HTML5 version.

Each of these templates can be customized to fit your site's design needs. You can create your own Joomla templates or find one from the thousands of free and commercial templates available for Joomla.

Template parameters, positions, and customization levels will vary between template developers. Some templates are easy to use, whereas others require more HTML and CSS expertise to match the template demos.

A A clean Joomla installation using the Beez2 default template

Using Joomla Templates

Take your time when selecting a template. Remember, you can create your entire site, and then with a few clicks and module repositioning, change the look and feel simply by installing a new template. You can also use multiple templates within a single web site.

Many template providers include "quick start" packages that include a complete Joomla installation with the template and all of its demo content. These packages offer a great way to learn how to configure and use your new template.

To use a third-party template:

1. Download the template.
2. Install the template.
3. Set the new template as the default .
4. Set your template parameters.
5. Customize your logo.

See Appendix B, "Joomla Resources," for a recommended list of the most popular template providers.

See Chapter 7, "Working with Templates," to learn how to install and configure a Joomla template.

Home

B The new template applied as the default for the site

Ⓐ During installation, Joomla creates the first category for you, the "Uncategorised" category.

Organizing the Main Pages

We know that Joomla, or any CMS for that matter, does not actually create static pages but dynamically retrieves various content from the database and displays it on the page. You can still think of your site's structure in terms of what should appear on a given page.

This is where a site's main navigation comes into play. You may have thousands of pages or only a few. You may have thousands of links or simple pagination between articles. In any case, you will need a main source of navigation to help users instantly identify and navigate to the web page on which their information, product, or form can be found. Your main menu should represent the main sources of your site's information.

There are as many ways to construct your content hierarchy as there are web pages. However, by structuring your categories in the beginning, the menus and linked content will be simpler for your users to navigate and for you to manage.

To create the main categories:

1. Log in to the back end of Joomla.

2. Choose Content > Category Manager.

   In a clean installation of Joomla, one with no sample data, your first category is automatically created for you and is titled Uncategorised Ⓐ.

   You may delete this category, but an uncategorized category has a multitude of uses.

continues on next page

3. On the toolbar, click New to create a new category.

   You should have a basic site map to reference when creating categories. In our example site, we use the site map from Table 11.1. Because we are thinking in terms of our main site structure and main navigation, these are the categories we can create now.

4. In the Title field, enter a title for this category.

   We are first creating a parent or root category. The title does not have to be the same as the one you will use for your menu items, but it should be descriptive of the types of content the category will contain. This title can also be used in your URLs.

5. Leave the Alias field blank, or type in an alias to be used if you are using search engine–friendly URLs.

6. From the Parent drop-down menu, choose No parent.

   This is a root category, and it is a parent category.

7. From the Status drop-down menu, choose Published.

   A category that is not published will not display on the site. Articles assigned to an unpublished category also will not display.

8. From the Access drop-down menu, choose Public.

   We want our blog page to be viewable by everyone, so this category needs to be set to public.

Categories, subcategories, and sub-subcategories!

If you have been working with web site design and development for a few years, you probably remember when CSS divs replaced table layouts. The introduction of the <div> tag had everyone going a bit div crazy. We created divs for everything to gain absolute control over our designs. After that bout of fun, we all calmed down and learned how to minimize our divs to maximize our design layouts.

The same is true when creating your category structure. You can create hundreds of categories and nest them infinitely deep, but doing so will make your page design far more difficult than it needs to be. Make a plan, create a site map, and think of the logical structure of your site content and how users will navigate it. Don't just randomly create containers to hold content. Creating additional categories as your site grows is far simpler than back-tracking and removing extraneous categories.

B In the Category Manager: Add a New Articles Category details screen, you create your category information.

C In the new categories publishing options, you can select another user. If you leave this field blank, the system will automatically assign your username in the "Created by" field.

9. Leave all other settings at their default values.

   Our blog page will not have a category description, so we will not enter any text in the Description area **B**.

10. If you want to set the user who created this category to someone other than yourself, under Publishing Options in the "Created by" field, click the Select User button.

    If you leave this field blank, the system will automatically fill in your user name as the created-by user for this category **C**.

11. Click the Basic Options link to open the Basic Options settings for this category only.

12. In the Alternative Layout field, choose the layout option for this category:

    ▸ **Global:** Uses the system-wide global option settings.

    ▸ **Blog:** Uses a blog layout along with overrides from your template, if the template supports com_content overrides.

    ▸ **List:** Uses a list layout along with overrides from your template, if the template supports com_content overrides.

    Template override styles included in your template can be found in the templates/templatename/html/com_content directory.

continues on next page

13. If you want to add an image to this category, click the Select button.

Clicking the Select button in the image field opens the Media Manager. From the Media Manager, you can choose an image or upload and insert a new image .

Images that are assigned to categories and not embedded in the category description will display beside the category title. The styling is based on your template and whether the image and title are set to show in the Category global options or in the Menu Item Category layout options.

14. Select an image, and then click Insert.

15. In the Note field, you can enter a note for administrators that identifies the purpose of this category, or leave the field blank .

16. Click the Metadata Options link.

It may be tempting to rapidly create your categories and articles with every intention of later adding your site's metadata. This rarely works. Take the time now to add basic metadata to every category and article as you create them. You can always add or change metadata later 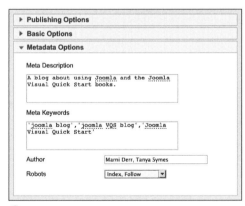.

17. In the Meta Description field, enter a short sentence to describe this category.

18. In the Meta Keywords field, enter a few descriptive keywords to identify what this category is about.

19. In the Author field, enter an author's name.

20. From the Robots drop-down menu, choose a search engine index option.

21. On the toolbar, click Save & New and continue adding your main categories.

Ⓓ You can add an image to a category through the Media Manager.

Ⓔ Using the new category Basic Options settings, you can select an alternative layout provided by your template, add an image, and a note describing this category to administrators.

Ⓕ The new category metadata options

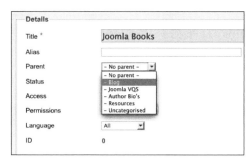

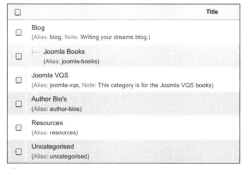

G Making a new subcategory by assigning it to a parent category

H The Category Manager displaying parent categories and their associated subcategories

To create subcategories:

1. Log in to the back end.

2. Choose Content > Category Manager.

3. On the toolbar, click New.

4. In the Title field, enter a title for this subcategory.

5. From the Parent drop-down menu, select the parent category for this subcategory.

   Categories can be nested as deeply as your site requires. Moving categories is as easy as using the batch processing feature to move multiple categories, or simply opening the category and changing its parent category **G**.

6. Fill in any additional details for this subcategory.

7. On the toolbar, click Save & Close.

   Once a subcategory is created, it will be listed beneath its parent in the Category Manager **H**.

8. Add the rest of your subcategory items to their parent categories.

   When you have created your highest level category and subcategory structures, you can create the main navigation by creating menu items for the Main Menu.

Creating the Main Menu

Content cannot be displayed on the site until you create menu items. A site can have multiple menu modules to help a user navigate and find content, or just a single menu that links to the main site categories. Either way, understanding how to create menus is one of the most important aspects of using Joomla.

All web sites use at least one high-level navigation menu. In Joomla, this is generally called the Main Menu, although you can give it any title you want. Presenting too many links and options can send users searching for a less-complicated site. You have only a few seconds to point users to what they need before they move on, so make your Main Menu count.

In this section, you create the menu items for the Main Menu module, assign it to a template position, and enable the display of secondary menu navigation.

To add categories to the main menu:

1. Log in to the back end.

2. Choose Menus > Main Menu.

    The Menu Manager: Menu Items screen opens displaying all the menu items created and assigned to the Main Menu **A**.

    The first menu item in the Main Menu is automatically created and links to all articles marked as "featured." The Home page menu item is the default page that a user will see when opening your site in a browser. You can set any menu item as the default, but you can have only one default item.

A The Menu Manager: Menu Items assigned to the Main Menu

B The Menu Item details screen

Select a Menu Item Type:

Contacts
List All Contact Categories
List Contacts in a Category
Single Contact
Featured Contacts

Articles
Archived Articles
Single Article
List All Categories
Category Blog
Category List
Featured Articles
Create Article

Newsfeeds
List All News Feed Categories
List News Feeds in a Category
Single News Feed

Search
List Search Results

Users Manager
Login Form
User Profile
Edit User Profile
Registration Form
Username Reminder Request
Password Reset

Weblinks
List All Web Link Categories
List Web Links in a Category
Submit a Web Link

Wrapper
Iframe Wrapper

Xmap
HTML Site map
XML Sitemap

C The list of all available menu item types installed on your site

In our example, we want our latest blog posts to display on the home page, so we have left the default Home menu item set to Featured Articles. When we post a new blog article, we will mark it as featured so that it displays on the home page.

3. On the toolbar, click New to open the Menu Manager: New Menu Item details screen.

   Before a menu item can be created and saved, it must have a type, a title, and be assigned to a menu module. All other fields are optional **B**.

4. Next to the Menu Item Type field, click the Select button.

   Every available menu item type is listed in this pop-up window, including any menu items provided with extensions you have installed. Notice the Xmap menu item types in the lower-right corner. These were added when we installed the Xmap component **C**.

5. Choose Category Blog.

   The second page of our site will link directly to our full blog, so we are selecting the Category Blog menu item type.

6. Enter a title for this menu item.

   This title will appear as the link in the Main Menu.

7. From the Menu Location drop-down menu, choose Main Menu.

continues on next page

8. Under Required Settings, in the "Choose a category" drop-down menu, choose the Blog category.

This menu item links to a category, so we must select the category to which we are linking.

Every category created on the site will be in this list 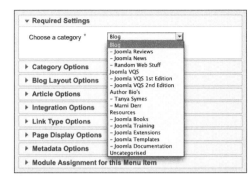.

9. On the toolbar, click Save & New.

10. Continue by adding each of your top-level main menu item types.

We won't yet worry about the menu item layout options. Right now, we only want to create the basic framework for our site.

To add submenus to the main menu:

1. Choose Menus > Main Menu.

2. On the toolbar, click New.

3. In the Menu Item Type field, click the Select button to select the menu item type for this link.

4. In the Menu Title field, enter the name of this link.

5. From the Menu Location drop-down menu, choose Main Menu.

6. From the Parent Item drop-down menu, choose the parent menu item for this link.

Secondary navigation or submenus are created as you would any other menu item; the exception is that it must select the parent item 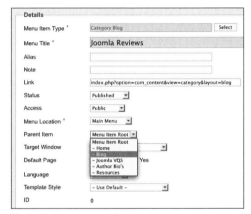.

7. Under Required Settings, choose the category for this link.

8. Continue adding each submenu item for your main menu.

D All options and settings are based on the menu item type you choose. The required settings for a Category menu item type is to select the category to which this menu item links.

E Creating a submenu item requires that you assign the submenu to a parent menu item.

To edit or change a menu item:

1. Log in to the back end.

2. Choose Menus > Main Menu.

   You can change a menu item type, settings, or layout options at any time.

   In our example we created a Category Blog menu item type for Resources. We want to change this to a list of categories **F**.

3. From the Menu Item Manager, select the menu item you need to change or edit.

4. Make any desired changes.

5. On the toolbar, click Save & Close.

   The Resources menu item is changed to a List All Categories layout **G**.

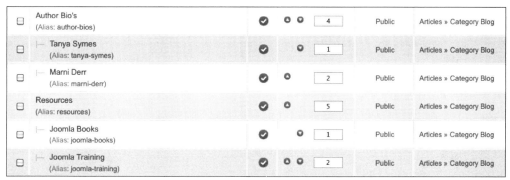

F The Resources menu item type is currently a Category Blog layout.

G Changing the Resources menu item type to a List All Categories layout is reflected in the Menu Item Manager.

Styling the Main Menu

Menu styling is provided by your Joomla template. Many third-party template providers give you access to multiple menu styles. For example, mega-menus and suckerfish-menus are JavaScript-enabled menus that let you create stylish menus using images and secondary text information. If you want to avoid using JavaScript, templates will generally have the option to use a pure CSS menu. Some templates have only one type of menu style for the main menu, but every template will have multiple menu styles. When customizing your Main Menu, consult your template provider's documentation.

If your template does not contain additional menu styles, you can add custom styling through the menu item itself. To see the Main Menu on your site, you need to assign the Main Menu module to the correct position.

To position the main menu module:

1. Log in to the back end.

2. Choose Extensions > Template Manager.

3. On the toolbar, click Options.

4. From the Templates tab, set Preview Module Positions to Enabled.

   This allows you to view all the available positions provided by your template .

5. Click Save & Close.

6. Choose Extensions > Template Manager.

Ⓐ In the Template Manager Options, you enable the Preview Module Positions.

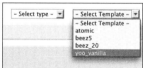

B The Template Manager: Templates link provides you with access to your template's source files and the ability to preview a template's positions.

C The Main Menu module details screen allows you to select the position for the Main Menu module.

D The position pop-up window has sort filters to display only positions used in a specific template.

E Our Main Menu module uses the menu template position.

7. Click the Templates link.

The Template Manager: Templates screen lets you view template positions, if enabled, and access the template's index and CSS files **B**.

Clicking the Styles link lets you view a template's parameters.

8. Click the Preview link below your template's title.

Doing so opens the front end of your site displaying each position contained in your template.

9. Choose Extensions > Module Manager.

10. Click the Main Menu title to open the Main Menu module details.

The Beez2 template is the default Joomla template, so the default position of the Main Menu is position-7, a position contained in the Beez2 template. If you are using another template as your site's default, you need to change this position **C**.

11. In the Position field, enter the position name for your main menu as provided by your template, or click the Select Position button to assign the correct position.

12. If you opt to click the Select Position button, all available template positions are listed. Use the sort fields, if necessary, to display only your current template's positions **D**.

Once a new position is entered or selected, the Position field will display the new position for the Main Menu **E**.

continues on next page

13. Click Save & Close.

14. Click View Site.

Your Main Menu now displays as the main navigation for your site .

15. Click through your new pages using your main menu navigation.

If you experience issues with submenus in the main menu—for example, your submenus either don't appear at all, or they are not styled correctly—you need to configure the menu module to display the submenus correctly. Unfortunately, the procedure for doing this varies greatly from template to template. All template developers should provide documentation on how to use their menu systems.

To display submenu items:

1. Log in to the back end.

2. Choose Extensions > Module Manager.

3. Click Main Menu to open the Main Menu module details screen.

4. Under Basic Options, set the Start Level to 1.

This tells the system to begin rendering the menu items at level 1, or the parent menu item.

F The Main Menu module is displayed correctly in our template's menu position on the front end of the web site.

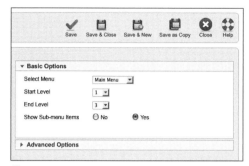

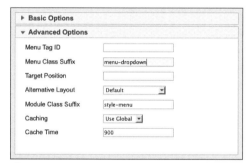

G Select the Start and End levels for your Main Menu module.

H Your template's menu and module class suffixes allow you to style your menus and submenus using your template's CSS class styles.

I The Main Menu now displays submenu items according to the styles in our template.

5. For the End Level, choose the number of submenu items you want the system to display beneath the parent menu item.

Choosing 0 will display no submenus. Choosing 1 will display the first submenu item. Choosing 2 will display the next two levels of submenus, and so on **G**.

Note that some template providers require that the Show Submenu Items option must be set to Yes to allow submenus to work correctly. If you enter the correct module and menu class suffixes and your submenus still don't display properly, try changing this option to Yes.

6. Click Advanced Options to open the advanced menu module option settings.

7. Enter the module and/or menu class suffixes required to correctly render your template's menu module.

To use your template's custom menus, you generally assign the menu module a specific menu class suffix and/or a module class suffix. Again, your template provider should provide this information **H**.

8. On the toolbar, click Save & Close.

The Main Menu module now displays our submenus **I**.

To add images to menu items:

1. Log in to the back end.

2. Choose Menus > Main Menu.

3. Select the menu item you want to add an image to.

   This will open the menu item details screen for this menu item.

   In our example, we will add the book covers for both the first and second editions of our Joomla VQS book, so users aren't confused about which edition they are looking for.

4. Click the arrow next to Link Type Options to open it.

   The Link Type Options allow you to add title attributes, special CSS styling for menu items, and images .

5. Next to the Link Image field, click Select.

   Doing so opens the Media Manager in which you can select an image to display next to your menu item link .

   If you have not already uploaded the image, you will want to use the Media Manager to upload the image.

6. Select an image to display next to this menu item.

   Menu item images should be sized relative to the menu. Small links should have smaller images. In this example, the image is 30x38 pixels.

7. With the image selected, click Insert.

8. Click Save & Close.

9. Select any images you want to add to your other menu items.

J The menu item link type options

K The Media Manager stores all images used on the site, including images associated with menu items.

L The new submenu items with images

M The menu item details screen. Adding || to separate text in the menu title will display any text after the symbols as subtext.

N The Main Menu submenus with subtext added

10. Click View Site.

Our Joomla VQS submenus now include images that show users which book cover is associated with each edition **L**.

You can further help your users by adding subtext to your menu items, if your template supports this feature.

To add subtext to menu items:

1. Log in to the back end.

2. Choose Menus > Main Menu.

The Menu Manager: Menu Items manager opens displaying all the menu items assigned to your main menu.

Most templates support adding subtext to your menu items, but you will need to check the documentation to verify this for your template.

3. Select a menu item to open the menu item details.

In our example, we want the 1st and 2nd edition menu items to have the Joomla VQS title followed by the edition reference as subtext.

4. In the Title field, add subtext using the straight line symbol: **Joomla VQS || 1st Edition** **M**.

5. Click Save & Close.

6. Click View Site.

The menu item now displays subtext below the menu title **N**.

Putting It All Together

1. **Create a site map.** Make the site map as extensive and thorough as you can in the beginning. Changing things later is fine, but a good site map helps make site creation easier.

2. **Create wireframes for your main pages.** Wireframes help lay out your main pages and identify where your content and modules are created and displayed.

3. **Install a *clean* copy of Joomla.** The Joomla sample data is great for learning how to use Joomla; however, it is difficult to remove all of that content. The sample data also uses many advanced techniques that you may not want to replicate on your site.

4. **Install third-party extensions.** When constructing your web site, install extensions before adding content to save time and avoid possible conflicts down the road.

5. **Install and configure your template.** Create your own templates, use the ones that come with Joomla, or download one of the thousands of third-party templates.

6. **Create your main categories.** Create your main categories and subcategories from your original site map.

7. **Add menu items to the Main Menu.** To display your content, you will need to add menu items to the Main Menu. First create the main navigation for your site, then create other menus as you add content.

8. **Style the Main Menu module.** You can create simple or advanced menu links. Position your menu and then style it using your template's menu and module class suffixes. Add images or subtext to help your users further identify your content.

Creating Portfolios and Galleries

In some respects, every site on the web is a great example of a portfolio. If you sell products, your site is a portfolio of your products and customer service. If you sell services, your site lists the types of services you provide and offers samples of your work. A personal CSV or resume web site is a portfolio of your expertise and work history.

In This Chapter

In our example site, we are promoting this book (product), the authors (resume and services), and Joomla (product and services). In this section, you will lay out the following portfolio pages:

- Product and personal portfolio pages **A**
- An image gallery and slideshow **B**

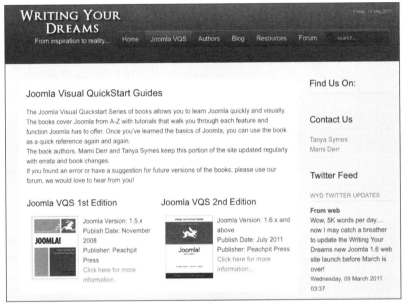

A Product portfolio

B Image gallery

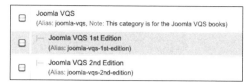

A The parent category and subcategories for our book pages

Showcasing Products and Services

When you begin using Joomla, first add categories and articles and then work on your page layouts. As you get started, laying out your pages will take most of your time. The more content you initially have to work with, the easier it will be to choose menu item types, set global options, and refine individual content options.

To display articles on category pages:

1. Log in to the back end.

2. Choose Content > Category Manager.

   We currently have one product category, the Joomla Visual QuickStart books, and two subcategories: Joomla VQS 1st Edition and Joomla VQS 2nd Edition Ⓐ.

   First we will add two articles to the parent category, Joomla Visual QuickStart Guides:

   ▸ Joomla VQS 1st Edition

   ▸ Joomla VQS 2nd Edition

   Then we'll add three articles to each subcategory:

   ▸ About This Book

   ▸ Table of Contents

   ▸ Errata

3. Choose Content > Add New Article.

4. Add a Title for this article.

5. Enter an alias for this article, or if you leave the field blank, the system will use the Title field as the alias.

   continues on next page

6. Select a category for this article.

   Every article must be assigned to a single category. After an article is assigned to a category, it displays using any Category menu item link or a Single Article menu item link.

7. Leave Status set to Published, Access to Public, Featured to No, and Language to All.

8. In the Article Text box, enter the article's full text and any associated images  **B**.

9. On the toolbar, click Save & New.

10. Place any additional articles in your parent and subcategories.

11. Click View Site.

    If you assigned this article to a parent category, select the parent category link.

    If the article was assigned to a subcategory, select the subcategory link.

TIP If your articles are not displaying, it is either because the global layout options or your category blog menu items are not set to display articles. Don't panic, we will cover display options shortly.

   In our example the parent category, Joomla Visual QuickStart Guides, displays with its category description.

   Next to display are our two new articles, assigned to the Joomla Visual QuickStart Guide category **C**.

TIP There is nothing wrong with setting your global layout options before you create content or setting your menu item layout options while creating menu items. Once you are comfortable using Joomla, you will develop your own workflow for laying out pages.

TIP When you are creating a new site, we recommend first creating content, and then setting layout options, because you can inadvertently turn settings off and find that your content does not display at all.

B The new article details screen. An article must have a title and be assigned to a category before it can be saved.

C The Joomla VQS category page displaying the parent category description and the two new articles

D Articles created for the books' portfolio pages

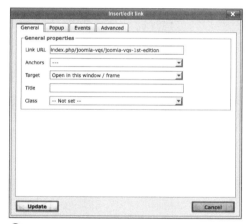

E You must select the text you want to turn into a hyperlink and then click the Link button in the editor.

To add hyperlinks to articles:

1. Log in to the back end.

2. Choose Content > Article Manager.

   We created a total of 10 articles for our Joomla VQS category and its subcategories **D**.

3. Select an article you want to add a link to and open it for editing.

   In our example, our parent category articles will link to the subcategory articles.

4. In the Article Text box, type a line of text for your link and select it **E**.

5. In the editor, click the Link button.

6. In the Insert/Edit link pop-up window, enter the URL for this link **F**.

7. Click Update.

   The text is now a hyperlink.

8. On the toolbar, click Save.

9. Click View Site.

10. Open the article page to which you added the link.

   Providing users with multiple ways to navigate your content is a sign of good web design and usability **G**.

F The Insert/Edit link pop-up window

Joomla VQS 1st Edition

Joomla Version: 1.5.x
Publish Date: Nov 2008
Publisher: Peachpit Press
Click here for more information.

G The text in the article is now a hyperlink to a subcategory page.

To add a Read More link to an article:

1. Choose Content > Article Manager.

   The Article Manager opens displaying all articles created on the site.

   Because we are showcasing a product, we don't want to require a user to scroll through long pages of text. You can isolate intro text using a Read More button. When a user visits the product's category page, she can click the article title or the Read More link to view the complete article.

2. Open one of your articles.

3. In the Article Text box, place your cursor where you want the intro text to end.

4. At the bottom of the edit box, click the Read More button.

   This inserts a Read More link into the article text. Only the text above the Read More link will display on the category page .

5. Add other Read More links to long articles that will display on a category page.

6. On the toolbar, click Save & Close.

7. Click View Site and navigate to the category page.

   The article on the category page now displays only the intro text and a link below it to the full article .

8. Click the Read More link to open the full article.

   The Read More link is styled by your template. The text that displays on the Read More link can be changed using article options.

9. Return to the back end.

10. Open any article with a Read More link.

H Add a Read More link to separate the article intro text from the full article.

I A cleaner and shorter article sample on a category page, displaying only the intro text and a Read More link to the full article text

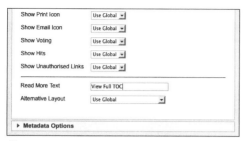

J You can add your own text to the Read More button.

K You can customize the text that displays on a Read More button.

L Inserting an article index using the page break pop-up window

11. Click Article Options to display all the layout options for your article.

12 In the Read More Text field, enter the text you want to display on the Read More link button **J**.

13. Click Save, and then click View Site.

The article's Read More button displays the text you entered in the Read More Text field **K**.

To add an article index using a page break:

1. Log in to the back end.

2. Choose Content > Article Manager.

One of the articles on the category page is extremely long. We could divide the article into individual articles, but we want the user to click only once to find the full article so we will create an article index using the page break function.

3. Open any article (the longer the better).

We are using our Errata article for the first edition of this book. The article is divided by chapter, so we will create an index to make it easier for the user to quickly find each chapter.

4. Select a place in the article text to begin your index, and then click the Page-break button at the bottom of the editor to open the Insert Page Break pop-up window **L**.

5. Enter a Page Title to be used in the article index to identify the page.

6. Enter a Table of Contents Alias to be used with your SEF URLs.

7. Click Insert Page Break to insert the page break and add it to the article.

continues on next page

8. On the toolbar, click Save.

9. Click View Site.

A complete index is available for the article content, allowing the user to click through a single article, but avoid scrolling through a long page of content .

If the user wants to view the full article, he can click the All Pages link at the bottom of the index.

The page break index is styled by your template. You can style the index using the CSS DIV ID `.article-index` located in your template's CSS files.

10. Continue adding as many page breaks as you need, and save the article.

To remove a page break or Read More link from an article:

1. Open the article from which you want to remove the page break or Read More link.

2. In the Article Text editor, click the "Toggle editor" button.

The only way to remove a page break or Read More link is to directly remove its code. Toggling the editor switches from WYSIWIG mode to pure code mode .

3. Select the page break code:

```
<hr id="system-pagebreak title=
"title" alt="alias title">
```

or the Read More code:

```
<hr id="system-readmore">
```

and then delete it.

4. Save the article.

Errata (1st Edition)

- Errata (1st Edition)
- Chapter 2
- Chapter 3
- Chapter 4
- Chapter 5
- Chapter 6
- Chapters 7,8,9
- All Pages

Page 1 of 7

The errata and additions are sorted by chapter and pag

Chapter 1:Installing Joomla

We received many emails regarding our choice to docu around hosting issues user's face when implementing a vary, it is not possible for us to cover all the necessary i

M An article using the page break article index function

N Selecting the page break HTML code in pure code view

A The Global Options for all content: categories, subcategories, articles, and lists

Creating Category Pages

Category pages can display category titles, images and descriptions above articles, or only the articles. They can display sub-category titles, images, and descriptions below the parent category information but above category and subcategory articles. Further, you can choose a specific number of subcategories and articles for display.

Category pages come in two formats: blog and list. Blog formats display categories, subcategories, and articles. Category lists display a list of categories and/or a list of articles assigned to those categories.

All default settings for articles and menu items are originally set to the Use Global settings. These settings are customized in your content manager's Options settings **A**.

When customizing the layout of your web pages, you have three options:

- Set the global content options to suit the majority of your site content, and then override these settings at the article and menu item level as needed.

- Set all global content options to Hide, and then override these settings on a per article or menu item basis.

- Set all global content options to Show, and then override these settings on a per article or menu item basis.

Best practice is to decide how you want the majority of your content to display and set the global options accordingly. All content layouts will inherit these settings automatically and save you time when creating new content.

Each of the content global settings are described in Chapter 6, "Controlling Content Layouts." In this section, you'll refine your layouts using articles and menu items.

To set the global order of articles:

1. Log in to the back end.

2. Choose Content > Article Manager.

   When setting ordering options, consider the main purpose of your content. On a blog, it is normal for the most recently published articles to display first. On pages with static or rarely updated information, you would set the ordering according to the order of the article in the Article Manager. News web sites will set the order of articles so that the most popular or most read articles appear first.

3. On the toolbar, click Options.

4. Click the Shared Options tab.

   This tab includes settings that apply to all content types: categories in blog or list layouts, and articles whether featured or not .

   These global options can be overwritten for categories at the menu item level, and for articles at the article or menu item level.

5. Set the Category Order and Article Order you want to use for the majority of your site content.

6. Set the Date for Ordering, if you want to order by date at the menu item level or article level.

   You can order by the following date types:

   ▸ **Created:** The date the article or category was created.

   ▸ **Published:** The date the article or category was published.

   ▸ **Modified:** The date the category or article was last modified.

B In the global content shared options, you set the ordering of articles and globally turn pagination on or off.

More Articles...

- Errata-2nd Edition
- Table of Contents-2nd Edition
- About the Book-2nd Edition

C Pagination is located at the bottom of a page, below the articles and any article links. The pagination links are styled by your template.

Page 1 of 2

Start   Prev   1   2   Next   End

D An example of the Beez2 template styling for pagination links

E The category options

7. Set the global Pagination option:

   ‣ **Hide:** Will not display pagination at the bottom of a page even if more articles are assigned to this category.

   ‣ **Show:** Will display pagination at the bottom of the page even if no more articles are assigned to this category.

   ‣ **Auto:** Links will display if more articles are in this category. If the category contains no more articles, pagination links will not display.

8. Set the Pagination Results.

   If Pagination is set to Show or Auto, the number of pages containing articles will display **C**.

   Pagination is styled by your template. The default Beez2 template pagination would look like figure **D**.

To set menu item category options:

1. Log in to the back end.

2. Choose Menus > Main Menu.

   We are going to finalize our product portfolio pages.

   For our Joomla VQS product page, we applied a Category Blog menu item type. This is the most common menu item type to use on pages with article content.

3. Open the parent category.

   To style the categories and subcategories on our category pages, we need to use the category options **E**.

4. Set Category Title to Show to display the category title above the category description.

5. Set Category Description to Show to display the category description.

continues on next page

6. Set Category Image to Show.

   If you linked an image to the category using the advanced options, the image will display.

7. Set Subcategory Levels to None.

   You don't want the subcategory articles to display on this page.

   If you do want the subcategory articles to display on this category page, you would set the number of subcategories beneath this parent category.

8. Set Empty Categories to Hide to hide subcategories with no articles assigned to them.

9. Set No Articles Message to Hide.

   If the category or subcategories are set to show but contain no articles, the message "There are no articles to display" appears.

10. Set Subcategories Descriptions to Hide.

    This setting hides or shows the subcategory description.

    At the time of this writing, subcategory titles and descriptions will only appear vertically beneath the parent categories articles. You cannot control where or how they display. For example, you cannot place subcategory descriptions above the parent category articles, and you cannot set subcategory descriptions to display in columns.

11. Set # Articles in Category to Hide to display the total number of articles assigned to the category next to the category title.

12. Leave the Page Subheading field blank.

    The page subheading will display any text in this field as an H2 heading below the category title.

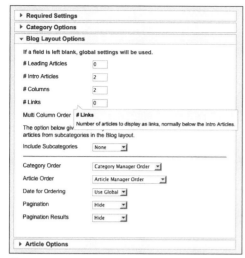

F Blog layout options

13. On the toolbar, click Save.

Category menu item options control the display of category and subcategory information. To control the layout of articles assigned to categories, you use the blog layout options.

To set menu item blog layout options:

1. Choose Menus > Main Menu.

In this example, we will lay out the articles assigned to our Joomla VQS parent category.

2. Open your category menu item for editing.

3. Click the arrow next to Blog Layout Options.

Blog layout options control the number of articles that will display on a page and how they will appear **F**.

For our product portfolio page, we will display the products in even rows and columns.

4. Set # Leading Articles to 0 to prevent any article from spanning across the main body of the page.

5. Set # Intro Articles to 2.

Intro articles display beneath any leading articles. Intro articles do not control intro text or how much of an article will display.

6. Set # Columns to 2.

Columns place articles side by side in evenly-spaced columns. For example, if you set columns to 2 and had six intro articles, the system would display three rows of two articles each.

continues on next page

7. From the Multi Column Order drop-down menu, choose Across to order the articles horizontally, or Down to order the articles vertically.

8. From the Include Subcategories drop-down menu, set the number of subcategory articles you want to display.

The parent category and subcategory articles share the # Leading and # Intro totals. The articles that appear in a category or its subcategories are controlled by the ordering settings.

9. From the Category Order drop-down menu, set the order in which the categories will appear on this page.

The parent category, and any included subcategories, display their titles and descriptions in the order you choose **G**:

▸ **Use Global:** Uses the global content Shared Option settings to determine the category ordering.

▸ **No Order:** Categories are unordered.

▸ **Title Alphabetical:** Order the categories alphabetically by title sorted A to Z.

▸ **Title Reverse Alphabetical:** Order the categories alphabetically by title sorted Z to A.

▸ **Category Manager Order:** Order the categories according to the ordering set in the Category Manager.

10. From the Article Order drop-down menu, set the order in which the articles appear on the page **H**:

▸ **Use Global:** Use the global content shared options settings to determine article order.

▸ **Featured Articles Order:** Use the Featured Article Manager ordering.

▸ **Most recent first:** Order the articles by publish date.

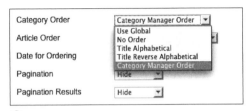

G Category ordering options

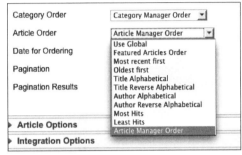

H Article ordering options

Joomla Visual QuickStart Guides

The Joomla Visual Quickstart Series of books allows you to learn Joomla quickly and visually. The books cover Joomla from A-Z with tutorials that walk you through each feature and function Joomla has to offer. Once you've learned the basics of Joomla, you can use the book as a quick reference again and again.

The book authors, Marni Derr and Tanya Symes keep this portion of the site updated regularly with errata and book changes.

If you found an error or have a suggestion for future versions of the books, please use our forum, we would love to hear from you!

Joomla VQS 1st Edition	Joomla VQS 2nd Edition
Joomla Version: 1.5.x Publish Date: Nov 2008 Publisher: Peachpit Press Click here for more information.	Joomla Version: 1.6.x and above Publish Date: July 2011 Publisher: Peachpit Press Click here for more information...

① A category blog layout page

▸ **Oldest first:** Order the articles by publish date.

▸ **Title Alphabetical:** Order the articles according to their titles sorted A to Z.

▸ **Title Reverse Alphabetical:** Order the articles according to their titles sorted Z to A.

▸ **Author Alphabetical:** Order the articles by the author name sorted A to Z.

▸ **Author Reverse Alphabetical:** Order the articles by the author name sorted Z to A.

▸ **Most Hits:** Order the articles based on the number of views.

▸ **Least Hits:** Order the articles based on the lowest number of views.

▸ **Article Manager Order:** Order the articles according to the settings in the Article Manager.

11. From the Date for Ordering drop-down menu, set the date to use for ordering if you have chosen to order by date in the Article Order drop-down menu.

12. From the Pagination drop-down menu, choose Show, Hide, or Auto.

13. From the Pagination Results drop-down menu, choose Show, Hide, or Auto.

14. Click Save.

15. Click View Site.

Based on our blog layout options the parent category—Joomla Visual QuickStart Guides—the title, and the description display at the top of the page followed by two intro articles in two columns. No subcategories or subcategory articles are set to display on this page **①**.

To set menu item article options:

1. Choose Menus > Main Menu.

2. Open a category menu item.

3. Click the arrow next to Article Options to open the article option settings.

   Menu item article options will overwrite your global content settings and the individual article's settings 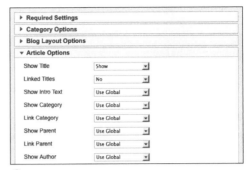.

   Because we are creating a product portfolio page, we want only the title and article content to appear on this page. If a user wants more information, she can click the Read More link or the hyperlink embedded in the content.

   Because each of our books has more than one article of information associated with it, we will turn off the ability to click the title. Instead, we want the user to click the For More Information link to navigate to each book's category page.

4. From the Show Title drop-down menu, choose Show.

5. From the Linked Titles drop-down menu, choose No.

6. Leave all other settings at the global defaults.

   Our books have their own subcategory pages with multiple articles, so it would be pointless to have the user click the article titles. A linkable title would open only to that article and add an extra step for our users.

7. On the toolbar, click Save & Close.

   Using global content options and menu item options, you can create complete product listings and product portfolios. You have total control over what appears on every page of your site and can combine these options to make your site easy to navigate.

① The article options

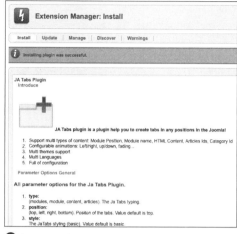

A A successful installation of the JA Tabs plug-in

Using Tabs and Slides

Using Joomla's global content and menu item layout options, you can style and display your web site content in hundreds of ways. But what if you want to augment current content with more advanced features such as accordions, tabs, or slides?

In future versions of Joomla, these features will become available as part of the core framework. In fact, the new Contact module already has these capabilities. Unfortunately, these features are not yet available for article content.

At the time of this writing, you need a third-party plug-in to present your content using accordions, tabs, or slides. A quick search of the Joomla Extension Directory will locate dozens of tab and slide plug-ins.

In our example, we will use the Tabs plug-in from www.joomlart.com.

To install a tab and slide plug-in for content:

1. Download a tab plug-in to your computer.

2. Log in to the back end.

3. Choose Extensions > Extension Manager to open the Extension Manager: Install screen.

4. Next to the Upload Package File field, click the Browse button.

5. Select the tab plug-in, and click Open.

6. Click Upload & Install.

   After the plug-in successfully installs, information on using the plug-in is displayed. We recommend that you copy and print this information A.

continues on next page

7. Choose Extensions > Plug-in Manager to open the Plug-in Manager.

8. In the Select Type drop-down list, choose system.

This sorts the Plug-in Manager to display only system plug-ins. The JA Tabs plug-in is currently disabled .

9. Select the System - JA Tabs title to open the plug-in settings.

10. From the Enabled drop-down menu, choose Enabled to turn on this plug-in.

Notice that the plug-in Details area also contains information on how to use this plug-in. You can return to the Plug-in Manager at any time to view the plug-in settings 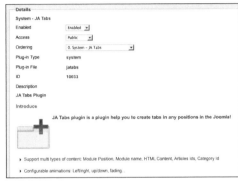.

11. Under Basic Options, set Disable Tabs to No.

12. From the "Default style" drop-down menu, choose a style for your tabs.

The styles available to this plug-in are based on the templates produced by Joomlart. You may have to try out a few styles before you find one that works best for your site 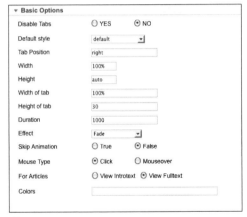.

13. In the Tab Position field, enter top, left, right, or bottom to set the position of the tabs in the article.

14. Set For Articles to View Introtext or View Fulltext.

15. Leave all other settings at their defaults.

When styling tabs, you may tweak these settings to try to achieve the precise layout you desire.

16. On the toolbar, click Save & Close.

B In the Plug-in Manager, you enable the JA Tabs system plug-in.

C The JA Tabs plug-in details screen

D In the JA Tabs plug-in basic options, you style and configure the plug-in.

E The beginning of the tabs code

To add the tabs to article content:

1. Choose Content > Article Manager.

    We will change our Errata article from using a page break index to using tabs so a user can navigate through each chapter.

2. Open the article for editing.

3. Delete the page breaks, if any.

4. Click the "Toggle editor" button.

    When using this type of plug-in, you need to be in code view, otherwise your editor could strip out the code you are entering.

    The Joomla editor window is small and can be difficult to read. When working with code, we recommend copying all the code into a text editor such as BBEdit or Coda. Then when you are done editing, copy the code back into the Joomla editor. If you try to do this in a WYSIWYG editor, you run the risk of having some code elements stripped out!

5. Below the Read More link code, type:

    ```
    {jatabs type="content" position=
    "top" height="auto" mouseType=
    "click" animType="animFade"}
    ```

    This tells the plug-in to begin the tabs here, position the tabs at the top, set the height of the content automatically, change the tabs when a user clicks them, and use the fade animation when changing tabs **E**.

6. For each tab you want to add to your article, type:

    ```
    [tab title="titlefortab"]
    ```

    at the beginning of the content to be separated.

continues on next page

7. At the end of the content to be contained on a single tab, type:

`[/tab]`

The final code might look like →this:

[tab title="Title"]<p>My text</p> →[/tab]

8. Continue until you reach the end of your content.

9. At the very end of all text and tags, type:

{/jatabs}

to end the tabs plug-in.

10. On the toolbar, click Save & Close.

Now view your tabbed content on the site **F**.

You can insert tabs and slides to present long bits of information. These elements work especially well when selling products.

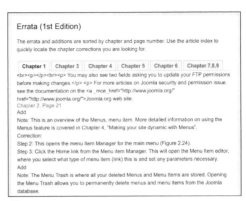

Errata (1st Edition)

The errata and additions are sorted by chapter and page number. Use the article index to quickly locate the chapter corrections you are looking for.

Chapter 1	Chapter 3	Chapter 4	Chapter 5	Chapter 6	Chapter 7,8,9

<p></p>
<p> You may also see two fields asking you to update your FTP permissions before making changes.</p> <p> For more articles on Joomla security and permission issue. see the documentation on the <a _mce_href="http://www.joomla.org/" href="http://www.joomla.org/">Joomla.org web site.

Chapter 2, Page 21
Add
Note: This is an overview of the Menus, menu item. More detailed information on using the Menus feature is covered in Chapter 4, "Making your site dynamic with Menus".
Correction:
Step 2: This opens the menu Item Manager for the main menu (Figure 2.24).
Step 3: Click the Home link from the Menu Item Manager. This will open the Menu Item editor, where you select what type of menu item (link) this is and set any parameters necessary.
Add
Note: The Menu Trash is where all your deleted Menus and Menu Items are stored. Opening the Menu Trash allows you to permanently delete menus and menu items from the Joomla database.

F Our new book errata information split into tabs on a single page.

A Select the template to duplicate in the Template Manager.

Personalizing Portfolios

A personal portfolio can constitute an entire web site dedicated to your work or services, a single page listing your experience and work history, or a combination of both. In each case, a personal portfolio should contain a snapshot of everything you want a potential employer or client to know about you. Portfolios should reflect your individual style and be clean and professional looking.

In this section, you will apply a different template style to the author pages, add a contact module, and create custom HTML modules.

To assign different templates or styles to a page:

1. Log in to the back end.

2. Choose Extensions > Template Manager.

   The Template Manager opens displaying each template installed on the site.

   You can apply template styles to individual pages in many ways. Most commercial templates come with multiple color schemes. Some templates include parameters you can set based on page assignment; others allow you to modify code using PHP.

   We are going to show you one method that works with all templates: duplicating the template and then selecting a theme or preset to apply to a specific page.

   The template in this example includes eight color presets (styles). We will apply a different template preset to each of our author pages.

3. Click the checkbox next to the template you want to duplicate **A**.

continues on next page

4. On the toolbar, click the Duplicate button.

The system displays an exact copy of the template. Even though it adds "(2)" to the title to identify it as a copy, you'll want to give it a more descriptive title **B**.

5. Click the title of the duplicate template.

6. Under Details, in the Style Name field, enter a new title for this duplicated template **C**.

You can change the name of any template so that administrators can easily identify which template is the default, and which templates are assigned to other pieces of the web site.

7. Under Basic Options, set the styles you want to use **D**.

8. Under Menu Assignment, select the pages you want to style using this template **E**.

The template is now assigned to those menu item pages. You can select a single menu item or multiple menu items.

9. On the toolbar, click Save & Close.

10. Click View Site and navigate to the page to which you assigned the template. The duplicate template styles are applied to the individual page.

TIP Using a duplicate template ensures that modules appearing on every page of your site are still in their proper positions. If you want to use an entirely different template on a page, you may have to create duplicate modules and assign them to the positions used by another template.

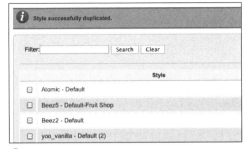

B The Template Manager contains links to duplicates of your template. Here you can change styles and assign templates to individual menu items.

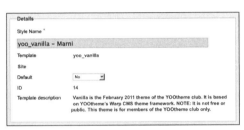

C When creating a duplicate template, add a descriptive title to identify the copy.

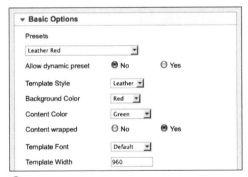

D Change the template styles using the duplicate template's basic options.

E Assign the duplicate template to the menu item.

Creating Galleries and Slideshows

You can use Joomla articles to display images with articles or next to text. You could create articles that consist of images only, and then build your pages to display those images like a gallery. Those are the basic options.

For more advanced applications, you can download a third-party image gallery or slideshow extension and create visual effects to dynamically showcase your work, products, or photos.

In this section, we will add a slideshow to our home page and create a Joomla web site gallery to showcase the sites we have built.

Every extension is different and contains various features and settings. We will be using the RocketTheme template and the RokStories slideshow extension on our front page and the GavickPro Image Show GK4 to showcase our web site examples.

To add a front page slideshow:

1. Install a slideshow module.

   Simple slideshows are generally modules that you use to call article content into and then display those articles in a module position on your site.

   More elaborate slideshow components don't use articles but let you create entire albums of content to display.

2. Choose Extensions > Module Manager.

3. On the toolbar, click New.

4. In the "Select a Module Type" pop-up window, select the Slideshow module.

continues on next page

5. Under Details, in the Title field, type a title for your slideshow.

6. Set Show Title to Hide.

   We do not want to display a title with the slideshow.

7. In the Position field, choose a position for your slideshow.

8. From the Status drop-down menu, choose Published.

   These are the basic settings appropriate for any module you create for your site .

9. Under Basic Options, configure your slideshow module according to the developer's documentation 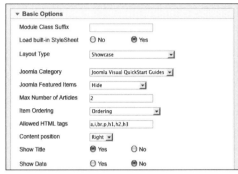.

10. Under menu assignment, select the pages on which you want the slide show to appear.

11. On the toolbar, click Save & Close.

12. Click View Site to see an example of a slideshow that showcases our book 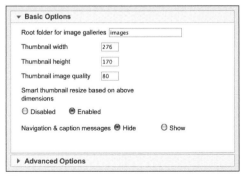.

To create an image gallery:

1. Log in to the back end.

2. Install an image gallery component, module, or plug-in.

   There are three types of image gallery extensions: component, module, and plug-in. The one you select depends on your site needs. Components and modules offer the most elaborate image galleries; plug-ins work with modules or articles.

3. Enable the image gallery plug-in in the Plug-in Manager and configure any basic options .

   We use the Simple Image Gallery plug-in from JoomlaWorks, which pulls the images from the Media Manager. Images is the Media Manager's root folder.

Ⓐ The Slideshow module details

Ⓑ In the basic options, you set slideshow module options.

Ⓒ An example of our slideshow module on the Home page

Ⓓ The basic options for the Simple Image Gallery plug-in

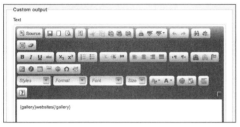

E The Custom HTML module details

F The code to call the image gallery is written in the custom output editor.

G The image gallery on the web site

4. Upload your gallery images to the Media Manager.

5. Choose Extensions > Module Manager.

6. On the toolbar, click New.

7. In the Select Module Type pop-up window, choose Custom HTML to open the Module Manager: Module Custom HTML edit screen.

8. Enter a title for your gallery and assign it to a position **E**.

9. Set any basic or advanced options according to the extension provider's instructions.

10. In the Custom Output edit box, the editor, enter the code to call the images **F**.

In our example we add:

`{gallery}websites{/gallery}`

This calls the plug-in and tells it where the images are located in the Media Manager.

11. Under Menu Assignment, select the pages on which you want the gallery to appear.

12. On the toolbar, click Save & Close.

13. Click View Site.

Your new image gallery is displayed on the pages you selected **G**.

Putting It All Together

1. **Create your article content.** Content is everything on a web site, and laying out your pages is far easier if you first create the article content.

2. **Set your global content options.** Think about how the majority of your content should be displayed, and then set your global options accordingly.

3. **Style your pages using menu item options.** When styling individual page layouts, use the menu item options.

4. **Use a slideshow extension.** Showcase your content on the Home page using a slideshow extension.

5. **Use a tab and slide extension.** Break up long articles using a tab or slide extension.

6. **Use a media gallery extension.** To showcase multiple images or a portfolio, use an image gallery extension.

13

Going Social

Over the last decade the web has seen monumental changes: from table layouts to CSS, from static pages to dynamic, from hiring a web team to a do-it-yourself CMS. The greatest change in the web, however, was the rise of social media. Facebook, LinkedIn, and Twitter attracted the masses, and in the simplest sense, almost everyone now has a web site in one form or another.

Before the big three though, there was the web log, more commonly known as the blog. Blogs may have started as personal journals or a way for writers to strut their stuff, but they have evolved into so much more.

Blogs share, teach, promote, provide news and information, and are now earning money. Every site from Amazon to the local PTA has some form of a blog, and yes Virginia, you can create your own blog with Joomla.

TIP Why should you use Joomla when Word-Press or Blogger are the blogging platforms of choice? If you only want a blog to do blog things, you should look into WordPress, Blogger, or even MoveableType. If, however, you want your site to expand beyond blogging, Joomla is the perfect solution.

In This Chapter

Creating a Blog Page

Creating a blog using Joomla involves creating all the elements of a good blog site. Begin with blog categories. Decide if you want a single blog category or if you will organize your blog posts into multiple categories. If you do want to organize your blog posts into several categories, create the parent Blog category, and then create your subcategories.

Once you have created a category structure for your blog page, create the menu item. The menu item type for blog categories should be a Category Blog type. After creating your categories and menu items, you can add articles and standard blog modules.

The only blog features missing from Joomla are a commenting system and a tag cloud. For these features, you will need to add a third-party extension.

Ⓐ The blog category details

To create blog categories:

1. Log in to the back end.

2. Choose Content > Category Manager.

3. On the toolbar, click New.

4. Under Details, in the Title field, enter **Welcome to Our Blog**.

   The category title does not appear in your menu item. It appears only at the top of the category page when the category title is set to show.

5. Leave all other options at their defaults.

   This is the parent category for your blog page. All other subcategories and articles will appear on or link from this page Ⓐ.

   Generally a blog does not need a description, but you can add a category description at the top of your blog page.

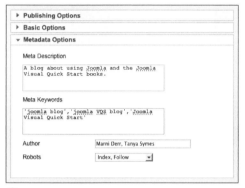

B The Blog category basic options

C The metadata options for the blog category

6. Under Publishing Options, leave all options at their defaults.

7. Under Basic Options, from the Alternative Layout drop-down menu, choose Blog **B**.

8. Under Metadata Options, enter a description for your blog, keywords, and any author names for SEO **C**.

9. On the toolbar, click Save & Close.

10. Continue adding subcategories to the main blog category, as desired.

   For this example blog, we have two categories: Joomla Stuff and Web Stuff.

To create the blog menu item:

1. Choose Menus > Main Menu.

   We will add the blog parent category to the web site's Main Menu.

2. On the Menu Manager: Menu Items toolbar, click New.

3. Under Details, for the Menu Item Type field, click the Select button.

4. In the "Select a Menu Item Type" pop-up window, choose Category Blog.

   The Category Blog menu item type allows you to style this page using a typical blog format.

continues on next page

5. In the Menu Title field, type **Blog**.

This is the title that will appear in your main menu .

6. Leave the Alias field blank.

7. In the Note field, enter a note that describes this menu item for administrators using the back end.

8. Leave the Status set to Published and the Access level set to Public.

9. From the Menu Location drop-down menu, choose Main Menu to assign this menu item to the Main Menu.

10. From the Parent Item drop-down menu, choose Menu Item Root. This is the parent or root category for the blog page.

11. From the Target Window drop-down menu, choose Parent.

When a user clicks the Blog link on the main menu, the blog page will open in the parent window and not in a new tab or window.

12. Set the Default Page to No.

If your blog page is to be the Home or Default page of your site, you should choose Yes.

13. From the Language drop-down menu, choose All.

14. From the Template Style drop-down menu, choose the template you want to use for this page.

15. Click Save.

16. Click View Site to look at your blog page .

Before styling the blog page, add a few articles. If you have subcategories, add at least one article to each to use when laying out the page.

D The category blog menu item type details for the Blog page

E The blog page added to the main menu on the web site

Styling a Blog Page

When creating a blog site, you could set the global content options and let the menu item options inherit those settings. In our example, only one portion of the site should be formatted as a blog page layout. We will control the layout of the blog page using the menu item layout options **A**.

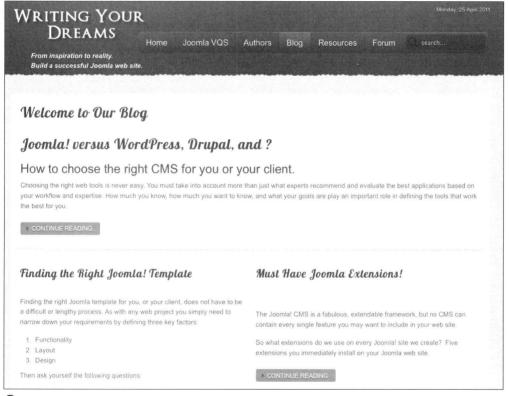

A The blog page using our site-wide global layout options

To set the menu item category options:

1. Log in to the back end.

2. Choose Menus > Main Menu to open the Menu Manager: Menu Items.

3. Select the menu item for the blog page to open it for editing.

4. Click the arrow next to Category Options to open it.

    All menu items are set to use global options by default. By setting options at the menu item level, you can customize individual pages.

    The category options control the display of category information 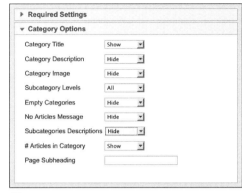.

5. Set the category options:

    ▸ **Category Title:** Show or hide the parent category title.

    ▸ **Category Description:** Show or hide the parent category description.

    ▸ **Category Image:** Show or hide the parent category image.

    ▸ **Subcategory Levels:** Set the level of subcategory articles allowed to appear on the parent category page. Choosing All displays any article in any subcategory on the parent page based on the blog layout options.

    ▸ **Empty Categories:** Show or hide categories with no articles.

    ▸ **No Articles Message:** Show or hide a message that displays a "No articles found in this category" message.

    ▸ **Subcategories Description:** Show or hide the subcategory descriptions.

B The menu item category options

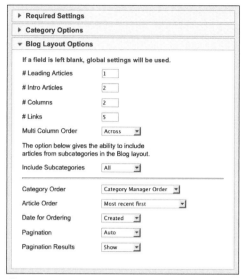

The following is the content within the figure:

▶ Required Settings

▶ Category Options

▼ Blog Layout Options

If a field is left blank, global settings will be used.

Leading Articles [1]

Intro Articles [2]

Columns [2]

Links [5]

Multi Column Order [Across ▼]

The option below gives the ability to include articles from subcategories in the Blog layout.

Include Subcategories [All ▼]

Category Order [Category Manager Order ▼]

Article Order [Most recent first ▼]

Date for Ordering [Created ▼]

Pagination [Auto ▼]

Pagination Results [Show ▼]

C The menu item blog layout options

▸ **# Articles in Category:** Show or hide the number of articles assigned to each category. This number will appear next to the category title.

▸ **Page Subheading:** Enter a subheading for this page or leave it blank.

6. On the toolbar, click Save.

7. Click View Site to make sure the category settings are set the way you want them.

To set the menu item blog layout options:

1. Log in to the back end.

2. Choose Menus > Main Menu.

3. Open your blog page menu item for editing.

4. Click the arrow next to Blog Layout Options to open it **C**.

5. In the # Leading Articles field, type **1**.

   The leading article will display in a single column and span the entire width of the main body of the page.

6. In the # Intro Articles field, type **2**.

   Intro articles will display beneath any leading articles.

7. In the # Columns field, type **2**.

   The # Columns value creates evenly spaced columns for each Intro article.

8. In the # Links field, type **5**.

   This will add links to any additional articles. Each link text will be the article's title.

9. From the Multi Column Order drop-down menu, choose Across.

10. From the Include Subcategories drop-down menu, choose All.

    We want all articles for subcategories to appear on the blog page.

continues on next page

11. From the Category Order drop-down menu, choose Category Manager Order.

    This will sort blog subcategories and their articles according to the order in which they appear in the Category Manager.

12. From the Article Order drop-down menu, choose Most Recent First.

    Blogs are updated regularly and always display the most recent post as the first article.

13. Set "Date for Ordering" to Created or Published.

    This helps ensure that the most recently added blog article will appear first.

14. From the Pagination drop-down menu, choose Auto.

    Doing so allows users to navigate to additional articles that are not displayed on the main blog page.

15. From the Pagination Results drop-down menu, choose Show or Hide.

    Pagination results display how many additional pages of articles are available.

16. On the toolbar, click Save.

17. Click View Site.

    Your blog page should now be formatted according to your layout choices .

    Blog articles, normally referred to as *posts*, generally provide more information than a standard informational article. Standard blog posts contain the date and author, and sometimes voting tallies or hit counts. You control the posts using the article options.

D The new blog page

E Article options for category and article titles

F Article option details

To set the article options:

1. Log in to the back end.

2. Choose Menus > Main Menu.

3. Open your blog page menu item for editing.

4. Click the arrow next to Article Options to open it **E**.

   Article options inherit the global settings first, then the individual article settings, then the menu item settings. To completely control what appears on the blog page, use the menu item Article Options.

5. From the Show Title drop-down menu, choose Show.

6. From the Linked Titles drop-down menu, choose Yes to turn the title into a hyperlink to the full article.

7. From the Show Intro Text drop-down menu, choose Show.

   Blog articles can be of any length. By showing the intro text, the user can click a Read More link, if any, to open the full article.

8. Set Show Category, Link Category, Show Parent, and Link Parent to Use Global.

9. Set Show Author to Show to display the author's name with articles **F**.

10. From the Link Author drop-down menu, choose Yes to make the author's name a hyperlink to her contact form.

11. From the Show Create Date drop-down menu, choose Show.

12. Set Show Modify Date, Show Publish Date, and Show Navigation to Use Global.

13. Set Show Voting to Show to add a user voting or rating feature to each article.

continues on next page

14. From the Show "Read More" drop-down menu, choose Show.

If an article has a Read More link inserted, this will add the Read More button to the end of the article's intro text.

15. Set "Show Title with Read More" to Use Global.

If you set this to Show, the article's title will appear on the Read More button.

16. Set Show Icons, Show Print Icon, and Show Email Icon to either Show or Hide.

Choosing Hide for Show Icons and choosing Show for Show Print Icon and Show Email Icon will display Print and Email text.

Choosing Show for Show Icons and choosing Show for Show Print Icon and Show Email Icon will use icon images for Print and Email 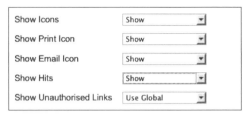.

17. On the toolbar, click Save & Close.

18. Click View Site to see your blog article layout **H**.

G Print and email icon or text options

TIP Make sure your individual article settings match your article option menu item settings. This way the articles are styled the same whether a user clicks the article's title or a Read More link.

TIP When you want to control the word count on your article's intro text and have the Read More buttons align vertically on your pages, you can use the global article options Read More Limit option instead of inserting a Read More link in the article text. Doing so sets the maximum word count for intro text and allows you to visually balance two-column article layouts.

We've Upgraded to Joomla 1.6!

| Print | Email

Written by Marni Derr on Saturday, 23 April 2011 20:11.

User Rating: ○○○○○ / 0
After weeks of testing Joomla 1.6, and writing the second edition of our Joomla Visual Quickstart Guide, we have finally gotten around to finishing the new Writing Your Dreams Joomla 1.5 and 1.6 site.

The site is now using the latest version of Joomla! 1.6.3.

So how hard or easy was the update?

> CONTINUE READING

H Articles on the web site

I Setting articles as featured

J In the Featured Articles Manager, you can control the order of your featured articles.

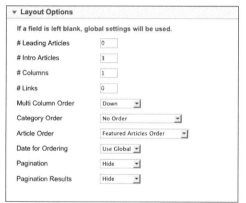

K The Home page featured articles menu item layout options

To display featured articles on the Home page:

1. Log in to the back end.

2. Choose Content > Article Manager.

   We want to display three of our most recent blog posts on the home page. Our home page is using the Featured Article menu item type, so we will select three articles and set them as Featured.

3. Select three articles by clicking the checkbox next to each of the article titles, and then on the toolbar, click Featured.

   The selected articles are now marked as Featured Articles **I**.

4. Click Featured Articles to open the Featured Articles Manager.

   We will set the order of these articles by using this manager **J**.

5. Click the Ordering column title to select it.

   Selecting a column's title enables it for sorting or ordering.

6. Use the up and down arrows to set the order of the featured articles, or enter the order number in the field. Then click the Save icon next to the Ordering column title.

7. Choose Menus > Main Menu.

8. Click Home to open the menu item for editing.

9. Click the arrow next to Layout Options to open it.

10. In the # Leading Articles field, type **0**.

    You could set the leading articles to 3 or the intro articles to 3 to accomplish the same thing (displaying three articles as leading articles across the entire page) as long you use a single column **K**.

continues on next page

11. In the # Intro Articles field, type **3**.

12. In the # Columns field, type **1**.

13. In the # Links field, type **0**.

14. From the Multi Column Order drop-down menu, choose Down.

We are not using columns, so the article order should be from top to bottom, or Down.

15. From the Category Order drop-down menu, choose No Order.

We do not want the article's category ordering to be used for featured articles on the home page.

16. From the Article Order drop-down menu, choose Featured Articles Order.

17. From the "Date for Ordering" drop-down menu, choose Use Global.

18. Set Pagination and Pagination Results to Hide.

We do not want pagination to appear on the Home page.

19. Click the arrow next to Page Display Options to open it.

Currently the top of the Home page reads, "Home." In the Page Display Options, you can change this to use category titles, the menu title, no title, or a custom title 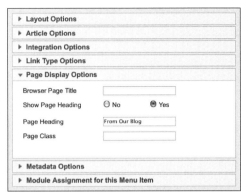.

20. Set Show Page Heading to Yes.

21. In the Page Heading field, type **From Our Blog**.

22. On the toolbar, click Save & Close.

23. Click View Site to see the blog posts on the Home page .

L Menu item page display options

M Featured articles as displayed on the web site's Home page

A The Module Manager: Module Archived Articles edit screen

Adding Blog Modules

The majority of your time so far has been spent creating your site structure through categories, adding content through articles, and laying out your blog page using a combination of global, individual, and menu item layout options. You will now use modules to add more dynamic and interactive pieces on the site pages.

Modules surrounding the main body of your content can showcase content, link to content, and provide user interaction. All modules are created within the Module Manager, assigned to positions used by your template, and then assigned to specific menu items.

In this section, you will create the most common modules for a blog page.

To add an archive module:

1. Log in to the back end.

2. Choose Extensions > Module Manager.

   The Module Manager opens with a list of each module created for the site.

3. On the toolbar, click New.

4. In the Select Module Type pop-up window, choose Archived Articles.

   The Archived Articles module displays only the months that contain articles set as archived. It will not display any other articles, no matter how old.

5. Under Details, in the Title field, type **Blog Archives** **A**.

6. Set Show Title to Show.

   Module titles appear at the top of the module block and are styled by your template using the h3 .moduletitle CSS class.

continues on next page

7. In the Position field, choose a position for this module by clicking the "Select position" button.

8. Leave all other options at their default values.

9. Under Basic Options, in the # of Months field, enter the number of months to display in the module.

   Based on the # of Months field, all months containing archived articles, as determined by publication date, will display a hyperlink to those articles based on month and year **B**.

10. Under Advanced Options, select an Alternative Layout, or keep the default template layout.

11. In the Module Class Suffix field, you can enter a special CSS class used by your template to style this module.

    Templates can come with many module styles. See your template provider's documentation for a list of special module class suffixes **C**.

12. Under Menu Assignment, choose "Only on the pages selected."

    You can choose all pages, selected pages, no pages, or all pages except selected pages **D**.

13. Select the menu items (pages) that should display this module **E**.

14. On the toolbar, click Save & Close.

15. Click View Site.

    Your new Archived Articles module displays on your blog page **F**.

TIP Some module extensions let you style archived articles as a calendar.

B Setting the number of months to display for archived articles

C In the archived article advanced options, you can style the module.

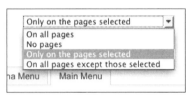

D Assign the module to appear only on the pages selected under menu assignment.

E Select the menu items (pages) on which to display the module.

F The Archived Articles module

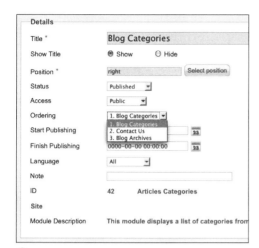

G The Article Category module details

H The Article Category module basic options

To add a category menu:

1. Log in to the back end.

2. Choose Extensions > Module Manager.

3. On the toolbar, click New.

4. In the Select Module Type pop-up window, choose Articles Categories.

5. Under Details, in the Title field, type **Blog Categories**.

6. Set Show Title to Show.

7. In the Position field, choose a position for this module.

8. Leave all other options at their defaults.

9. On the toolbar, click Save.

   Until a module is saved, you cannot select the ordering. All modules default to the top. After you save the module, you can assign the order in which it appears.

10. From the Ordering drop-down menu, set this module to appear after the Blog Archive module.

   The Ordering menu displays all modules assigned to the same position, even if those modules are not assigned to the same page. When setting the module order, choose the module that should appear directly above this module on this page **G**.

11. Set the Basic Options **H**:

   ▸ **Parent Category:** Choose the top-level category for the blog categories.

   ▸ **Category Descriptions:** Choose Yes to display the category descriptions in the module, or choose No to display only the category titles.

   ▸ **Show Subcategories:** Choose Yes to display the subcategories of the parent blog category, or choose No to hide subcategory titles.

continues on next page

- ▸ **# First Subcategories:** Choose the level of subcategories assigned to the blog parent category that you want to display.

- ▸ **Maximum Level Depth:** Set the number of categories assigned to the subcategories of the parent blog category that you want to display.

12. Set the Advanced Options 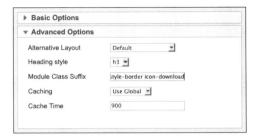 :

- ▸ **Alternative Layout:** If your template supports alternative layout styles, you can choose the style here; otherwise, use the default.

- ▸ **Heading style:** Choose the style for the category and subcategory titles that will display in the module. Note that this style is not used by the module title.

- ▸ **Module Class Suffix:** If your template has additional module classes, enter the class name in this field.

- ▸ **Caching:** Enable or disable browser caching for this module.

- ▸ **Cache Time:** Enter the amount of time the browser should cache this module before refreshing.

Note that cache settings apply only if you have the Joomla system cache plug-in enabled. Generally, you should enable caching only after completing the main development of the web site.

13. Under Menu Assignment, select the pages this module should appear on.

14. On the toolbar, click Save & Close.

15. Click View Site.

Look at the module as it appears on the site  .

Ⓘ The Article Category module advanced options

Ⓙ The Article Category module on the blog page of the web site

TIP You can add many other modules to your blog pages. For example, when you have many more posts and readers, you can add a related articles module, which lists articles with metadata that matches the article being viewed. You can add a most read content module that will display articles with the most hits (views).

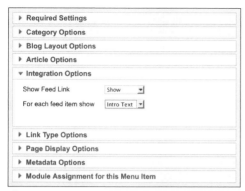

| ▶ Required Settings |
| ▶ Category Options |
| ▶ Blog Layout Options |
| ▶ Article Options |
| ▼ Integration Options |
| Show Feed Link |
| For each feed item show |
| |
| ▶ Link Type Options |
| ▶ Page Display Options |
| ▶ Metadata Options |
| ▶ Module Assignment for this Menu Item |

A The menu item category blog page integration options

Adding an RSS Feed

There are many ways to market your site using newsletters, email, and RSS feeds. These techniques can deliver your content directly to readers. You should use all three delivery methods to address each user's preference for following a favorite site. The Joomla Extension Directory contains many varieties of each.

To enable an RSS feed:

1. Log in to the back end.

2. Choose Menus > Main Menu.

3. Select the menu item to which you want to add the feed.

4. Click the arrow next to Integration Options to open it.

5. From the Show Feed Link drop-down menu, choose Show.

6. From the "For each feed item show" drop-down menu, choose to show only the intro text or the full article in the user's feed reader **A**.

   This will add an RSS icon to the user's browser address bar when reading articles assigned to this category **B**.

TIP You can also insert a feed icon into a custom HTML module so users can click the icon directly and subscribe to your site's feed.

B The RSS feed icon in the browser toolbar

Adding a Comment System

Blogs rely on interaction between you and your readers. Comments, links, trackbacks, and tweets all play an important part in keeping a blog relevant and stimulating. Joomla does not have a comment feature but you can choose from dozens of comment extensions.

A comment extension for Joomla can be as simple as a plug-in that adds comments to all your articles or a full-featured component that can be configured to allow comments only on specific articles.

There are also comment systems available that integrate with Disqus, Instant Debate, Digg, or Posterous blog networking accounts.

In our example, we will use the Joomlart JA Comment component.

To enable commenting:

1. Download and install the comment extension.
2. Choose Extensions > Plug-in manager.
3. Enable the plug-in .
4. Select the categories and menu items (pages) where you want to allow commenting on articles 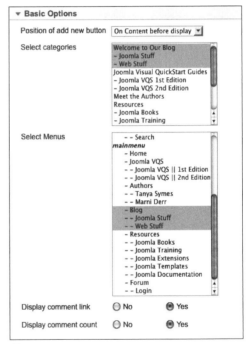.

A Enable the comment plug-in

B Select the pages and categories where the comment form should display.

We've Upgraded to Joomla 1.6!

Written by Marni Derr on Saturday, 23 April 2011 20:11.

💬Add comment (0)

After weeks of testing Joomla 1.6, and writing the second ed
Quickstart Guide, we have finally gotten around to finishing
Joomla 1.5 and 1.6 site.

The site is now using the latest version of Joomla! 1.6.3.

So how hard or easy was the update?

> CONTINUE READING

⊙ A link to add a comment on your intro text

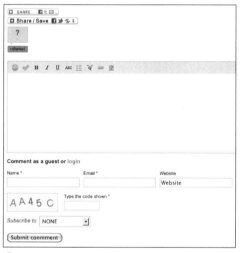

⊙ The comment form added to the end of full articles

5. Click Save & Close.

6. Click View Site and open your blog page.

   A comment counter is placed at the top or bottom of intro articles, depending on your configuration **⊙**.

7. Open the full article to see the comment form displayed at the end of the full article **⊙**.

   You can configure the extension to allow comments from the public at large or only registered users. You can turn on anti-spam features to prevent undesired comments and you can enable social networking features.

Putting It All Together

1. **Create a blog category.** Create your blog page using a blog category and any subcategories.

2. **Style the blog menu item.** If the entire site is a blog, set your global options accordingly. If only a section of the site is for your blog, style the blog pages using the menu item layout options.

3. **Add blog modules.** Blogs have standard modules: an archive, category menu, and so on. Add these modules to your blog pages.

4. **Enable an RSS feed.** Turn on the RSS feed to your content using the integration settings, either globally or in your menu item.

5. **Add a comment extension.** Install and configure a comment system to interact with your readers.

Creating Joomla Templates

The template system in Joomla is one of the main reasons that Joomla is gaining so rapidly in popularity. If you are not comfortable with HTML and CSS, you can create your site using one of the thousands of free or commercial Joomla templates available for download.

However, for those knowledgeable in HTML and CSS, this chapter shows how to take a standard web site design and convert it into a Joomla template.

Programs such as Artiseer can help you customize your own Joomla templates in a variety of ways. You can start by duplicating an existing Joomla template and then modifying its images and CSS files. You can create your own template entirely from scratch, or you can add your CSS styles and images to using one of the Joomla template frameworks we list at the end of this chapter.

This chapter will show you the base file requirements needed to create a working Joomla template. Before you begin, be aware that the chapter assumes basic familiarity with CSS and HTML.

In This Chapter

Understanding Joomla Template Requirements

Joomla allows developers and designers to keep site content and style separate, so it is easy to update the look and feel of your web site by simply selecting a new template. To create your own template, you need only a text editor—such as Notepad, Text Edit, or BBEdit—and an application capable of creating web graphics, such as Adobe Fireworks or Photoshop.

The following files and folder structures are required for a Joomla template to function properly. You can find all Joomla templates in the /templates folder **A**.

- **index.php file:** Contains all the HTML/XHTML information. It tells Joomla where the components, modules, and content are to be placed on the web page. This file must be named index.php. If you use any other file type (.htm or .html, for example), the template won't work.

A The Joomla templates folder

- **templateDetails.xml file:** Lists all files and folders used by the template. This file must be complete for Joomla to render the template correctly. Every template filename, folder name, and all positions must be listed in this file.

- **CSS folder:** Contains all the CSS stylesheets used by the template. You can have a single template.css file or any number of CSS files according to your design preferences.

- **Images folder:** Contains all the images used by the template.

- **template_thumbnail.png:** A small .png thumbnail image of the site design, generally at a resolution of 150 x 150 pixels. The Template Manager uses it to display a thumbnail image of the site design.

- **template_preview.png:** The preview image is used in the Joomla template styles page to show a preview of the template.

In addition to these minimum requirements, most templates contain the following, though Joomla can operate without them:

- **favicon.ico:** This icon is used in the browser's address bar to identify the site. It is generally a smaller version of the site's logo or brand.

- **js folder:** You can have a js (JavaScript, or JavaScript libraries such as jquery or mootool) folder.

- **html folder:** Contains custom system style overrides for components, modules, extensions, and so on.

- **fonts folder:** Contains any special fonts to use on the web site.

- **index.html**, **compontent.php**

- **language folder**

To create the base template files and folders:

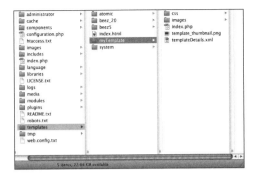

B The new myTemplate file and folder structure for a new Joomla template

1. Create a new folder called **myTemplate** to contain all the template files needed for your design.

2. Inside the myTemplate folder, create two new folders: **css** and **images**.

   You can also add a js folder to contain JavaScript files, and an include folder to contain includes if your design incorporates custom JavaScript or PHP. These folders are not required for a basic template to work.

3. Using a plain text editor, such as BBEdit, Notepad, Espresso, or Coda, to create files named **index.php** and **templateDetails.xml**, and then save them to the myTemplate folder.

4. Create files named **template.css** and **layout.css** and save them in the css folder.

   Don't worry about the thumbnail images or the favicon icon yet. You will create these later. You folder structure should look like image **B**.

   You can create the new Joomla template on your computer and then install it, or you can create the files within your Joomla template folder, and as you will learn at the end of this chapter, "discover" the template so it is recognized with your site.

Creating the index.php File

In this section, you will add basic HTML/XHTML tags to define your template structure and use the `<div>` tag to create containers. Although there are no hard and fast rules for creating the **divs**, you should keep best practice guidelines in mind.

When you first design a web site, you usually create a sketch or wireframe that represents your content layout **A**.

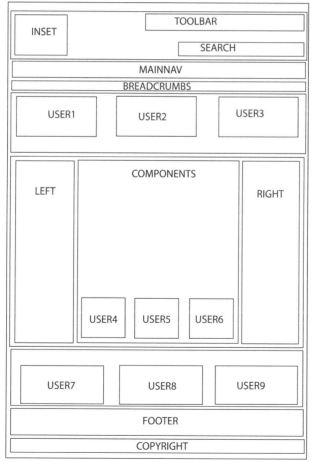

A An example wireframe layout

To create the index.php file:

1. From the myTemplate folder, open the index.php file in any text editor.

   All of the examples in this section can be downloaded from the authors' website, www.writingyourdreams.com, or you can type in the code manually.

2. Type the following code in the index.php file:

```php
<?php
/**

* @package myTemplate

* @file index.php

* @version 1.0 April 2011

* @author Your Name

* @copyright Copyright (C) 2007
- 2011

* @license Enter your license
 information, GPL, GNU,
 or commercial

*/
```

   The index page begins immediately with a PHP function that calls the Joomla copyright and details the GNU/GPL licensing. It also tells Joomla whether this is an admin or site template.

3. Begin a new line and type the following:

```php
// no direct access
defined( '_JEXEC' ) or
 die( 'Restricted access' );
?>
```

   This ends the first PHP function. The page should look like **Code 14.1**.

Best Practices

- Do not place any standard XHTML tags (**h1**, **h2**, **p**, and so on) in the index.php file. Everything will be styled using a CSS stylesheet. It is a pure CSS layout. To help you style your content, you will find a list of the Joomla core class styles at the end of this chapter. These classes must be styled in your CSS, or they will use a browser's default styling.

- When creating your index.php file, organize your **div** containers in a logical order. Remember that a browser reads from top to bottom. To a browser, you are just creating a large stack of boxes, one on top of another. Consider where you want elements placed on the web page and create the **div** containers accordingly. This makes it easier to later read the code in the template and make changes.

- Give similar descriptive names to your **divs** and positions. For example, a left column **div** should have a name such as left_col. Doing so will make it easier when you are assigning positions to your content and adding code.

- Although you can name positions in any way you choose, it is best practice to use common Joomla names. Most template designers use the standard Joomla positions such as top, mainnav, footer, user1 through user9, and so on. This practice helps when your site already contains content and modules. If the positions in the new template vary a great deal, you will need to reassign all those modules to new positions. User1 may not seem very descriptive, but it is a standard used throughout the Joomla community.

Code 14.1 The first PHP function used to identify information about this template

```php
<?php
/**
 * @package    myTemplate
 * @file       index.php
 * @version    1.0 April 2011
 * @author     Your Name
 * @copyright  Copyright (C) 2007 - 2011
 * @license    Enter your license information,
 → GPL, GNU, or commercial
 */
// no direct access
defined( '_JEXEC' ) or die( 'Restricted access' );
?>
```

Code 14.2 The !DOCTYPE declaration is required for every web site or the HTML content cannot be rendered in your browser.

```html
<!DOCTYPE html PUBLIC "-//W3C//DTD XHTML 1.0
 → Transitional//EN" "http://www.w3.org/TR/
 → xhtml1/DTD/xhtml1-transitional.dtd">

<html xmlns="http://www.w3.org/1999/xhtml"
 → xml:lang="<?php echo $this->language;
 → ?>" lang="<?php echo $this->language; ?>">
```

4. Press Enter twice to create a blank line, and then type the following:

```html
<!DOCTYPE html PUBLIC "-//W3C//
 → DTD XHTML 1.0 Transitional//EN"
 → "http://www.w3.org/TR/xhtml1/DTD/
 → xhtml1-transitional.dtd">

<html xmlns="http://www.w3.org
 → /1999/xhtml" xml:lang="<?php
 → echo $this->language; ?>" lang=
 → "<?php echo $this->language; ?>">
```

This is the **!DOCTYPE** declaration required by all sites that tells the browser what DOCTYPE is being used for the HTML code in this document.

The next code statement contains the **PHP** function used by Joomla to identify which language to use on this site. It is pulled from the global configuration page in Joomla.

All of this code is placed before the **<head>** tag (**Code 14.2**).

5. Type **<head>**, add a few blank lines, and close the head of the document with **</head>**.

Included in the head of the index page are the paths to the CSS files, custom PHP files, and JavaScript files or libraries used by this template.

6. Between the **<head>** **</head>** tags, type **<jdoc:include type="head" />**.

The **jdoc:include** (object:method) is the primary method to call all the objects used in Joomla.

The line **<jdoc:include type="head" />** inserts the **<meta>** tags on a standard web page. It tells Joomla to use the meta tag information entered in the back-end administrative global configuration pages.

continues on next page

7. To call the CSS files, type the following directly below the **jdoc**, but before the **</head>** closing tag:

```
<link rel="stylesheet" href="<?php
→ echo $this->baseurl;?>/templates
→ /<?php echo $this->template;?>
→ /css/template.css" media="screen"
→ type="text/css" />
```

If your template contains more than one stylesheet, repeat this line and replace the **/template.css** filename with the name of the other CSS file.

If you have PHP includes, special parameter files, or JavaScript files, the paths to these files also need to be contained in the **<head> </head>** tags of the index page.

8. To tell the browser the character set, type the following:

```
<meta http-equiv="Content-Type"
→ content="text/html; charset=
→ UTF-8" />
```

Joomla versions 1.5, 1.6, and later are UTF-8 compliant and, therefore, use the Unicode character set.

9. To display your favicon in the browser address bar, add the line:

```
<link rel="shortcut icon"
→ href="<?php echo "$GLOBALS
→ [mosConfig_live_site]/templates
→ /$GLOBALS[cur_template]/favicon.
→ ico"; ?>" />
```

Your index.php file should now look like **Code 14.3**.

Code 14.3 The <head> of the index.php document, with links to the CSS stylesheets and any other files used by your template

```
<head>
<jdoc:include type="head" />

<meta http-equiv="Content-Type"
→ content="text/html; charset=UTF-8" />

<!-- This links to the main layout CSS
→ stylesheet. The layout CSS file calls all
→ of your other stylesheets -->
<link href="templates/<?php echo $this->
→ template ?>/css/layout.css" rel="stylesheet"
→ type="text/css" media="all" />
<link href="templates/<?php echo $this->
→ template ?>/css/template.css" rel=
→ "stylesheet" type="text/css" media="all" />

<!-- These links will call in javascript
→ files being used in your template -->
<script>
</script>

</head>
```

10. To finish the base HTML code needed for the index.php file, add the following tags:

```
<body>

</body>

</html>
```

All remaining tags and functions will go inside the **<body> </body>** tags.

11. Save the index.php file.

To add the HTML/CSS layout structure:

1. Open the myTemplate index.php file in any plain text editor.

2. Type the following lines of code between the body tags:

```
<body>

  <div id="wrapper">

    <div id="header">

    <div id="toolbar"></div>

    <div id="inset"></div>

    <div id="search"></div>

  </div>

</div>

</body>

</html>
```

These lines add a wrapper that will enclose the entire design. They place a header container inside the wrapper that contains positions for a toolbar, an inset, and a search box.

continues on next page

3. After the closing **</div>** for the header, but before the closing **</div>** for the wrapper, type the following:

```
<div id="left_col">
</div>
<div id="main_content">
</div>
<div id="right_col">
</div>
<div id="footer">
</div>
```

Containers for the left column position, main body (for components), right column position, and the footer position are added and contained within the main wrapper. Creating a Joomla template is not so different from creating any standard web design; the only difference will be where and how to use the PHP functions so that Joomla can render your site correctly.

4. Add the rest of the code, as shown in **Code 14.4**, or download the completed index.php file from the companion web site.

In this example, we have added all the positions we want used in our Joomla template.

5. Save the file.

TIP What you currently have is no different than any standard **HTML** web page. The template at this stage cannot communicate directly with Joomla, because the php functions required to render the template need to be added. Don't panic, these functions are very easy and basic at this point. If you already have a working design, continue adding the PHP. You can tweak the layout at any time.

Code 14.4 All of the div containers to render and organize your web page content. All containers need to be between the **<body></body>** tags.

```
<body>
<div id="wrapper">
    <div id="toolbar">
    <div id="header">
        <div id="inset">
        </div>
        <div id="search">
        </div>
    </div>
    <div id="mainnav">
    </div>
    <div id="breadcrumbs">
    </div>
    <div id="top">
    </div>
    <div id="maincontentwrap">
        <div id="left_col">
        </div>
        <div id="main_content" >
        </div>
        <div id="right_col">
        </div>
    </div>
    <div id="bottom">
    </div>
    <div id="footer">
    </div>
</div>
<br clear="all" />
</div>
</body>
</html>
```

Code 14.5 Add three additional positions to the top div container.

```
<div id="breadcrumbs"></div>
    <div id="top">
        <div id="user1"></div>
        <div id="user2"></div>
        <div id="user3"></div>
    </div>
```

Code 14.6 Add additional positions below the main content area and the bottom container.

```
<div id="breadcrumbs"></div>
    <div id="top">
        <div id="user1"></div>
        <div id="user2"></div>
        <div id="user3"></div>
    </div>
<div id="maincontentwrap">
    <div id="left_col"></div>
    <div id="main_content"></div>
        <div id="user4"></div>
        <div id="user5"></div>
        <div id="user6"></div>
    <div id="right_col"></div>
</div>
<div id="bottom">
    <div id="user7"></div>
    <div id="user8"></div>
    <div id="user9"></div>
</div>
<div id="footer"></div>
```

To add multiple positions to a single horizontal or vertical container:

1. Open the myTemplate index.php file in any plain text editor.

   In this section, you will add multiple positions to the template so you can assign modules to display side-by-side vertically or horizontally. You can display module content in many ways. You can style your modules in CSS or use the following examples.

   In our example, we tell Joomla to display a module *if* it is assigned to this position. If only one position is used, use the entire width. If two positions are used, split the width evenly. If all three positions are used, space them evenly with each position using one-third of the horizontal or vertical space.

2. Inside the `<div id="top"> </div>` container, add three more positions (**Code 14.5**):

   ```
   <div id="top">

       <div id="user1"></div>

       <div id="user2"></div>

       <div id="user3"></div>

   </div>
   ```

3. Add three additional positions beneath the `main content` area and the `bottom` content areas (**Code 14.6**).

Adding jdoc:include statements to the index.php file (positions)

The PHP functions render your Joomla template positions. Your positions are built using PHP jdoc:include statements. Without these functions, the template will not work in Joomla. The jdoc method tells Joomla what to place in the positions used by your template.

In our example wireframe, we create a one-to-one correlation between our container div tags and our template positions. It is best practice to give your positions and your div IDs the same name. Then, when you are choosing the positions for your menus, modules, and components, you will find it easier to locate the right position.

The jdoc:include statement contains four parts:

- **jdoc:include**: The object:method function that tells Joomla to display the type being called.

- **type="modules"**: Tells Joomla what type of object to include: head, module, or component.

- **name="location"**: The head and component functions do not include a location, as this is defined by the system. The head is the metadata to be displayed dynamically on each page. A component can be called only into the main body of the page. A module can be placed into any location you specify—for example, left, right, top, bottom, user1, and so on.

- **style="optional"**: The style call is optional and applies only to modules. You can create your own styles to use—such as xhtml, rounded, container, or none—or leave off the style statement completely. This is an advanced method and won't be covered in this book.

In our next wireframe, we map out the jdoc:include code statements to include in the index.php for our div containers. Joomla uses these to identify and render the template positions **B**. Remember that the style statements are optional.

TIP The `jdoc:include type="component"` and `jdoc:include type="head"` statements are the only two include statements that do not have a name or style.

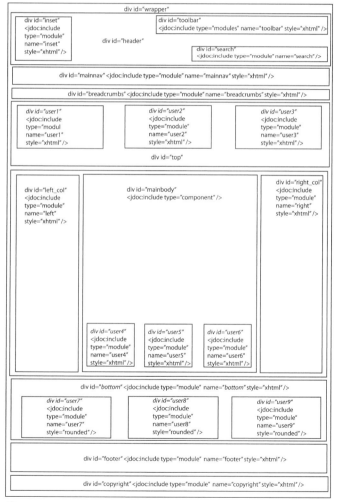

B Our wireframe with the j:doc include statements mapped out

To add the required jdoc:includes:

1. Open the index.php file in any text editor.

   Note that the first div container—**`<div id="wrapper">`**—is used to contain the entire layout. You do not need to add any statements to the wrapper because it is not a position used by Joomla.

2. Add a blank line between **`<div id="toolbar">`** and its closing **`</div>`**, and then type the following:

   `<jdoc:include type="modules"`
   ` name="toolbar" />`

   This statement tells Joomla that the toolbar is a module and its position name is toolbar (**Code 14.7**).

3. Scroll down and find the **`<div id="main_content">`** container. Add the following line:

   `<jdoc:include type="component" />`

   The main content area is not a position you can use for modules. It used to display components. Remember that content, categories, and articles are components. Because of this, no name is required (**Code 14.8**).

4. Continue adding all the jdoc:include statements to your index.php file positions (**Code 14.9**).

TIP Watch out for typos; they are the number one reason code fails to work properly.

Code 14.7 Adding jdoc:include statements tells Joomla what and where the position is, and displays any module assigned to that position.

```
<body>
    <div id="wrapper">
    <div id="toolbar">
    <jdoc:include type="modules"
     name="toolbar" />
    </div>
........
```

Code 14.8 The main content area contains components; because it does not use module positions or names, no name is required.

```
<div id="maincontentwrap">
<div id="left_col"></div>
<div id="main_content">
    <jdoc:include type="component" />
</div>
    <div id="user4"></div>
```

Code 14.9 All jdoc:include statements must be created for every position available to the template.

```
<body>

<div id="wrapper">
    <div id="toolbar">
        <jdoc:include type="modules"
         name="toolbar" />
    </div>
    <div id="header">
        <div id="inset">
            <jdoc:include type="modules"
             name="inset" />
        </div>
        <div id="search">
            <jdoc:include type="modules"
             name="search" />
        </div>
    </div>
    <div id="mainnav">
        <jdoc:include type="modules"
         name="mainnav" />
    </div>
    <div id="breadcrumbs">
        <jdoc:include type="modules"
         name="breadcrumbs" />
```

code continues on next page

```
        </div>
    <div id="top">
            <div id="user1">
            <jdoc:include type="modules" name="user1" />
            </div>
            <div id="user2">
            <jdoc:include type="modules" name="user2" />
            </div>
            <div id="user3">
            <jdoc:include type="modules" name="user3" />
            </div>
    </div>
    <div id="maincontentwrap">
        <div id="left_col">
            <jdoc:include type="modules" name="left" />
        </div>
        <div id="main_content">
    <jdoc:include type="component" />
            </div>
            <div id="user4">
            <jdoc:include type="modules" name="user4" />
            </div>
            <div id="user5">
            <jdoc:include type="modules" name="user5" />
            </div>
            <div id="user6">
            <jdoc:include type="modules" name="user6" />
            </div>
        <div id="right_col">
            <jdoc:include type="modules" name="right" />
        </div>
      <br clear="all" />
    </div>
    <div id="bottom">
        <div id="user7">
            <jdoc:include type="modules" name="user7" />
        </div>
        <div id="user8">
            <jdoc:include type="modules" name="user8" />
        </div>
        <div id="user9">
            <jdoc:include type="modules" name="user9" />
        </div>
    </div>
    <div id="footer">
        <jdoc:include type="modules" name="footer" />
    </div>
<br clear="all" />
</div>
</body>
</html>
```

Adding the PHP Functions

The basic index.php file combined with CSS stylesheets and the templateDetails.xml file can render your Joomla template. However, without PHP functions, every position created in the index.php will appear on your pages, with or without content, leaving large areas of blank space all over your web site. Even if you place as many usable positions in the template as possible, it does not mean that you are going to use all of them.

The basic PHP **if** functions covered in this section tell Joomla to hide or display modules based on whether or not modules are assigned to this specific position. Assigning the modules to positions is done through the Joomla administrative back end.

To add the basic PHP functions:

1. Open the index.php file in any text editor.

2. Locate the first div after the wrapper div container.

   In our example, this is the toolbar.

3. Right above the **<div id="toolbar">**, type:

   ```
   <?php if ($this->countModules
   → ('toolbar')): ?>
   ```

   Joomla reads the PHP **if** function, and if a module is assigned to this position, Joomla renders it. If no modules are assigned to this position, Joomla ignores the position and moves on to display the next position that contains content.

Code 14.10 Adding the php if statements tells Joomla to render only a position that contains content.

```
<body>
<div id="wrapper">
    <div id="toolbar">
    <?php if ($this-   >countModules
     ➝('toolbar')): ?>
        <jdoc:include type="modules"
        ➝ name="toolbar" />
        </div>
        <?php endif; ?>
......
```

Code 14.11 All positions, except the header and main_content, need the php if statements.

```
<div id="wrapper">
<div id="toolbar">
<?php if ($this->countModules('toolbar')): ?>
<jdoc:include type="modules" name="toolbar" />
</div>
<?php endif; ?>

<div id="header">
<?php if ($this->countModules('inset')): ?>
<div id="inset">
<jdoc:include type="modules" name="inset" />
</div>
<?php endif; ?>

<?php if ($this->countModules('search')): ?>
<div id="search">
<jdoc:include type="modules" name="search" />
</div>
<?php endif; ?>
</div>

<?php if ($this->countModules('mainnav')): ?>
<div id="mainnav">
<jdoc:include type="modules" name="mainnav" />
</div>
<?php endif; ?>

<?php if ($this->countModules('breadcrumbs')): ?>
<div id="breadcrumbs">
<jdoc:include type="modules"
 ➝ name="breadcrumbs" />
</div>
<?php endif; ?>
```

code continues on next page

4. Right after the closing **</div>** for the toolbar, type:

   <?php endif; ?>

   to end the PHP function. You can place any other **if** or **else if** statements between these functions. Make sure that the closing php endif statement is after the closing div for the position.

   Your code now looks like **Code 14.10**.

5. The following div containers are all positions that you want available to display modules, so each needs an appropriate PHP **if** statement:

   ▸ insert

   ▸ toolbar

   ▸ search

   ▸ mainnav

   ▸ breadcrumbs

   ▸ user1, user2, and user3

   ▸ left_col (position left)

   ▸ right_col (position right)

   ▸ user4, user5, and user6

   ▸ user7, user8, and user9

   ▸ footer

   Add the php **if** statements to all positions. The header and main_content positions do not need these statements as they should always be rendered, even if they contain no content (**Code 14.11**).

```
<div id="top">
<?php if ($this->countModules('user1')): ?>
<div id="user1">
<jdoc:include type="modules" name="user1" />
</div>
<?php endif; ?>

<?php if ($this->countModules('user2')): ?>
<div id="user2">
<jdoc:include type="modules" name="user2" />
</div>
<?php endif; ?>

<?php if ($this->countModules('user3')): ?>
<div id="user3">
<jdoc:include type="modules" name="user3" />
</div>
<?php endif; ?>
</div>

<div id="maincontentwrap">

<?php if ($this->countModules('left')): ?>
<div id="left_col">
<jdoc:include type="modules" name="left" />
</div>
<?php endif; ?>

<div id="main_content">
<jdoc:include type="component" />
</div>

<?php if ($this->countModules('user4')): ?>
<div id="user4">
<jdoc:include type="modules" name="user4" />
</div>
<?php endif; ?>

<?php if ($this->countModules('user5')): ?>
<div id="user5">
<jdoc:include type="modules" name="user5" />
</div>
<?php endif; ?>
```

```
<?php if ($this->countModules('user6')): ?>
<div id="user6">
<jdoc:include type="modules" name="user6" />
</div>
<?php endif; ?>

<?php if ($this->countModules('right')): ?>
<div id="right_col">
<jdoc:include type="modules" name="right" />
</div>
<?php endif; ?>
</div>

<div id="bottom">
<?php if ($this->countModules('user7')): ?>
<div id="user7">
<jdoc:include type="modules" name="user7" />
</div>
<?php endif; ?>

<?php if ($this->countModules('user8')): ?>
<div id="user8">
<jdoc:include type="modules" name="user8" />
</div>
<?php endif; ?>

<?php if ($this->countModules('user9')): ?>
<div id="user9">
<jdoc:include type="modules" name="user9" />
</div>
<?php endif; ?>
</div>

<?php if ($this->countModules('footer')): ?>
<div id="footer">
<jdoc:include type="modules" name="footer" />
</div>
<?php endif; ?>
</div>
</body>
</html>
```

Creating the templateDetails.xml File

The index.php page now has all the fundamental pieces of information that it needs to function as a Joomla template. Without the templateDetails.xml file, however, the template will not work. The templateDetails.xml file lists everything your template contains so that Joomla can render it properly. Creating the XML file can be a bit tedious, but it's not difficult. The main rule to keep in mind is that if it exists in your template folder, it must be listed in the XML file.

The templateDetails.xml file is organized into six areas:

- Joomla version
- Template and designer details
- List of files and folders
- List of positions
- List of images
- List of parameters (optional)

TIP XML and XHTML files are case-sensitive. It is best practice to use only lowercase when naming images and files. The one exception is the templateDetails.xml file, as this is the required filename used by Joomla.

To create the templateDetails.xml file:

1. Open your templateDetails.xml file in a plain text editor.

2. At the top of the page, type:

   ```
   <?xml version="1.0" encoding=
   ⤷ "utf-8"?>
   ```

   This identifies the type of document (XML), the version of XML (1.0), and the encoding type (UTF-8).

   continues on next page

3. On the next line, type:

```
<!DOCTYPE install PUBLIC "-//Joomla!
→ 1.6//DTD template 1.0//EN">
→ "http://www.joomla.org/xml/
→ dtd/1.6/template-install.dtd">
```

This is the code required to render and install the template.

4. On the next line, type:

```
<extension version="1.6"
→ type="template" client="site">
```

5. Enter the following template information, by replacing the text with your information:

```
<name>myTemplate</name>

<creationDate>05/05/11</
→ creationDate>

<author>MarniDerr</author>

<authorEmail>marni@webcafeclub.
→ com</authorEmail>

<authorUrl>http://www.web
→ cafeclub.com</authorUrl>

<copyright>Copyright (C)
→ 2005 - 2011 Open Source
→ Matters, Inc. All rights
→ reserved.</copyright>

<license>GNU General Public
→ License version 2 or   later;
→ see LICENSE.txt</license>

<version>1.6.0</version>

<description>TPL_MYTEMPLATE_XML_
→ DESCRIPTION</descrip tion>
```

This tells Joomla that it is an extension for version 1.6, that the extension type is a template, and that the template is a site template.

Each item must be on its own line. These are the details for your template; they will display in the Template Manager fields. When finished, your file will look like **Code 14.12**.

Code 14.12 XML code necessary for Joomla to install and use the template

```
<?xml version="1.0" encoding="utf-8"?>
<!DOCTYPE install PUBLIC "-//Joomla! 1.6//DTD
→ template 1.0//EN" "http://www.joomla.org/
→ xml/dtd/1.6/template-install.dtd">
<extension version="1.6" type="template"
→ client="site">
    <name>myTemplate</name>
    <creationDate>05/05/11</creationDate>
    <author>MarniDerr</author>
    <authorEmail>marni@webcafeclub.com
    → </authorEmail>
    <authorUrl>http://www.webcafeclub.com
    → </authorUrl>
    <copyright>Copyright (C) 2005 - 2011
    → Open Source Matters, Inc. All rights
    → reserved.</copyright>
    <license>GNU General Public License
    → version 2 or later; see LICENSE.txt
    → </license>
    <version>1.6.0</version>
    <description>TPL_MYTEMPLATE_XML_
    → DESCRIPTION</description>
```

Code 14.13 All files and folders used by the template must be listed in the templateDetails.xml file in order to work properly.

```
<description>TPL_MYTEMPLATE_XML_DESCRIPTION
  ‣ </description>
<files>
    <folder>html</folder>
    <folder>css</folder>
    <folder>images</folder>
    <folder>js</folder>
    <filename>index.php</filename>
    <filename>index.html</filename>
    <filename>favicon.ico</filename>
    <filename>templateDetails.xml</filename>
    <filename>template_preview.png
    ‣ </filename>
    <filename>template_thumbnail.png
    ‣ </filename>
    </files>
```

6. Save the file.

7. After the **`</description>`** closing tag, on a new line, type **`<files>`**, then enter each folder and file contained in the myTemplate folder, and close the file tag with **`</files>`** (**Code 14.13**).

   Every file and folder used by the template must be listed in the templateDetails.xml file.

   In the xml file, you need to identify all the positions that will be used by the template.

8. Add the following lines directly below the closing **`</files>`** tag:

   `<positions>`

      `<position>header</position>`

      `<position>toolbar</position>`

      `<position>inset</position>`

      `<position>search</position>`

      `<position>mainnav</position>`

      `<position>breadcrumbs</`
      ‣ **`position>`**

      `<position>left</position>`

      `<position>right</position>`

      `<position>user1</position>`

      `<position>user2</position>`

      `<position>user3</position>`

      `<position>user4</position>`

      `<position>user5</position>`

      `<position>user6</position>`

      `<position>user7</position>`

      `<position>user8</position>`

      `<position>user9</position>`

      `<position>footer</position>`

   `</positions>`

   `</extension>`

continues on next page

Notice that in the example index.php file, header, top, bottom, and wrappers are not listed because these are not positions we need to assign content to in this template. They are simply layout containers. The same applies to the main_content position, as this is always used by Joomla to display components (**Code 14.14**).

At this point you can save and close the XML document using the **</extension>** closing tag.

In addition, you could add custom parameter files, language files, and so on.

9. Save the file.

Code 14.14 All template positions need to be listed in the templateDetails.xml file.

```
</files>
<positions>
    <position>toolbar</position>
    <position>inset</position>
    <position>search</position>
    <position>mainnav</position>
    <position>breadcrumbs</position>
    <position>left</position>
    <position>right</position>
    <position>user1</position>
    <position>user2</position>
    <position>user3</position>
    <position>user4</position>
    <position>user5</position>
    <position>user6</position>
    <position>user7</position>
    <position>user8</position>
    <position>user9</position>
    <position>footer</position>
    <position>debug</position>
</positions>
</extension>
```

Installing or Discovering the Template

If you created the files outside of your Joomla installation, you can compress the files into a .zip package and install it through the Extension Manager.

If you worked directly in the template folder, Joomla knows that the template is there, but you need to install it properly using the new Joomla 1.6 Discover feature.

To install and use your new template:

1. Log in to the back end.

2. Choose Extension > Extension Manager.

3. Select Discover, and then click the Discover icon on the toolbar.

    This screen allows you to discover any extensions that were not installed by the normal Joomla extension installation process 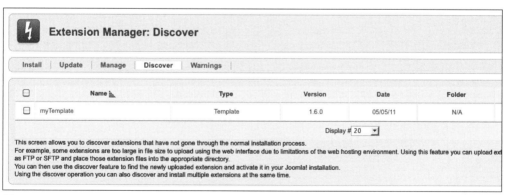.

continues on next page

⚡ Extension Manager: Discover

| Install | Update | Manage | Discover | Warnings |

☐	Name ≛	Type	Version	Date	Folder
☐	myTemplate	Template	1.6.0	05/05/11	N/A

Display # 20 ▼

This screen allows you to discover extensions that have not gone through the normal installation process.
For example, some extensions are too large in file size to upload using the web interface due to limitations of the web hosting environment. Using this feature you can upload ext as FTP or SFTP and place those extension files into the appropriate directory.
You can then use the discover feature to find the newly uploaded extension and activate it in your Joomla! installation.
Using the discover operation you can also discover and install multiple extensions at the same time.

Ⓐ Using the Extension Manager Discover feature to install your new Joomla template

The system will look for any extensions that are available but not installed. As long as your new template is located in your Joomla templates folder, and not already installed through the Extension Manager, it will appear in the discovery list.

4. Select the checkbox next to your template.

5. On the toolbar, click Install.

6. Choose Extensions > Template Manager.

   Your new template is installed and ready for use on the site .

   To verify that the files are coded properly, let's look at the template details.

7. From the Template Manager: Styles, select Templates.

   The new template appears at the end of the template list in the Template Manager: Templates. Notice the details that are pulled from the XML file **C**.

   Since we have not created the thumbnail image previews, the template does not contain a preview. After you have styled your template with CSS, you can take a screenshot of the web site and use an image editor to create thumbnails for your template.

8. Click the Preview link under the myTemplate Details.

   If your code is error free, all template positions will display **D**.

   To use your new template, make it the default and change any existing modules to positions used in the new template.

B An installed template will appear in the Template Manager lists.

C The template details are pulled from the XML file, and the preview image is the thumbnail.png file.

D If all template files are free of errors, the position previews will work.

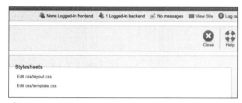

A The Template Manager: Customise Template screen provides access to all template CSS files.

B The new code mirror editor in Joomla highlights code, which makes editing files within Joomla far easier than in prior versions of Joomla.

Editing Template CSS Stylesheets

Any standards-based CSS design can work within Joomla, as long as your index.php page has the correct **jdoc** commands and the templateDetails.xml file lists all template files, folders, and .css files.

Most Joomla template designers like to keep the layout separate from the core Joomla CSS styles. To do so, you should create a separate layout.css file to style your layout, and a template.css file to style your content. This method makes it easier to adjust the layout of the template.

We can't teach you CSS within the scope of this book, but we can show you where to access and modify your stylesheets.

To modify template CSS files:

1. Log in to the back end.
2. Choose Extensions > Template Manager.
3. Select Templates to open the Template Manager: Templates.
4. Click the title of myTemplate Details to open the Template Manager: Customise Template screen **A**.
5. Click the title of the .css file you want to edit. You can edit your .css and index.php files directly in Joomla **B**.

Joomla Base CSS Style Tables

We cannot walk you through creating each CSS style—that process depends entirely on your particular design and CSS knowledge. You can find a list of Joomla classes at http://docs.joomla.org/List_of_Joomla!_generated_core_CSS_classes.

The following tables include a basic list of the core CSS classes used by default in Joomla. The descriptions are generalizations intended to give you an idea of where to style default classes and are by no means exclusive.

TIP To view the styles in use, open your web browser, navigate to the front end of your web site, and choose View Source. You will see the classes in the source code for the pages. Or use a browser plug-in like Firebug or Web Developer toolbars for Firefox and Safari.

TABLE 14.1 Global CSS Styles

Class Name	Description
a	Global styles to be used unless a more specific style is specified
a:hover	
a:active	
a:visited	
a.image	
a.image:hover	
h1	
h2	
h3	
h4	
h5	
li	
p	
td	
th	
ul	

TABLE 14.2 Banners

Class Name	Description
.bannerfooter	Styles used when creating the banner component and module
.bannergroup	
.bannerheader	
.banneritem	

TABLE 14.3 Breadcrumbs Styles

Class Name	Description
.pathway	Styles used with the breadcrumb navigation
a.pathway:link	
a.pathway:visited	
a.pathway:active	
a.pathway:hover	

TABLE 14.4 Articles = Content Styles

Class Name	Description
Section	
.sections	Styles used for a section layout
.sectiontableentry	
.sectiontablefooter	
.sectiontableheader	
Category	
.category	Styles used for category list and links
a.category	
.subcategory	
.categorydescription	
.subcategorydescription	
.category img	
.subcategory img	
Articles	
.article_separator	Styles used in article layouts
.author	
.blog	
.blogsection	
.blog_more	
.blog_heading	
.content_rating	
.content_vote	
.contentdescription	
.contentheading	
.contentpagetitle	
.contentpane	
.contentpaneopen	
.contenttoc	
.createdate	
.created-date	
.date	
.hastip	
.highlight	
.intro	
.title	
.modifydate	
.mosimage	
.mosimagecaption	
.readon	
.small	
.smalldark	
.wrapper	Style used when selecting the wrapper layout

TABLE 14.5 Components

Class Name	Description
.componentheading	Style used for the main component heading

TABLE 14.6 Forms and Input Boxes

Class Name	Description
.button	Styles used for all buttons and form fields unless otherwise specified
.buttonheading	
.contact_email	
.fieldset	
.input	
.inputbox	
.search	
.searchintro	
.selectbox	
.text_area	

TABLE 14.7 Main Menu Navigation Styles

Class Name	Description
Main Menu	
.mainlevel	Styles used by the main menu
a.mainlevel	
a.mainlevel:visited	
a.mainlevel:hover	
a.mainlevel:active	
Submenu	
a.sublevel	Styles for submenus under the main menu
a.sublevel:visited	
a.sublevel:active	
a.sublevel:hover	

TABLE 14.8 Modules — General

Class Name	Description
.latestnews	Styles for individual modules
.mostread	
.newsfeed	
.pollstableborder	

TABLE 14.9 Modules — Table Styles

Class Name	Description
table.moduletable	Styles used for modules that use a table layout
table.moduletable	

TABLE 14.10 Modules

Class Name	Description
div.module	Styles used to create rounded or pure table-less modules
div.module h3	
.module li	
.module ul	
.module a:link	
.module a:visited	
.module a:hover	
.module a:active	
Rounded Corners	
.module	
.module div	
.module div div	
.module div div div	
.module div div div div	

TABLE 14.11 Page Navigation (Pagination)

Class Name	Description
a.pagenav	Styles for the page navigation, previous, next, page count, and so on
a.pagenav:hover	
.back_button	
.pagenav	
.pagebar	
.pagenav_prev	
.pagenav_next	
.pagenavcounter	

TABLE 14.12 Tabbed Edits

Class Name	Description
.adminform	Styles used to override the background styling
.code	
.edit-tabs	
.message	
.moscode	
.pagetext	
.ontab	
.offtab	
.tabheading	
.tabpadding	

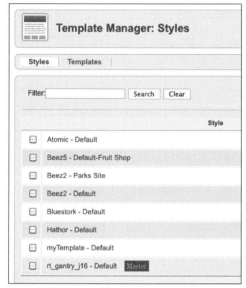

A The Gantry template framework installed

B The new template framework listed in the Template Manager

Using Template Frameworks

If you aren't a PHP or JavaScript code developer, but you're a killer CSS designer, you can create your own templates by downloading one of the many template frameworks available to Joomla and then adding your own images and CSS styles. These template frameworks come complete with customized PHP parameters and JavaScript menus.

Three of the most popular frameworks for Joomla 1.6 and later are:

- Gantry framework by www.rocketheme.com

- ZenGrid by www.joomlabamboo.com

- Joomlart T3 by www.joomlart.com

To install a Joomla template framework:

1. Download the framework to your computer.

2. Log in to the back end of Joomla.

3. Choose Extensions > Extension Manager.

4. Install the framework **A**.

   When the framework is installed, it will appear in your Template Manager **B**.

   All frameworks have a plug-in that you must enable in order to use the framework.

continues on next page

5. Choose Extension > Plug-in Manager and enable the framework plug-in **C**.

6. To view the details of your new template framework, choose Extension Manager > Template Manager, and click the template's title.

The new template with all its fancy PHP and JavaScript features is installed and ready for you to configure and style according to your own web designs **D**.

7. To access the template files, choose Extensions > Template Manager.

8. Select the Templates link.

9. Click the template's title in the list.

10. Select the file you want to edit **E**.

Using template frameworks to create custom Joomla template designs can save you an incredible amount of development time and expense.

TIP When working with template frameworks and modifying files, it is best practise to first create a duplicate of the template. If something should go wrong with your edits, you always have access to the original files.

C Enable the framework plug-in in the Plug-in Manager or the framework will not work properly.

D The RocketTheme Gantry framework is incredibly powerful, fully customizable, and easy to work with when developing your own design.

E Accessing the template source files

Putting It All Together

1. **Create the Joomla template folder.** You can create your new Joomla template locally or directly on your Joomla site.

2. **Add the css, image, and html folders.** All images and .css files need to be in their own folders.

3. **Create the index.php file.** The index.php file is the HTML and PHP code that defines the layout of your web site and what positions are available for your content.

4. **Create the templateDetails.xml file.** Include all the required information in the XML file; Joomla uses this information to install and render your template.

5. **Create the .css stylesheets.** Create your .css files to style your Joomla content.

6. **Install your new template.** Before a template can be used by the system, you must install or discover it using the Extension Manager.

7. **Create the thumbnail.png and template_preview.png images.** When your site design is complete, including images and CSS, take a snapshot and use an image editor to create a thumbnail preview image.

Updates and Maintenance

Other than adding content to your site, Joomla requires only basic maintenance to keep it running smoothly and hacker free.

The Joomla development group releases regular security and maintenance releases in the form of "dot revisions." For example, if you are currently using Joomla 1.6.0, when the Joomla 1.6.1 patch or security release is announced, you can immediately install the new patch. Security releases are considered to be minor updates and not major upgrades.

Security patches and bug releases do not require a migration of your site extensions and content and will not alter site functionality. However, when installing any patch or extension, it is best practice to perform a complete site backup just in case something goes wrong during the installation process.

An upgrade is a major release that constitutes a revision of the core software. In the past, migrating a site from 1.0.x to 1.5.x to 1.6.x was a major undertaking. The Joomla team is working on making this a less complex process with shorter releases and fewer core code modifications.

In This Appendix

Updating Joomla

You can update Joomla manually using an FTP client or through cPanel. Update extensions are also available that make the update process much easier. We will explain both processes.

To download the latest patch:

1. Log in to the back end of Joomla and verify your current version number.

   The Joomla version number is located at either the bottom of the screen or on the top toolbar, depending on your version **A**.

2. Go to www.joomla.org.

3. Click Download or "Download latest version" to find all currently supported Joomla versions and upgrade packages **B**.

   The Joomla web site uses the term "upgrade" even though these are simply patches.

4. Select and download the package upgrade based on your current version. For example, if you are running Joomla 1.6.0, you would download the Joomla 1.6.0 to 1.6.1 upgrade package.

5. Using your cPanel account or an FTP program, upload the .zip file to your web server's root folder.

6. Extract the files to your Joomla installation's root folder.

   Upgrade packages are designed to overwrite only those files that require modification.

7. Log back in to the back end of Joomla to verify that the upgrade was completed successfully.

Joomla!® is free software released under the GNU General Public License.   Version 1.6.1

A The current Joomla version reported by the system in the back end

B The www.joomla.org site where you can download the latest upgrade patch

> **TIP** At this time upgrades between major Joomla versions 1.5 to 1.6 require a migration script.

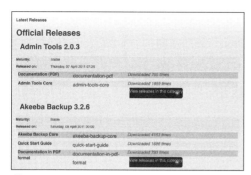

C At the Akeeba web site, you can download Akeeba extensions.

D Akeeba backup control panel

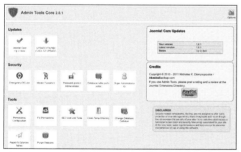

E Akeeba control panel reporting an upgrade has been found for the site

To use an update extension:

1. Go to www.akeebabackup.com.

2. Download Akeeba backup and Akeeba admin tools.

   These are two extensions we recommend for every Joomla site. Akeeba has both free and commercial versions of their software **C**.

   Akeeba backup creates full or partial backups of your entire Joomla site.

   Akeeba admin tools allow you to:

   ▸ Repair and optimize your database.

   ▸ Secure permissions on your files and directories.

   ▸ Update Joomla with one click.

3. Log in to the back end of your site.

4. Choose Extensions > Extension Manager.

5. Install Akeeba Backup and Akeeba Admin Tools.

6. Choose Components > Akeeba Backup.

   The Akeeba Backup: Control Panel screen opens **D**.

   In this control panel, you can configure your backups, set when to back up the site, and check for the latest version of Joomla.

7. Choose Components > Admin Tools.

   The Admin Tools control panel opens. If any upgrades are available, the Updates buttons will read, "UPDATE FOUND" **E**.

8. Click the Update button.

continues on next page

9. To update Joomla or the extension, on the following screen, click the "Update to the latest version" button **F**.

   When the update is completed successfully, the Admin Tools will report that you have the latest versions **G**.

   Using an update extension is the easiest way to keep your site up to date, optimized, and secure. It also helps avoid possible overwrite issues when manually updating files and directories.

   TIP The Akeeba admin tool extension provides many more features to optimize, maintain, and protect your Joomla site. Take the time to read through the documentation on the Akeeba site and learn about all of its features.

F Akeeba update selection screen

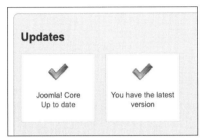

G Akeeba reporting that Joomla and the Akeeba extensions are all up to date

Migrating from Joomla 1.5.x to Joomla 1.6 and Later

A few extensions in the Joomla Extension Directory allow you to migrate from one Joomla version to the next. These migration tools are for major upgrades, not simple security or patch releases.

The most popular extension is jUpgrade, which has versions for Joomla 1.5 and Joomla 1.6.

1. Go to www.joomla.org.

2. Choose Do More > Extensions.

3. Choose Migration & Conversions.

4. Choose jUpgrade, and then click website.

   jUpgrade provides migration tools for Joomla 1.0.x to Joomla 1.5.x and Joomla 1.5.x to Joomla 1.6+.

   At the time of this writing, jUpgrade is still in beta, which means that they still have some bugs to resolve. However, many people have successfully used the jUpgrade tool, and by the time this book is released, the extension should be fully tested and stable.

5. Download the jUpgrade extension.

6. Follow the directions on the jUpgrade site to install the extension.

   When you use a migration tool, it is very important that you first read through the documentation and instructions.

   Always create a full backup of your working site before trying any extensions, especially a migration tool.

Joomla Resources

As with all open source applications, Joomla's supporting community is vast—including developers, extension creators and template designers, personal bloggers, and tutorial writers.

This appendix offers a brief overview of the new features in Joomla 1.6 and later, and it lists the most popular documentation, blog, extension, and template provider links.

What's New in Joomla 1.6+

The Joomla development group is working hard to make upgrades and migrations less difficult for the masses. Until the next long term support release, the new development strategy is to support Long Term Support cycles (LTS), such as Joomla 1.5, and Short Term Support for Joomla 1.6, 1.7, and so on.

The objective is to create much more stable and modular upgrades that allow Joomla site administrators to click and upgrade. This means that a site running on Joomla 1.6 and later will have an easier transition or upgrade path to Joomla 1.7 than a site currently running Joomla 1.5.

This strategy is new to Joomla and the development team. To lend your support, you are encouraged to join some of the Joomla groups and add your voice.

Joomla 1.6 New Features

This content is quoted from the documentation at www.joomla.org/announcements/general-news/5348-joomlar-16-has-arrived.html:

- **ACL** = **Finer access controls** for viewing and editing content with configurable user groups and viewing levels

- **Categories** = **A user-defined category structure**, from simple one-level to complex multi-level categories. Gone is the Section > Category > Article hierarchy.

- **Installation improvements** allowing for multiple extension installations in one package, updatable with a single click. Manage and update your extensions from a single manager.

- **Expanded language support** for easy production of multi-lingual sites

- **Layout control**

- **Start and end publishing times** for modules with more control over where they display, many more customizable elements for complete modular control and design.

- **Fresh new templates and semantic markup** to please the eye as well as the search engines. Multiple copies of a single template for individual page styling.

- **More creative control** through template styles, category and article options, and menu item options.

Finding Documentation and Help

Multiple resources on the web provide information on using Joomla and its many third-party extensions.

Joomla Documentation and Resources

Log in to the back end of Joomla and select the Help menu.

- **Support Forum:**
  http://forum.joomla.org/
- **Documentation wiki:**
  http://docs.joomla.org/
- **Resources:**
  http://resources.joomla.org/
- **Joomla Community Portal:**
  http://community.joomla.org/
- **Security:**
  http://developer.joomla.org/security.html
- **Developer resources:**
  http://developer.joomla.org

Joomla Extensions Directory

- http://extensions.joomla.org/

Joomla Template and Template Frameworks

- www.joomlart.com
- www.joomlaxtc.com
- www.joomlashack.com
- www.gavick.com
- www.yootheme.com
- www.rockettheme.com
- www.joomlabamboo.com

- www.adminpraise.com
- www.pixelpointcreative.com
- www.youjoomla.com

Joomla Content Construction Kits

- www.seblod.com
- www.flexicontent.com
- www.yoozoo.com
- www.getk2.org

Joomla Editors

- **JCE Editor:**
  www.joomlacontenteditor.net
- **JCK Editor:**
  www.joomlackeditor.com
- **CK Editor:**
  www.joomlacode.org/gf/project/ckeditor
- **Artof Editor** (a plug-in for the CK Editor):
  www.theartofjoomla.com/extensions/artof-editor.html

Joomla Security, Update, and Backup Tools

- Akeeba Backup and Admin tools:
  www.akeebabackup.com
- jUpgrade migration tool: www.matware.com.ar/joomla/jupgrade.html

Joomla File Management

- **eXtplorer:**
  http://extplorer.sourceforge.net/
- **ninja Xplorer:**
  http://ninjaforge.com/

Manager Options Quick Reference

Joomla 1.6 and later introduces new options features in each of the Joomla managers. They allow you to configure functions and customize your content display with increased control over display and layouts.

Because it is not possible to cover every situation in a single book, we have compiled a complete list of layout options organized by manager: user, content, components, and menu items. Use this appendix as a quick reference to quickly locate specific layout and functional options.

User Manager Options

User options help control user interaction on the front end of your site, such as account creation, logging in, and emailing site users. To access the User Manager options, choose Users > User Manager, and then on the toolbar click the Options button.

User Manager Options
These options control front-end user registration and account creation.

Name	Description
Allow User Registration	Choose Yes or No. Choosing Yes will allow users to register and create a user account on the site.
New User Registration Group	Choose a default group from the list. A newly registered user will be assigned to this group after creating a site account. These groups are created in the User Groups Manager.
Guest User Group	Choose the default user group for visitors who have not registered an account on the site.
New User Account Activation	Choose the account activation method you want to use for newly registered users: None creates an account immediately; Self requires users to access a link provided in an email to verify they are real users; Admin requires administrative approval before a user can log in to the front end of the site.
Front-end User Parameters	These turn on users' abilities to choose front-end language, editor, and help preferences from their profiles. Choosing No disables these parameters and allows users access to only their registration information.

User Manager Mass Mail Options

Name	Description
Subject Prefix	Text added to the subject line of the email.
MailBody Suffix	Text added to the end of the email.

Article (Content) Manager Global Options

Global content options are set once and inherited by your content and should be set according to how you want the *majority* of your content to display. You can then override these settings at the individual article and/or category level using the menu item layout settings. To access the Article Manager options, choose Content > Article Manager, and on the toolbar click Options.

Articles Global Options

These options control the global article display and layout settings. They can be inherited or overwritten by individual article and menu item settings.

Name	Description
Choose a layout	Choose a default layout for articles. This option can be used to create custom article styling and templates.
Show Title	Show or hide an article's title.
Linked Titles	Choose Yes to make the article title a link to the full article. Choose No to display the article title, but not as an active link to the full article.
Show Intro Text	Show or hide an article's intro text.
Show Category	Show or hide the title of the category an article is directly assigned to.
Link Category	Choose Yes to make the category a link to all articles assigned to this category. Choose No and the category title is not a link.
Show Parent	If the article is assigned to a subcategory, show or hide the parent category.
Link Parent	Choose Yes to make the parent category a link to all articles assigned to the category. Choose No and the parent category is not a link.
Show Author	Show or hide the author's name.
Link Author	Choose Yes to make the author's name a link to the author's contact page. Choose No and the author's name is not a link.
Show Create Date	Show or hide the date an article was created.
Show Modify Date	Show or hide the date an article was modified.
Show Publish Date	Show or hide the date an article was published.
Show Navigation	Show or hide the Prev and Next navigation buttons below articles.
Show Voting	Show or hide a five-star voting or rating feature.

table continues on next page

Articles Global Options *(continued)*

Name	Description
Show "Read More"	Show or hide a Read More button if the article's intro text is set to show.
Show Title with Read More	Display the title of the article on the Read More button or text.
Read More Limit	If an article's intro text is set to show, set the word count limit for the intro text.
Show Icons	Show or hide the Print and Email icons above an article.
Show Print Icon	If Show Icons is set to show, show or hide the Print icon.
Show Email Icon	If Show Icons is set to show, show or hide the Email icon.
Show Hits	Display the number of hits (views) on articles.
Show Unauthorized Links	Choose Yes to display links to articles that a front-end user cannot access. (Even though the user may not view the article, the title will still be displayed.) Choose No to hide links to articles that the user does not have the permission or access to view.

Category Global Options

These options control the global settings for category content for both parent and subcategories.

Name	Description
Choose a layout	Choose List or Blog layout. A list layout presents categories in a list. A blog layout displays categories and their articles in a blog format.
Category Title	Show or hide the category title.
Category Description	Show or hide the category description.
Category Image	Show or hide the category image used by the category image field (not those images embedded in the category description text).
Subcategory Levels	Choose the level of subcategories to display on a page.
Empty Categories	Show or hide categories that do not contain articles.
No Articles Message	Show or hide a message stating that a category contains no articles.
Subcategories Descriptions	Show or hide subcategory descriptions.
# Articles in Category	Show or hide the number of articles assigned to a category. The number will appear beside the category or subcategory title.

Categories Global Options

These options control the global settings for subcategory display.

Name	Description
Top Level Category Description	Show or hide the root level category description for this subcategory.
Subcategory Levels	Select the level of subcategories to display.
Empty Categories	Show or hide subcategories that do not contain articles.
Subcategories Descriptions	Show or hide the subcategory description.
# Articles in Category	Show or hide the number of articles assigned to a category. The number will appear beside the category or subcategory title.

Blog/Featured Global Layouts

These global options control the global display of articles when using the Category Blog or Featured Article menu items.

Name	Description
# Leading Articles	Enter the number of leading articles to display on the page. Leading articles are displayed using the full width of the main body of the page.
# Intro Articles	Enter the number of introductory articles to display on the page. Intro articles display beneath the leading articles.
# Columns	Enter the number of columns in which to display intro articles. The articles will display in columns beneath the leading article.
# Links	Enter the number of links to additional articles in this category. The article titles will display beneath the intro articles and link to the full article's content.
Multi-Column Order	If you entered more than one column in the # Columns field, choose the ordering of the intro articles, either down or across.
Include Subcategories	If you want to display articles assigned to subcategories of the parent category, select the level of subcategory articles to display.

Integration Global Options

Integration options control RSS feed options for your site content.

Name	Description
Show Feed Link	Show or hide a link that allows a user to subscribe to your content feed.
For feed item show	Control the amount of text to display in your content feed by choosing intro text only or the full text of the articles.

List Global Layouts

These options control the global display settings when using a category list menu item. Lists are displayed as tabular data.

Name	Description
Display Select	Show or hide the drop-down menu that allows a user to set the number of items that appear in the list on a single page.
Filter Field	Show or hide a filter field that allows a user to filter the items in the list.
Table Headings	Show or hide the table headings for the list.
Show Date	Hide the date column, or choose to display the created, modified, or published dates for the items in the list.
Date Format	Enter the format to use for the Show Date column.
Show Hits in List	Show or hide the total number of hits for an item.
Show Author in List	Show or hide the item author's name.

Shared Options

These options control the global display for settings shared by categories and subcategories.

Name	Description
Category Order	Set the order in which the categories appear on a page.
Article Order	Set the order in which the articles appear on a page.
Date for Ordering	If an article or category is set to display by date, set the date ordering option: Published, Created, or Modified.
Pagination	Display navigation at the bottom of the page that links to additional articles in this category or subcategory.
Pagination Results	Hide or show numeric navigation at the bottom of the page that tells the user how many more pages of articles are associated with this category or subcategory.

Text Filters Global Options

Text filter options control text filters for article content created by users. This helps prevent script attacks and hacks that can be uploaded to your site through the editor text.

Name	Description
Filter Groups	All user groups created on the site are listed in the Filter Groups column.
Filter Type	Choose Black List, White List, No HTML, or No Filtering.
Filter Tags	Enter any tags you want to block, each tag separated by a comma.
Filter Attributes	Enter any attributes you want to block, each attribute separated by a comma.

Component Managers

Each component has its own option settings. Unlike the content options, these settings help configure the way a component functions on the site.

Banner Component Options

Client Options

Name	Description
Purchase Type	Choose the purchase type for advertising banner clients: Unlimited, Yearly, Monthly, Weekly, or Daily.
Track Impressions	Choose Yes to track page impressions. Choose No to disable page impression tracking.
Track Clicks	Choose Yes to track click-throughs. Choose No to disable click-through tracking.
Meta Keyword Prefix	Enter the prefixes for keyword searching.

Contact Component Options

Single Contact Options
Global content options control the display of single contact information.

Name	Description
Choose Layout	Choose an alternate layout for contacts, if available.
Contact Category	Hide the contact category, show the category as a link, or show the category without a link.
Show Contact List	Show or hide the contact list.
Display Format	Choose between Global, Tabs, Sliders, or Plain for the contact information displayed on a page.

The following options can be set to Show or Hide on the single contacts page:

Name	Contact's Position	Email	Street Address	City or Suburb
State or County	Postal Code	Country	Telephone	Mobile Phone
Fax	Webpage	Misc. Information	Image	vCard
Show User Articles	Show Profile	Show Links		

The following labels can be customized. These labeled fields can be used to display additional web links or additional information for a contact, such as portfolio, blog, social media sites, and so on.

Link A Label	Link B Label	Link C Label	Link D Label	Link E Label

Contact Icons

Icon options are used to display custom icon settings and images.

Name	Description
Settings	Choose to use icons, text only, or no icons or text.

You can upload your own custom icons for:

Address icon	Email icon	Telephone icon	Mobile icon	Fax icon	Misc icon

Contact Category

These options are used for contact categories and subcategories.

Name	Description
Choose a Layout	If you use custom layouts for contact forms and pages, you can choose an alternate layout here.
Category Title	Show or hide the contact category title.
Category Description	Show or hide the contact category description.
Category Image	Show or hide the contact category images.
Subcategory Levels	Choose the number of contact subcategory levels to display.
Empty Categories	Show or hide categories or subcategories that do not contain any contacts.
Subcategory Descriptions	Show or hide subcategory descriptions.
# Contacts in Category	Show or hide the number of contacts in a category or subcategory. The number will display next to the title.

Contact Categories

These options apply to pages that display more than a single contact, such as a contact category page.

Name	Description
Top Level Category Description	Show or hide the root level contact category description.
Subcategory Levels	Select the level of contact subcategories to display.
Empty Categories	Show or hide subcategories that do not contain contacts.
Subcategories Descriptions	Show or hide the contact subcategory description.
# Articles in Category	Show or hide the number of contacts assigned to the category. This number will appear beside the category/subcategory title.

Contact List Layouts

These options control the display of contact list pages. The content is displayed in a table.

Name	Description
Display Select	A drop-down menu to set the number of contacts listed on a single page.

You can show or hide the following information in the table:

Table Headings	Position	Email	Phone	Mobile	Fax
City or Suburb	State or County	Country	Pagination	Pagination Results	

Contact Form

These options control the display of a single contact form.

Name	Description
Show Contact Form	Show or hide a contact form for a contact.
Send Copy to Submitter	Show or hide the button that allows the person filling out the contact form to receive an email copy of the message sent.
Banned Email	Enter email addresses that are banned from using a contact form on the site.
Banned Subject	Enter any subject text that is banned from entry in a contact form on the site.
Banned Text	Enter any text that is banned from entry in the contact form.
Session Check	Choose Yes to check for a session cookie. Choose No to disable session cookie checks.
Custom Reply	Choose Yes to send the user a customized reply message. Choose No to disable this feature.
Contact Redirect	Enter an alternate email address where a contact message should be sent. This allows you to use an email hidden from the public and spammers. Many spammers pull email information from web sites. This feature displays a public address with your contact information, and uses a private, hidden address to send you messages.

Messaging Component

My Settings

These options control the settings for the back-end administrator private messaging system.

Name	Description
Lock Inbox	Choose Yes or No to lock or unlock your message box from receiving private messages.
Email New Messages	Choose Yes or No to send (or not send) an email alert when you receive a private message.
Auto-purge Messages (days)	Enter the number of days to wait before purging your messages from the system.

News Feed Component

News Feed Options

These settings control the display of news feeds on the site.

Name	Description
Choose a layout	If custom layouts for news feeds are displayed on the site, you can select an alternate layout in this field.
Feed Image	Show or hide the news feed image.
Feed Description	Show or hide the news feed description.
Feed Content	Show or hide the news feed content.
Characters Count	Set the maximum number of characters to display with each news feed article.

News Feed Category Options

Name	Description
Choose a Layout	If custom layouts for news feeds are displayed on the site, you can select an alternate layout in this field.
Category Title	Show or hide the news feed category title.
Category Description	Show or hide the news feed category description.
Category Image	Show or hide the news feed category images.
Subcategory Levels	Select the number of news feed subcategory levels to display.
Empty Categories	Show or hide categories or subcategories that do not contain any news feeds.
Subcategory Descriptions	Show or hide news feed subcategory descriptions.
# Contacts in Category	Show or hide the number of news feeds in a category or subcategory. The number will display next to the title.

News Feed Categories Options

Name	Description
Top Level Category Description	Show or hide the root level news feed category description for this subcategory.
Subcategory Levels	Select the level of news feed subcategories to display.
Empty Categories	Show or hide the news feed subcategories that do not contain feed content.
Subcategories Descriptions	Show or hide the news feed subcategory description.
# Feeds in Category	Show or hide the number of news feeds assigned to the news feed category. This number will appear beside the category/subcategory title.

News Feed List Layouts Options

Name	Description
Display Select	Show or hide the drop-down menu that controls the number of feed items displayed on a single page.
Table Headings	Show or hide the news feed table headings.
# Articles	Show or hide the total number of articles in a news feed.
Feed Links	Show or hide news feed links.
Pagination	Show or hide pagination.
Pagination Results	Show or hide the number of news feed pages.

Search Component

Search Manager Options
These options control the internal search statistics for the web site. This feature is displayed in the back end only.

Name	Descriptions
Gather Search Statistics	Enable (Yes) or disable (No) the system from gathering search statistics for your site.
Use Search Areas	Enable (Yes) or disable (No) the checkboxes next to the system search area results.
Created Date	Show or hide the date that search statistics were created.

Web Links Component

Web Link Options
These options control the display and click features for the web link component.

Name	Description
Target	Choose whether a link opens in the Parent, New, or Pop-up window.
Count Clicks	Enable (Yes) or disable (No) a system count of the number of times a web link is clicked.
Text/Icon/Web Link Only	Display a web link text, icon, or a standard web link only.
Select Icon	Upload a custom icon for your web links.

Web Link Category Options

Name	Description
Choose a Layout	If custom layouts for web links are displayed on the site, you can select an alternate layout in this field.
Category Title	Show or hide the web link category title.
Category Description	Show or hide the web link category description.
Category Image	Show or hide the web link category images.
Subcategory Levels	Select the number of web link subcategory levels to show.
Empty Categories	Show or hide categories or subcategories that do not contain any web links.
Subcategory Descriptions	Show or hide web link subcategory descriptions.
# Contacts in Category	Show or hide the number of web links in a category or subcategory. The number will display next to the title.

Web Link Categories Options

Name	Description
Top Level Category Description	Show or hide the root level web link category description for this subcategory.
Subcategory Levels	Select the level of web link subcategories to display.
Empty Categories	Show or hide the web link subcategories that do not contain links.
Subcategories Descriptions	Show or hide the web link subcategory description.
# Web links	Show or hide the number of web links assigned to the web link category. This number will appear beside the category/subcategory title.

Web Link List Layouts Options

Name	Description
Display Select	Show or hide the drop-down menu that controls how many links will appear on a single page.
Table Headings	Show or hide the web link table headings.
Links description	Show or hide the web links description.
Hits	Show or hide the number of clicks a web link has.
Pagination	Show or hide pagination.
Pagination Results	Show or hide the number of web links pages.

Menu Item Options

Menu item options are specific to the type of menu item you are using. Each menu item type has its own options. For example, a Featured Articles menu item would not have Categories options and a Category Blog menu item would not have List layout options. Regardless of the menu item you are using, every type of layout option is listed in the following tables.

The options tables are listed in the order in which they generally appear in the menu item details screen. Any menu item option set to Use Global or left blank will use the global (default) options set in the Content and Component Managers. Any menu item layout option set in menu item details will override the global content and component options.

Menu Item Layout Options

Name	Description
# Leading Articles	Enter the number of leading articles to display on the page. Leading articles are displayed using the full width of the main body of the page.
# Intro Articles	Enter the number of introductory articles to display on the page. Intro articles display beneath the leading articles.
# Columns	Enter the number of columns in which to display intro articles. The articles will display in columns beneath the leading articles.
# Links	Enter the number of links to additional articles in this category. The article titles will display beneath the intro articles, and link to the full article content.
Multi-Column Order	If you entered more than one column in the # Columns field, choose the ordering of the intro articles, down or across.
Include Subcategories	If you want to display articles assigned to subcategories of the parent category, select the level of subcategory articles to display.
Category Order	Set the order in which the categories appear on a page.
Article Order	Set the order in which the articles appear on a page.
Date for Ordering	If an article or category is set to display by date, set the date ordering option: Published, Created, or Modified.
Pagination	Display navigation at the bottom of the page that links to additional articles in this category or subcategory.
Pagination Results	Show or hide numeric navigation at the bottom of the page that tells the user how many more pages of articles are associated with this category or subcategory.

Menu Item Article Options

Name	Description
Show Title	Show or hide the article's title.
Linked Titles	Choose Yes to make the article title a link to the full article. Choose No to display the article's title, but not as an active link to the full article.
Show Intro Text	Show or hide the article's intro text.
Show Category	Show or hide the title of the category to which an article is directly assigned.
Link Category	Choose Yes to make the category a link to all articles assigned to this category. Choose No and the category title is not a link.
Show Parent	If the article is assigned to a subcategory, show or hide the parent category.
Link Parent	Choose Yes to make the parent category a link to articles assigned to the parent category. Choose No and the parent category is not a link.
Show Author	Show or hide the author's name.
Link Author	Choose Yes to make the author's name a link to the author's contact page. Choose No and the author's name is not a link.
Show Create Date	Show or hide the date an article was created.
Show Modify Date	Show or hide the date an article was modified.
Show Publish Date	Show or hide the date an article was published.
Show Navigation	Show or hide the Prev and Next navigation buttons below articles.
Show Voting	Show or hide a five-star voting or rating feature.
Show "Read More"	Show or hide a Read More button if the article's intro text is set to show.
Show Title with Read More	Display the title of the article on the Read More button or text.
Read More Limit	If an article's intro text is set to show, set the word count limit for the intro text.
Show Icons	Show or hide the Print and Email icons above an article.
Show Print Icon	If Show Icons is set to Show, show or hide the Print icon.
Show Email Icon	If Show Icons is set to Show, Show or hide the Email icon.
Show Hits	Display the number of hits (views) on articles.
Show Unauthorized Links	Choose Yes to display links to articles to which a front-end user does not have access (even though a user cannot view the article, the title will display). Choose No to hide links to articles to which the user does not have permission and cannot view.

Menu Item Blog Layout Options

Name	Description
# Leading Articles	Enter the number of leading articles to display on the page. Leading articles are displayed using the full width of the main body of the page.
# Intro Articles	Enter the number of introductory articles to display on the page. Intro articles display beneath the leading article(s).
# Columns	Enter the number of columns to use to display intro articles. The articles will display in columns beneath the leading article.
# Links	Enter the number of links to additional articles in this category. The article titles will display beneath the intro articles, and link to the full article's content.
Multi-Column Order	If you entered more than one column in the # Columns field, choose the ordering of the intro articles, down or across.
Include Subcategories	If you want to display articles assigned to subcategories of the parent category, select the level of subcategory articles to display.
Category Order	Set the order in which categories appear on a page.
Article Order	Set the order in which articles appear on a page.
Date for Ordering	If an article or category is set to display by date, set the date ordering option: Published, Created, or Modified.
Pagination	Display navigation at the bottom of the page that links to additional articles in this category or subcategory.
Pagination Results	Show or hide numeric navigation at the bottom of the page that tells the user how many more pages of articles are associated with this category or subcategory.

Menu Item Category Options

Name	Description
Category Title	Show or hide the category title.
Category Description	Show or hide the category description.
Category Image	Show or hide the category image used by the category image field (not images embedded in the category description text).
Subcategory Levels	Select the level of subcategories to display on a page.
Empty Categories	Show or hide categories that do not contain articles.
No Articles Message	Show or hide a message stating that the category contains no articles.
Subcategories Descriptions	Show or hide subcategory descriptions.
# Articles in Category	Show or hide the number of articles assigned to a category. This number will appear beside the category/subcategory title.
Page Subheading	Enter a subheading to be used on this menu item page.

Menu Item Categories Options

Name	Description
Top Level Category Description	Hide or show the top level category description.
Top Level Category Description	Enter a custom category description in this field if you want to hide the category descriptions set at the category level. Or use it to add more information to this menu item.
Subcategory Levels	Select the level of subcategories to display.
Empty Categories	Show or hide subcategories that do not contain articles.
Subcategories Descriptions	Show or hide the subcategory description.
# Articles in Category	Show or hide the number of articles assigned to the category. This number will appear beside the category/subcategory title.

Menu Item Contact Display Options

Name	Description
Display Format	Choose between Global, Tabs, Sliders, or Plain for the contact information displayed on this page.
Contact Category	Hide the contact category, show the category as a link, or show the category without a link.
Show Contact List	Show or hide the contact list.

All of the following options can be set to Show or Hide on the single contacts page:

Name	Contact's Position	Email	Street Address	City or Suburb
State or County	Postal Code	Country	Telephone	Mobile Phone
Fax	Webpage	Misc. Information	Image	vCard
Show User Articles	Show Profile	Show Links		

The following labels can be customized. The fields can be used to display additional web links or other information for a contact, such as portfolio, blog, social media sites, and so on:

Link A Label	Link B Label	Link C Label	Link D Label	Link E Label

Menu Item Mail Options

Name	Description
Show Contact Form	Show or hide a contact form for a contact.
Send Copy to Submitter	Show or hide the button that allows the user filling out the contact form to receive an email copy of the message sent.
Banned Email	Enter email addresses that are banned from using a contact form on the site.
Banned Subject	Enter any subject text that is banned from entry in a contact form on the site.
Banned Text	Enter any text that is banned from entry in a contact form.
Session Check	Choose Yes to enable the system to check for a session cookie. Choose No to disable a session cookie check.
Custom Reply	Choose Yes to send a user a custom reply message. Choose No to disable this feature.
Contact Redirect	Enter an alternate email address where the contact message should be sent. Many spammers pull your email information off of web sites. This feature displays a public email address in your contact information, and uses a private, hidden email address to send you messages.

Menu Item Feed Display Options

Name	Description
Feed Image	Show or hide the news feed image.
Feed Description	Show or hide the news feed description.
Feed Content	Show or hide the news feed content.
Characters Count	Set the maximum number of characters to display per news feed article.

Menu Item Integration Options

Name	Description
Show Feed Link	Show or hide a link that allows a user to subscribe to your content feed.
For each feed item show	Set the amount of text to display in your content feed: intro text only, or the full article text.

Menu Item Link Type Options

Name	Description
Link Title Attribute	Add an optional HTML attribute to this menu item using this field.
Link CSS Style	Add custom CSS styling to this menu item.
Link Image	Assign an image to this menu item.
Add Menu Title	When using an image with the menu item, choose Yes to display the menu title next to the image.

Menu Item List Layout Options

Name	Description
Display Select	Show or hide the drop-down menu that allows the user to set how many items appear in the list on a single page.
Filter Field	Show or hide a filter field that allows a user to filter the items in the list.
Table Headings	Show or hide the table headings for the list.
Show Date	Hide the date column, or choose Show to display the created, modified, or published date for the items in the list.
Date Format	Enter the format to use for the Show Date column.
Show Hits in List	Show or hide the total number of hits for the item.
Show Author in List	Show or hide the item author's name.
# Articles to List	Select the number of articles to list in the table.
Pagination	Display navigation at the bottom of the page that links to additional articles in this category or subcategory.
Pagination Results	Show or hide the numeric navigation at the bottom of the page that tells the user how many more pages of articles are associated with this category or subcategory.

Menu Item Mail Options

Name	Description
Show Contact Form	Show or hide a contact form for a contact.
Send Copy to Submitter	Show or hide a button that allows the person filling out the contact form to receive an email copy of the message sent.
Banned Email	Enter email addresses that are banned from using a contact form on the site.
Banned Subject	Enter any subject text that is banned from entry in a contact form on the site.
Banned Text	Enter any text that is banned from entry in a contact form.
Session Check	Choose Yes to perform a system check for a session cookie. Choose No to display a session cookie check.
Custom Reply	Choose Yes to send a user a custom reply message. Choose No to disable this feature.
Contact Redirect	Enter an alternate email address where the contact message should be sent. Many spammers pull your email information off of web sites. This feature displays a public email address in your contact information, and uses a private, hidden email address to send you messages.

Menu Item Page Display Options

Name	Description
Browser Page Title	Enter an optional page title for this menu item.
Show Page Heading	Choose Yes to display the menu item title at the top of the body of this menu item's page content. For example, if the Home page displayed the title "Home" at the top, you would prevent the menu item title from displaying by choosing No.
Page Heading	Enter a custom page heading for this menu item's page.
Page Class	Use custom CSS styling for the content on this page.

Menu Item Metadata Options

Name	Description
Meta Description	Add a short sentence as the metadata description for this menu item.
Meta Keywords	Add keywords to this menu item.
Robots	Select the search engine robot setting for this menu item.
Secure	Select to Ignore, Turn on, or Turn off secure SSL settings for this menu item.

Menu Item Login Link Basic Options

Name	Description
Login Redirect	Enter the URL for the page that the user should be taken to after logging in to the site. This cannot be an external URL. When this option is left blank, users remain on their login page.
Login Description	Show or hide the login description.
Login Description Text	Enter any text you want to display on the login page. It will appear above the login form prior to a user's login.
Login Image	Assign an image to use on the login page.
Logout Redirect	Enter the URL of the page that a user will be taken to after logging out of the site.
Logout Text	Show or hide the logout text.
Logout Descriptions Text	Enter text that will appear on the page when a user logs out.
Logout Image	Select an image to display on the logout page.

Index